Teach Yourself VISUALLY™

WordPress®

2nd Edition

Visual

Janet Majure

WILEY

John Wiley & Sons, Inc.

Teach Yourself VISUALLY™ WordPress®, 2nd Edition

Published by
John Wiley & Sons, Inc.
10475 Crosspoint Boulevard
Indianapolis, IN 46256

www.wiley.com

Published simultaneously in Canada

Wiley publishes in a variety of print and electronic formats and by print-on-demand. Some material included with standard print versions of this book may not be included in e-books or in print-on-demand. If this book refers to media such as a CD or DVD that is not included in the version you purchased, you may download this material at http://booksupport.wiley.com. For more information about Wiley products, visit www.wiley.com.

Library of Congress Control Number: 2012933344

ISBN: 978-1-118-19787-5

Manufactured in the United States of America

10 9 8 7 6 5 4 3 2

Trademark Acknowledgments

Wiley, the John Wiley & Sons, Inc. logo, Visual, the Visual logo, Teach Yourself VISUALLY, Read Less - Learn More and related trade dress are trademarks or registered trademarks of John Wiley & Sons, Inc. and/or its affiliates. WordPress is a registered trademark of Automattic, Inc. All other trademarks are the property of their respective owners. John Wiley & Sons, Inc. is not associated with any product or vendor mentioned in this book.

Contact Us

For general information on our other products and services please contact our Customer Care Department within the U.S. at 877-762-2974, outside the U.S. at 317-572-3993 or fax 317-572-4002.

For technical support please visit www.wiley.com/techsupport.

Credits

Acquisitions Editor
Aaron Black

Sr. Project Editor
Sarah Hellert

Technical Editor
Donna L. Baker

Copy Editor
Scott Tullis

Editorial Director
Robyn Siesky

Business Manager
Amy Knies

Sr. Marketing Manager
Sandy Smith

Vice President and Executive Group Publisher
Richard Swadley

Vice President and Executive Publisher
Barry Pruett

Project Coordinator
Sheree Montgomery

Graphics and Production Specialists
Andrea Hornberger
Jennifer Mayberry

Quality Control Technician
Bryan Coyle

Proofreader
Nancy L. Reinhardt

Indexer
Potomac Indexing, LLC

Screen Artist
Jill A. Proll

Illustrators
Ronda David-Burroughs
Cheryl Grubbs
Mark Pinto

About the Author

Janet Majure is an author, writer, and editor with more than 30 years in the publishing industry. She writes or has written for three WordPress blogs (individual blogs Homecooking Revival.com and Foodperson.com plus group blog Ethicurean.com) and has written and edited books, newsletters, articles for daily newspapers, and technical white papers.

Author's Acknowledgments

The author gratefully acknowledges the WordPress community, which has made this remarkable software available, as well as the ongoing support of family and friends. In particular, she thanks friend, neighbor, colleague, and agent Neil Salkind, and Wiley editors Sarah Hellert and Aaron Black.

How to Use This Book

Who This Book Is For

This book is for the reader who has never used this particular technology or software application. It is also for readers who want to expand their knowledge.

The Conventions in This Book

① Steps

This book uses a step-by-step format to guide you easily through each task. **Numbered steps** are actions you must do; **bulleted steps** clarify a point, step, or optional feature; and **indented steps** give you the result.

② Notes

Notes give additional information — special conditions that may occur during an operation, a situation that you want to avoid, or a cross-reference to a related area of the book.

③ Icons and Buttons

Icons and buttons show you exactly what you need to click to perform a step.

④ Tips

Tips offer additional information, including warnings and shortcuts.

⑤ Bold

Bold type shows command names or options that you must click or text or numbers you must type.

⑥ Italics

Italic type introduces and defines a new term.

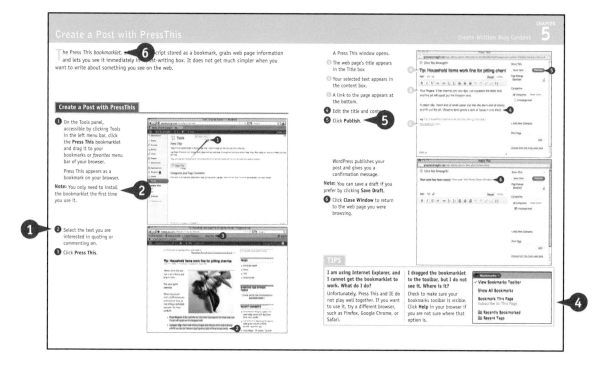

Table of Contents

Table of Contents

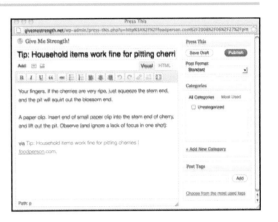

Chapter 6   Create Visual and Audio Content

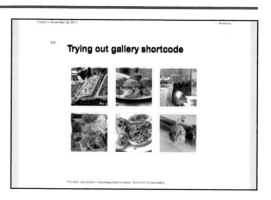

Chapter 7   Explore Widgets and Plugins

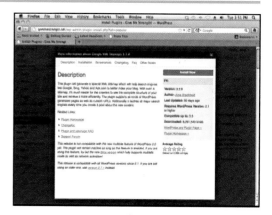

Table of Contents

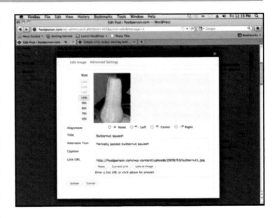

Chapter 10   Tweak Your Theme

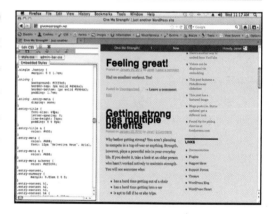

Table of Contents

Chapter 12 | Maintain Your WordPress Blog

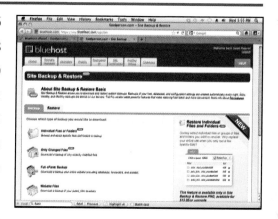

CHAPTER 1

Introducing WordPress

WordPress has become the platform of choice for new blogs, and increasingly it is the software chosen for websites of many different descriptions. WordPress lets you get your message out quickly and easily while giving you all the control you want.

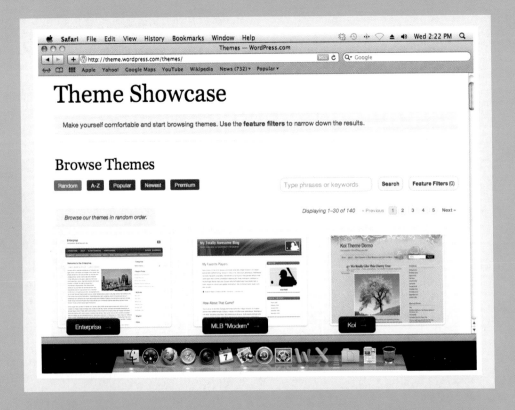

Choose a Version of WordPress

If you want to start a blog or create a website using WordPress, you can get up and running in very little time by using one of the two different WordPress varieties. First you must choose which one. At WordPress.com, you can get hosting service and standard site configurations. WordPress.org offers blogging software for self-hosted blogs, and even for blog networks. If you are on a WordPress.org blog network through, say, your school system, you will find your WordPress experience similar to that of WordPress.com users.

Whichever WordPress software option you choose, you can change it later!

About WordPress

WordPress is *open-source* software, meaning anyone can download it, use it, and change it, generally for free and with few restrictions. It has been around since 2003 as a program for self-hosted blogs, and this book uses versions 3.2.1–3.3.1. The organization that developed around the software, WordPress.org, later started WordPress.com for people who did not want to host their own blogs.

Why WordPress?

With other free blogging platforms available, you may wonder why you should choose WordPress. The answer largely comes down to control. With WordPress you own your content, and you can customize all you want. Also, WordPress allows use of static *pages*, which look and act like ordinary web pages, instead of simply showing content in chronological order as is typical for most blogs.

Hosted WordPress Blogs

WordPress.com is a blog host. Sign up with WordPress.com, and you can start blogging within minutes. The user interface is simple and similar to that of self-hosted WordPress.org blogs, and the host handles updates and maintenance. WordPress. com, however, limits your options in terms of your blog's content and performance.

Self-Hosted WordPress Blogs

Options for customizing your blog are near limitless when you have a self-hosted, or independent, WordPress.org blog. The tradeoff is that your independent blog takes a little more effort to start, and maintaining the software updates and content backups is your job.

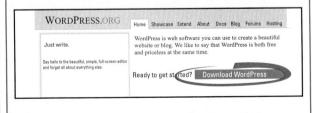

Key Differences: Appearance

WordPress.com offers more than 130 layout designs, called *themes*, but they are good ones. If you want to customize your theme by editing the *cascading style sheet*, or *CSS*, you must pay an annual fee. With a self-hosted WordPress blog, you can choose among countless free themes or purchased themes, or create your own.

Key Differences: Plugins

Plugins are program-like extensions that work with WordPress to add functionality. You can have as many as you want on your independent WordPress blog. WordPress. com does not let you add plugins, although many of the WordPress.com widgets provide plugin functions. A *widget* allows you to arrange sidebar information without writing code.

Key Differences: Ads

With a self-hosted WordPress blog, you can publish zero to endless amounts of advertising. At WordPress.com, the blog host itself occasionally posts ads on your blog, unless you pay a no-ad fee. Also, WordPress.com does not allow most types of ads, including AdSense, and only allows affiliate ads under special circumstances. However, in December 2011 WordPress.com introduced WordAds to allow some, but not all, bloggers to make money on their sites.

Key Differences: Cost

The blogging software is free, whether you host your own blog or put it on WordPress.com. If you self-host, you must pay for space on a web server, although that can be less than a dollar a month. If you go with WordPress. com, you may decide to pay fees to eliminate their ads, edit the CSS, or post videos — costs absent for independent blogs.

Key Differences: Support

WordPress.com has a clearly written support section, redesigned in 2011, plus forums and a contact form for support. The support documentation for WordPress.org blogs is called the *codex*. Written by WordPress volunteers, its quality gets better all the time, but it is inconsistent. At WordPress.org, no support contact exists except for the forums, but they are excellent.

Choose a Blog Topic

Y ou can choose anything as your blog topic, but doing a little research may help you identify the topic that you will love to write about and that readers will come looking for.

Expertise

If you are an expert in some field, your knowledge could make an excellent blog topic. By writing about your area of experience you will have plenty of content and confidence, and you may be able to use your blog to attract business and advertising.

Hobby

Perhaps you have a hobby that you avidly pursue and continue to learn more about. This, too, is a good subject for a blog. Fellow hobbyists may look to you for ideas and advice, and they can offer ideas and advice in return.

Business

A blog is a great way to keep in touch with your customers and to attract more customers. It is like a newsletter, only easier. As with a hobby, you surely have plenty of content to offer readers, whether news about products, special offers, or holiday hours.

Scattershot

One option is not to choose a topic at all and simply write your blog as you might write a diary. This is a fine approach as long as you are content to attract a small audience. Only a few people, by virtue of their fascinating lives or captivating writing styles, can write a scattershot blog and attract a large number of readers.

Focused

The more focused your topic, the easier it will be for search engines to find it. A focused blog also has greater potential to generate advertising revenues later, if that is one of your goals.

Competition

If you are unconcerned about developing an audience or if you want your blog to focus on your personal life, you need not worry about competition. For other subjects, however, check out the competition before you settle on a blog topic.

Useful and Entertaining

Whatever topic you choose, you will get more readers if your blog is useful or entertaining — or both. As you narrow your list of possible topics, think about which ones give you the greatest opportunity to be helpful or engaging. Those may be your best bets.

Research the Competition

You can get clues as to what is being written about and what is popular at these websites:

- http://wordpress.com/tags: See the most popular recent *tags,* which are like keywords, on WordPress.com blogs.

- www.alexa.com: Search for websites on your topic, and Alexa lists them and their traffic ratings.

- www.technorati.com: This page lists the 100 most popular blogs among Technorati users and most popular tags.

- www.stumbleupon.com: Sign up with this service, select your topic of interest, and then *stumble,* which takes you to blog post after blog post on that subject.

- http://google.com/blogsearch: Search on a topic to find existing blogs and blog posts on the topic.

Think Ahead about Passwords

Making a password plan now will make life easier as you go about setting up your WordPress site, because chances are you are going to need multiple usernames and passwords before you are done. You may use some all the time, such as your site's logon information, but you may use others less often. You, of course, are too smart to use the same password for all situations, right?

What Not To Do

Remember first what not to do: Do not use easily guessed words such as your spouse's or child's name, the word *password,* your license plate number, widely used combinations (such as qwerty or 123456), or any word in the dictionary spelled forward or backward. Also, do not put your password on a sticky note on your computer, and do not use the same word on multiple sites. Really.

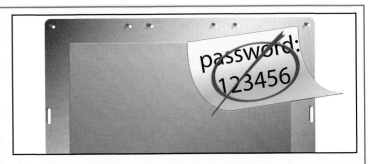

Choosing Passwords

Numerous strategies exist for choosing passwords. The basic approach is to choose a memorable phrase such as "My country tis of thee," use the first letters of the phrase's word — *Mctot* — and add numbers and special characters to get something like **Mctot!1*. The longer the password the better. Have four or five passwords ready before you start your WordPress experience.

Saving Passwords

Experts agree that having your computer or browser remember your password for you is generally a bad idea because the bad guys are good at cracking those bits of software. The most secure plan is to *remember* your passwords, but that is not possible for many of us. Although there is some debate, the idea of writing them down and putting the list in a safe place is considered more secure than doing any of the items on the what-not-to-do list.

Understanding WordPress and Blog Terms

Learning a few WordPress and blog terms before you dive in makes the process easier to follow. Terms in this section arise again and again.

Posts and Posting

Each entry in a blog is known as a *post*, and the usual presentation of posts is with the newest entry at the top of the screen. Variations are possible, though. *Post* is also what you do. That is, you post a new post to your blog.

Pages

You could think of a website as a collection of web pages, with each web page having its own content. With WordPress, the blog posting page typically — but not always — is the home page, which usually displays the last few posts chronologically. Themes provide page templates that are used to display posts by category. You can have other *static*, or unchanging, pages too. The most common static page on websites is an About page to explain the site to visitors.

Dashboard

The WordPress Dashboard is the online but behind-the-scenes control panel from which you create and modify your website. The Dashboard differs a little between the .com and .org versions of WordPress.

Permalinks

A permalink is the *permanent link* to a specific post or page. WordPress gives you options on what your permalinks look like, which may make it easier for search engines to find your post.

SEO

SEO is *search engine optimization*, and your interest in it depends on the purpose of your blog. SEO aims to improve your site's ranking in search results by search engines such as Google. A higher ranking leads more search engine users to find your site. SEO is based partly on making generous use of searched-for words.

9

Plan Your Blog's Content

Your blog will be easier to create and maintain and easier for readers to follow if you plan your content before you start blogging. By planning ahead, you can give your blog a consistent approach that works for you, your content, and your readers.

Words, Pictures, or Both?

Your choice of having content that is word heavy, picture heavy, or an even balance of words and pictures affects not only the appearance of your blog, but how you spend your time preparing your posts. Give thought now as to what medium best expresses the ideas you want to share.

Consider Post Length

Although there is no general ideal length, there may be an ideal length for you and your blog. Having a somewhat predictable post length enables you to know how long it may take to write a post, and lets regular readers know how much time to allow for reading. You can break up long subjects into a series of posts.

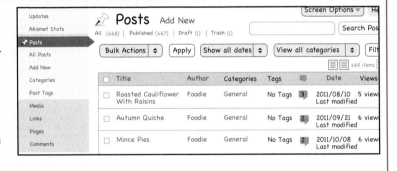

Consider Post Frequency

Some bloggers post multiple times a day; others post once a week. Your blog's topic and your time constraints may dictate how often you can post, and that is fine. *More* is not necessarily better, but *predictable* is definitely better!

Make Your Blog Stand Out

After you have studied other blogs in your subject area, ask what will make your blog unique, aside from its being written by you? If your topic is broad — cars, perhaps — yours will stand out better and be easier to plan if you narrow the subject to, say, restoring Chevrolets from the 1950s, or reviewing late-model two-seat sports cars.

Make Your Blog Accurate

Even if you are an authority in your subject area, you need to check your facts and, where possible, link to your sources. Yes, you can find popular sites, particularly on politics, that use dubious information, but if you want credibility with most readers, you need to get your facts straight. Include fact-checking as part of your content plan.

Suit the Content to the Subject

If your blog is about sculpture or carpentry or any other highly visual subject, you need to have pictures! Podcasts would be desirable on an interview blog. Make sure you have the equipment you need for the media you plan to use. If your blog is about grammar or creative writing, you can probably skip buying a top-flight digital camera.

Research Blog Titles

If you do not take care in naming your blog, you may find down the road that your choice does not serve you well. It may duplicate the name of an existing blog, or you may decide you want to get a domain name and find that a website with your blog's domain name already exists.

Blog Title versus Domain

Your *blog title* generally appears across the top of your blog's front page. A *domain name* is the part of a web address that includes *.com, .net, .info,* or one of the other domain name extensions. You can read about buying a domain name in the next section, "Buy a Domain Name."

Corresponding Names

It is helpful for the blog title and domain name to match, or at least to correspond, so that people can find you more easily. If you want to name your blog *In My Opinion*, it would be wise to see whether a domain such as *inmyopinion.net* or *imo.com* is available.

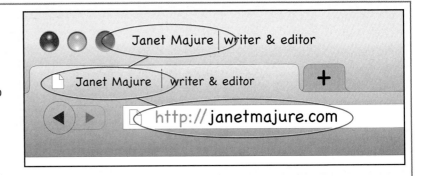

Consider the Long Term

If you are going to keep your blog private or are certain that you do not want to develop a significant audience, the blog title makes no difference. Most people start blogs, though, because they want to be heard. If you are one of those people, then consider the advice on these pages.

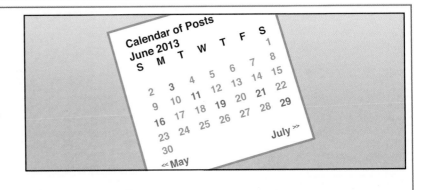

Brainstorm Names

Your blog topic is the place to start your search for blog titles. Write as many words and phrases as you can think of associated with your topic. If you have a personal blog, you may simply want to use your real name. But even your real name may not be as unique as you think, so write down many options. Narrow the options to a dozen or more, and then see whether another blog uses those names.

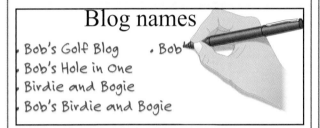

All the Good Names Are Taken!

So many sites are on the web these days that it may seem that all the good names are taken, but forge onward. You can try alternate spellings, whimsical expressions, or combinations of your name and your interest. If you can make the title memorable and easy to spell, all the better. You can get help at sites such as panabee.com, bustaname. com, or dotomator.com, which also tell you when related domain names are taken or available.

Try for a Unique Name

Increase your odds of having a unique blog title by:

- Typing your proposed title into the Google blog search engine, at http://google.com/blogsearch, to find blogs that use your title in full or in part.
- Typing your proposed title in your browser's address box followed by **wordpress.com**. For example, you could type **mythoughts.wordpress. com** to see if a WordPress.com blog by that name pops up.
- Typing the proposed title in the address box followed by **blogspot.com**, as in **mythoughts. blogspot.com**.

Avoid Duplication

If someone else has a website with your preferred title, you can still use it, but it is a bad idea. Besides the potential for legal conflict if someone decides to trademark the title, the bigger issue is that readers may get your blog and the other site confused.

Buy a Domain Name

If you are self-hosting your blog, you likely will want to buy a domain name to make it easier for readers to find you. You may want to buy one for a WordPress.com blog too.

You can buy a domain name from any number of *registrars* as a step independent of your hosting decision. However, web hosts often will register domains and give their customers a price break on the service. Therefore, if you are planning an independent blog, you may want to choose a web host before registering your domain.

Buy a Domain Name

1 Go to www.name.com in your web browser.

Note: This site is one of many where you can search for and buy domains. Your web host may give you a discounted price.

2 Type the name of your proposed domain in the box.

3 Click **Search** or press **Enter**.

A Domains with the name you searched appear at the top of the page. Those already registered are marked *Taken (Backorder)*. *Premium* domains are registered to someone else who is selling them at premium prices.

Choosing **Backorder** means Name.com will try to snag the domain for you when its registration expires.

Suggested alternative domain names appear farther down on the page.

If none of the available or suggested domain names satisfies you, repeat steps **2** and **3** until you find one you want.

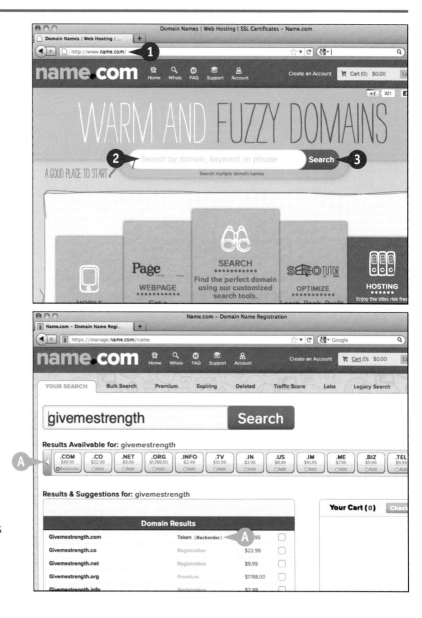

④ Click the domain name you want to register (☐ changes to ☑).

Ⓑ The domain also appears on the right side of the screen under Your Cart. You may select multiple domains if you want.

⑤ When you have selected all the domains you want to register, click **Checkout**.

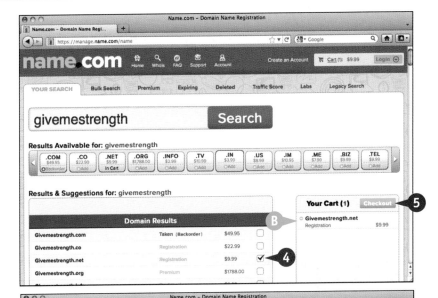

A new web page opens.

⑥ Review the information on the confirmation page.

⑦ If you are satisfied, click **Create an Account**.

The window expands to let you enter registration information. Complete it, and then click **Continue**.

Proceed through the remaining screens until your registration and purchase are complete.

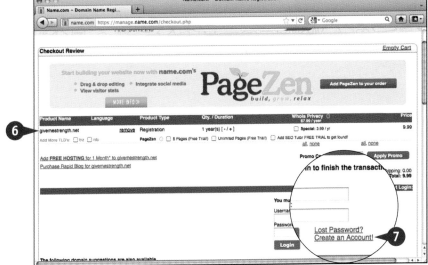

TIPS

Do I have to buy a domain name?
No. If you do not, however, your URL will be your web host's domain and directory listing, such as www.webhost.com/*myweblog*, or it could be a subdomain such as *myweblog*.wordpress.com.

Is the process the same for a WordPress.com blog?
It can be, or you can buy your domain name through WordPress.com. Doing so eliminates a few steps in setup.

CHAPTER 2

Set Up Your WordPress.com Blog

Once you have decided to run your blog on WordPress.com, getting set up is a snap. In this chapter, you sign up with WordPress.com, get familiar with its workings, choose among settings, and select a visual *theme* for your new blog's appearance.

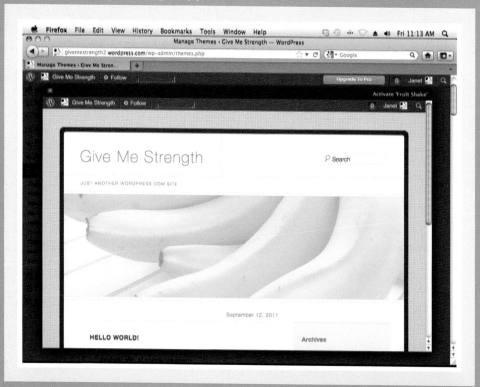

Sign Up with WordPress.com

With just a few simple steps, you can sign up with WordPress.com. When you do, you can start communicating, customizing, and getting in touch with the world as soon as you want.

Sign Up with WordPress.com

1 Navigate to http://wordpress.com in your web browser.

2 Click **Get started here**.

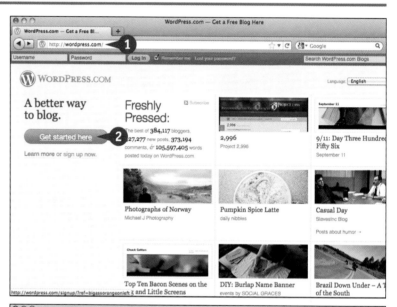

3 Type the name you want for your blog in the Blog Address box.

A A pop-up box tells you if the name is available or not and offers to sell you available, similar domains as an option.

4 Click **No thanks, I'll use the free wordpress.com address**.

5 Type a username in the Username box, or leave the blog name, the default, as your username.

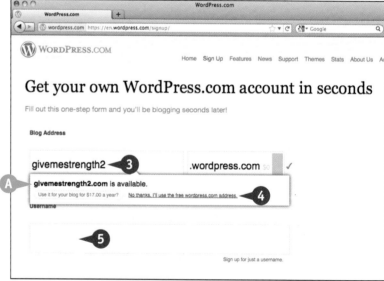

6 Type a password.

7 Retype the password.

Ⓑ A password strength indicator tells you how secure your password is.

8 Type the e-mail address where you want to receive WordPress.com notices.

Ⓒ Read the information at the terms of service link.

9 Click **Sign up**.

The next screen explains that you will receive a confirmation e-mail at the address you provided.

10 Click the link in the e-mail you receive to confirm your account.

A window opens the Dashboard in your browser confirming your account is now active and giving you introductory information. Click your blog's name to see your new site.

Note: WordPress sends you a second confirmation e-mail. Keep a copy of it because it contains your username and password as well as an API key that you will need later.

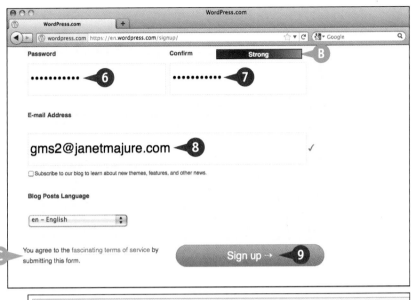

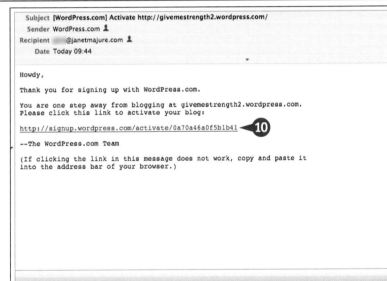

TIPS

Can I just sign up without starting a blog?
Yes. You can add your own blog or site later. To sign up without starting a blog, click **Sign up for just a username** under the Username box, and follow the signup instructions.

Now that I am a member, how do I sign in?
You can go to the home page at WordPress.com and sign in at the top of the page; you can type your blog's address plus **/wp-admin**, such as **example.wordpress.com/wp-admin**; or, if you have a Meta section on your blog, you can go to your blog's home page and click the **Log in** link.

View Your New Blog

Now it is time to learn the parts and pieces that make up your new blog. That general understanding will help you to make decisions as to your blog's appearance and content and help you understand the controls behind the scenes.

Ⓐ Header

The header, which runs across the top of the screen, displays the blog title and tagline, in this case "Just Another WordPress.com Site."

Ⓑ Admin Bar

As a WordPress.com member, you see the gray Admin Bar when you are signed in. It gives easy access to WordPress.com resources and tools.

Ⓒ Page List

Your initial site lists just one page, About.

Ⓓ Sidebar

Most themes include sidebars, and you get to choose items that appear in them.

Ⓔ Blog Post Date

Note the format of the date; it can be changed.

Ⓕ Blog Post Title

The post title is the headline for an individual post.

Ⓖ Blog Post

The main text section of your blog entry, known as a *post*.

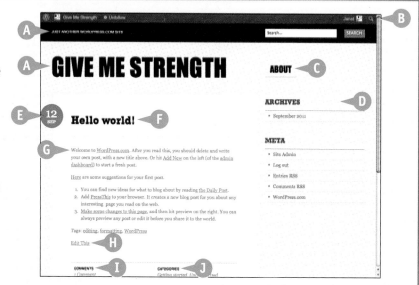

Ⓗ Edit Link

This link, or one very similar, appears only when you are logged in, and only on your own blog. It takes you "behind the scenes" to where you create your blog.

Ⓘ Blog Post Comments Link

This link takes you to comments on the post and shows how many comments are recorded.

Ⓙ Blog Post Category

You have the option of selecting categories for your blog. Categories, as explained in "Understanding Categories and Tags" in Chapter 8, are useful for organizing your blog's content.

About Your New Blog

A Complete Package

Your initial WordPress installation includes everything you need for a site. The home page shows a default post titled "Hello world!" with links to WordPress.com support pages, to your administrative location, or *Dashboard,* and to default content with sample text for your blog. That content includes a comment, an About page, and archives by date and by author.

Your First Theme

WordPress gives you a *theme*, a visual template, to start. Yours may differ from what you see here. Like many themes, your initial theme probably is a *two-column* theme, with the blog posts appearing in one column and a sidebar serving as the second column. Other themes offer one to four columns.

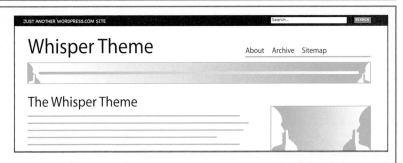

Practice Run

Spend a few moments clicking the various links to see what a default WordPress.com blog looks like and how to navigate through it. Doing so will help you make decisions about your blog's content and appearance, and you may want to follow some of the suggestions the default text offers.

Sidebar Terms

The starting sidebar contains two terms unfamiliar to blog newbies. They are *Blogroll*, which is simply a list of blogs that you favor, and *Meta*. *Meta* refers to *metadata*, or information about your blog and its contents. The Meta links vary, depending on whether you are logged in or not.

Get to Know Your Blog's Dashboard

Your blog's Dashboard is information central. The Dashboard's modules give you an overview of current and past activity on your blog, and you can add to your blog's content. WordPress includes introductory text and a video when you are new.

You can access your WordPress.com administrative panels by clicking Dashboard under Blog on the Admin Bar. Self-hosted WordPress.org users arrive at the Dashboard when they log on.

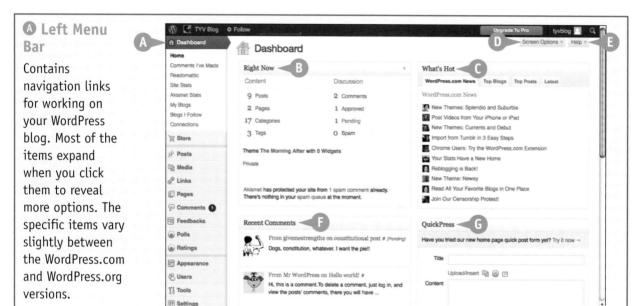

Ⓐ Left Menu Bar

Contains navigation links for working on your WordPress blog. Most of the items expand when you click them to reveal more options. The specific items vary slightly between the WordPress.com and WordPress.org versions.

Ⓑ Right Now

Provides the facts on how many posts, pages, and other content items your blog has.

Ⓒ What's Hot

Offers links to WordPress news and blogs. WordPress.org users have WordPress news modules with some similar information.

Ⓓ Screen Options Expand Button

Opens a box that lets you choose what content modules appear on your Dashboard.

Ⓔ Help

Provides links to WordPress.com support information.

Ⓕ Recent Comments

Reveals the names of recent commenters along with the name of the post that they commented on and the first line or two of the comment.

Ⓖ QuickPress

Lets you type up a blog post when you are in a hurry and do not need to do anything fancy.

Ⓐ Your Stuff

Lists your posts, edits, comments made, and comments received.

Ⓑ Recent Drafts

Shows posts and pages you have written but not published.

Ⓒ Stats

Gives a snapshot of how many times people are viewing your WordPress.com blogs and what blog posts are getting the most interest.

Ⓓ View All

Links to a page of detailed WordPress.com statistics.

Ⓔ Footer

Gives links to various WordPress.com support.

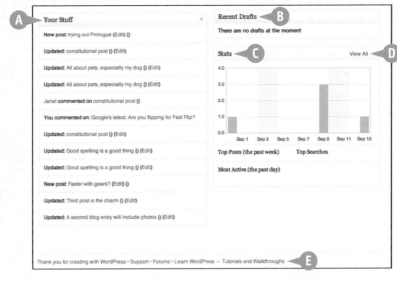

Ⓐ Show on Screen

Indicates with a checked box (☑) that the content item appears on your Dashboard.

Ⓑ Screen Layout

Shows with a selected radio button (◉) how many columns WordPress uses to display your Dashboard information.

Ⓒ Screen Options Collapse Button

Collapses the Screen Options box.

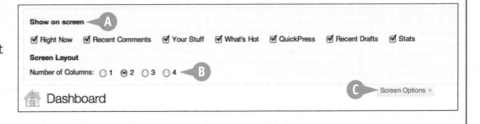

Understanding the WordPress.com Admin Bar

When you are logged in at WordPress.com, the Admin Bar provides a wealth of tools. With just a click, you can start a new blog post, visit other blogs, and do a whole lot more. Some Admin Bar offerings vary depending on where you are on your own blog or other WordPress.com blogs.

Simply position your mouse pointer over the menu of interest to reveal its options.

The WordPress.com Menu

A Opens a WordPress.com panel with these menu options.

B Opens a New Post panel in a general WordPress.com interface, rather than in your Dashboard.

C Opens list of WordPress.com blogs that you choose to follow.

D Goes to a showcase of featured posts on blogs hosted at WordPress.com.

E Reveals popular topics, or tags, in use at WordPress.com sites.

F Lists posts on which you chose to click the Like button.

G Lists all blogs you host at WordPress.com.

Blog Menu

A Shows name of blog you are visiting.

B Takes you to your Dashboard.

C Opens a menu to choose to add a new post, page, or blogroll link or to upload new media.

D Opens administrative panel associated with item named — comments, menus, and widgets, all explained in later chapters.

Note: The above menu items are visible only when you are visiting your own site.

E Provides a *shortlink* for current page or post, handy for Twitter or e-mail.

F Goes to a random post on the current site.

G Reports to WordPress.com that the post you are viewing — your own or on some other blog — should be marked as *mature*. WordPress.com allows some adult content.

H Lists theme name.

Note: When visiting others' blogs, you also see a Report Spam menu option.

Main Menu

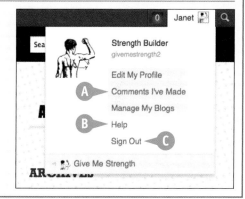

A Options for managing your account.

B Support page link.

C Sign out link.

Create Your WordPress.com Profile

Your WordPress.com public profile allows you to tell the world who you are through words, pictures, and links. This information is public and displayed at Gravatar.com, so do not include any information you want to keep private.

Create Your WordPress.com Profile

① Type your first name in the First Name box.

② Type your last name in the Last Name box

③ Type the name that you want to appear on your blog as your posts' author.

④ Type a sentence or paragraph about you that you think readers might want to know.

⑤ Click **Update Profile** to save changes, and scroll down to reveal more profile options.

⑥ Click **Change your Gravatar**.

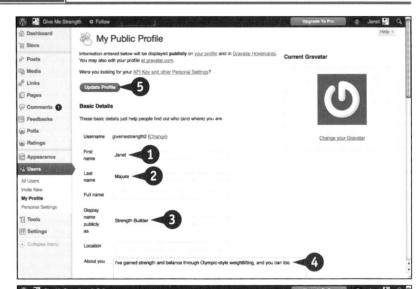

The Upload your Gravatar window opens.

⑦ Choose an option for uploading an image if you want, and follow the directions that appear.

⑧ Choose **Edit My Profile** from the Main Menu.

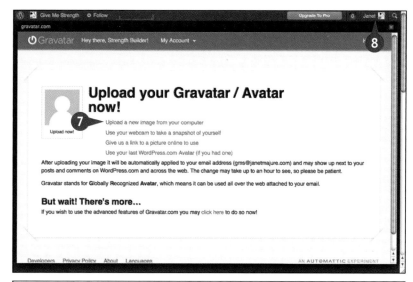

The My Public Profile page opens.

⑨ Type the web address in the URL box of any web page you like plus a name for the page in the Title box.

⑩ Click **Add Link**.

⑪ Click **Update Profile**.

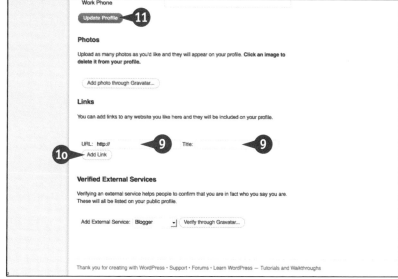

Where does my profile appear?

Several places, all served through Gravatar.com, which is operated by the same company, Automattic Inc., that owns WordPress.com. Your Gravatar and pop-up profile, or *hovercard*, appears with comments you make on WordPress.com blogs and on posts where you click **Like**. It is associated with your e-mail address.

I do not want my picture and information all over the place. Can I opt out?

Not exactly, because you automatically have a Gravatar account when you sign up with WordPress. However, you can leave your profile information blank, and only a symbol and your username appear when you comment or like a post.

Select Your General Settings

You can polish your site's title, add a tagline, and choose time formats, among other options, on the General Settings page. You can also upload an image to serve as a *favicon*, which appears in the address bar next to your blog's address. And if you do not like your choices, you can always change them later.

Select Your General Settings

1 On the Dashboard, click **Settings** to open the settings list.

2 If you want to modify your blog's title, type the new name in the Site Title box.

3 Type your blog's tagline in the Tagline box, which by default contains the tagline, "Just another WordPress.com site." Or, delete it and leave it blank.

4 In the Timezone box select a city in your time zone from the popup or your time relative to UTC, or *coordinated universal time*.

Note: Scroll up in the pop-up list to find cities. If you choose a UTC setting, you must manually reset the zone for daylight savings time.

5 Review the date and time formats and click to choose one other than the default (○ changes to ⦿).

6 Click **Browse** to find an image on your computer for your Blog Picture/Icon.

7 Once you have located an image, click **Upload Image** to upload it.

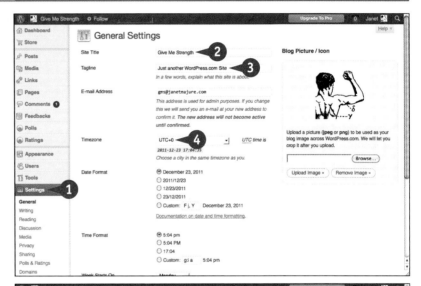

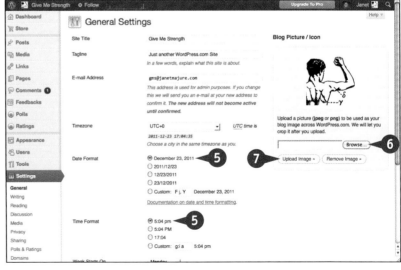

28

The image appears on a new screen.

8 Click and drag the white selection box to choose the area you want for your image.

Note: Click the box's edge to stretch or shrink the selection.

9 Click **Crop Image**.

10 A confirmation screen opens with a link, Back to Blog Options. Click it to return to General Settings.

11 Select the first day of the week you prefer for WordPress calendars from the drop-down menu.

12 If you plan to write in a language other than English, choose it from the drop-down menu.

13 Click **Save Changes**.

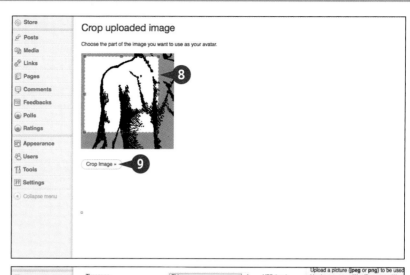

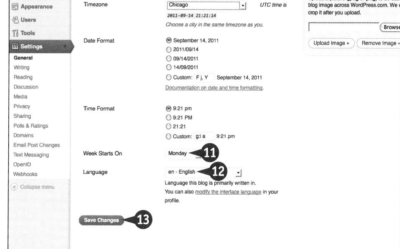

TIPS

What is the difference between the Gravatar on the profile page and the Blog Picture/Icon on the General Settings page?

The Gravatar is an icon, also known as an *avatar*, associated with your e-mail address and appears with comments you make. The Blog Picture/Icon on this page — known as *blavatar* to indicate a *blog* avatar — is an icon specifically for your blog. It appears as the favicon in your blog's URL when people visit as well as in the WordPress.com Admin Bar.

Can I have the same image for both Gravatar and blavatar?

Absolutely. Many people prefer to use the same image for consistency, but you must upload the image twice — once for each purpose.

Choose and Install a New Theme

You can give your blog a personal look by choosing a theme that corresponds with your purpose or personality. WordPress.com gives you many options, including themes for photo galleries and for social networking blogs, and you can customize those options further.

Choose and Install a New Theme

① On the Dashboard, click **Select your theme**, if available, or **Appearance** in the left menu bar.

WordPress opens the Manage Themes page.

Ⓐ The Manage Themes page lists the current theme and its options.

Ⓑ A selection of random themes appears at the bottom of the page.

Ⓒ WordPress gives you six ways to browse themes.

② Scroll down to view the currently displayed themes.

Each theme bears a brief description and *tags*, which serve as keywords. Clicking a tag displays all themes that bear that tag.

③ Click **Feature Filters** to search by particular theme elements.

The Theme Filters box opens.

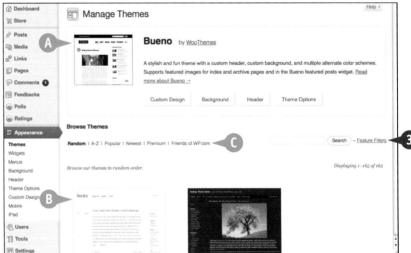

④ Click theme characteristics
(☐ changes to ☑).

Note: The selected options are
cumulative. If you select, for
example, **Green** and **Orange**, the
search finds only themes that use
both the Green and Orange tags.

⑤ Click **Apply Filters**.

WordPress presents the themes
that meet your criteria.

⑥ Scroll down to see filtered
themes. Try a theme by
clicking **Preview**.

WordPress displays a preview.

⑦ When you find a theme you
like, click **Activate**.

The Manage Themes page
returns, with your new theme
in the Current Theme section.

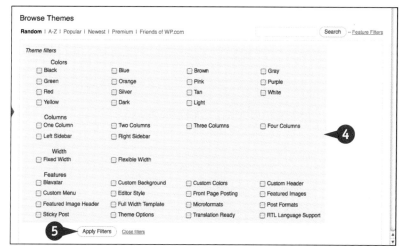

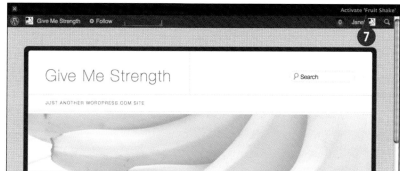

TIP

What do all those theme filters mean?

The colors and columns mean what you think they mean. Here is a guide to popular options whose meaning
may be unclear.

Theme Filter	What It Is
Fixed Width	Keeps column widths the same no matter how wide the window in which they are viewed.
Flexible Width	Lets columns grow wider or narrower to accommodate the screen width of the viewer.
Custom Menu	Allows you to alter your navigation menu's order and content.
Front Page Posting	Lets you post from the home page rather than the Dashboard.
Featured Images	Allows you to situate highlighted images on your home page.
Post Formats	Allows a choice of several display formats each time you post.
Theme Options	Contains nonstandard visual options, such as a variety of numbers of columns or different color schemes.
RTL Language Support	Supports use of right-to-left languages, such as Arabic and Hebrew.

Consider Premium WordPress.com Options

You can do more customizing of your WordPress.com site when you buy premium features. These let you use your own domain name, do a custom *cascading style sheet*, or CSS, and more.

A The Premium Features page, at http://en.wordpress.com/products, provides information about the available premium features and their prices:

B Using your own domain name. Domain names, which are discussed in Chapter 1, can be purchased or, if you already own one, can be mapped to your WordPress.com site.

C Buying more storage space.

D Customizing the type on your blog or editing the CSS if you know how.

E Using WordPress.com's VideoPress service.

F Blocking WordPress.com's occasional ads from your blog.

G Allowing more than 35 registered users if you have a private blog.

H Getting a premium theme for added theme customization and support.

Premium Features

Our free features are what makes WordPress.com such a great community, but we offer these optional upgrades to *really* help you stand out from the pack. Upgrades are pri

Be the master of your domain ($12.00 – $17.00/yr)
Your WordPress.com blog address is a sure sign of style, but what happens when you really get serious about controlling your online identity? It's easy to add your own domain name, like example.com, to your existing WordPress.com blog. Or if you already have your own domain name, it's easy to transfer it to your WordPress.com blog.

http:// mygr

Extra Storage ($19.97 – $289.97/yr)
If you find yourself running out of space, it's easy to add more storage to your blog. You can add 5, 15, 25, 50, or 100 gigabytes to your blog, so you'll have all the room you need to host tons of photos, videos, and music.

3 + 5 15 25
GB   GB GB GB

Custom Design ($30.00/yr)
The Custom Design upgrade lets you customize your blog's fonts with a point-and-click interface — no coding required. If you know your way around a cascading stylesheet, you can really put a personal touch on your blog with the CSS Editor. Need help crafting your

VideoPress ($59.97/yr)
Sometimes, you just have to say it with video. It's a great way to add a little liveliness to your blog. With VideoPress, it's simple—just upload your video and we'll convert it to the right formats for sharing on the web (including an HD option for high definition video). We'll present your videos in great style, with a minimalist player design that won't get in the way or clash with your blog's design. Adding VideoPress to your blog will instantly turn your blog's RSS feed into a video podcast you can drop right in to any podcast player such as Miro or iTunes.

To the right: an example of VideoPress in action. Turn on HD for the full experience!

Introducing VideoPress for WordPress.com

Go Ad-Free ($29.97/yr)
From time to time, we display text ads on your blog to logged-out users who aren't regular visitors. Doing this allows us to keep bringing you the free features you love. However, if you'd prefer your readers didn't see ads, you have the

Unlimited users ($29.97/yr)
The free limit of 35 users per private blog is enough for most people, but if you're building a private site that will have a large community or if

Premium Themes
Add more options for site custom exclusive designs, and support o theme authors with a Premium T Pricing for each theme can be fo your dashboard under the Premi

More about Upgrades

Custom Design

This upgrade lets you customize your site layout with Custom Fonts or with *Cascading Style Sheets*, or CSS. Try them for free before buying the upgrade by clicking **Custom Design** under Appearance in the Dashboard's left menu bar. Custom Fonts lets you choose from a selection of typefaces and sizes for your blog title, headings, and body type. CSS lets you create custom settings for the size, typeface, indention, color, and more, from headings to footers, posts to comments to links. CSS also gives the default style settings for images.

Adding Storage Space

Your free WordPress.com blog account includes 3 gigabytes of storage. You could blog for years and not use it up unless you use many big images. Because audio uses a lot of storage, however, WordPress.com requires a space upgrade if you want to upload audio or music to your blog.

VideoPress

VideoPress is a slick feature if you plan to use video, because it lets you host the video on your blog rather than on a separate site such as YouTube, and it makes your videos available as video podcasts. It automatically converts your uploaded videos to the MP4 and Ogg formats.

Text Messaging

The Text Messaging upgrade lets you use your mobile phone's text message capabilities to read and moderate comments and to add short posts. The option does not currently appear on the Premium Features page and is available only in the United States.

Buy an Upgrade

To buy an upgrade, go to your site's Dashboard and click **Store** near the top of the left menu bar. Click **Buy Now** under the upgrade you want to purchase, and follow the steps on the screens that follow. Except for Guided Transfer, which gives you help in transferring to a self-hosted site, all upgrades are for one year only and must be renewed annually to maintain them. Most upgrades can be canceled and refunded within 30 days.

Choose Your Personal Settings

Your personal settings let you choose among numerous options that affect how you work on your WordPress.com site.

You can find Personal Settings under Users in the left menu bar of the Dashboard.

Choose Your Personal Settings

① Click **Keyboard Shortcuts** (☐ changes to ☑) to enable keyboard shortcuts for comment moderation.

Ⓐ The More Information link leads to keyboard shortcuts explanation.

② Click **Enable Geotagging** (☐ changes to ☑) to allow your site to use geotags.

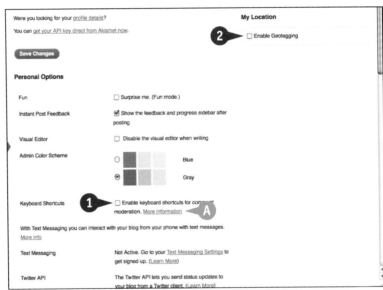

The geotagging box expands.

③ Type a ZIP code, city, or address.

④ Click **Find Address**.

Ⓑ WordPress shows a circle — not visible in some browsers — for an inexact address or a pointer for an exact address.

⑤ Review the privacy settings, which default to public geotags, and click to change them if you want.

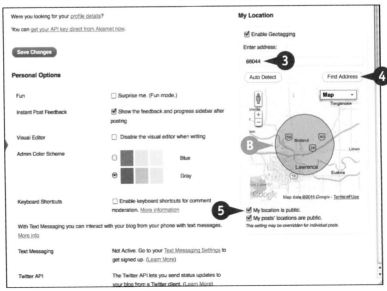

6 Scroll down the panel and click **Browser Connection** (☐ changes to ☑) if you access your blog via a public computer.

Note: This step helps protect your blog from hijacking by specifying use of a secure connection.

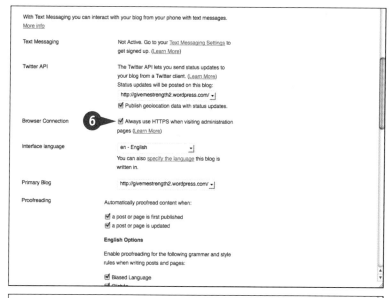

7 Confirm e-mail address for notices from WordPress.com is correct.

C This is where you change your password if necessary.

8 Click **Save Changes**.

Your new Personal Settings are saved.

TIPS

What are all those other settings on this panel?
The Personal Settings are a catchall for assorted WordPress.com options. Most are covered in other chapters in this book.

What about the Fun, Instant Post Feedback, and Snow settings?
If you select **Fun** mode, you may occasionally see messages or even brief animations cheering you on. **Instant Post Feedback** produces a sidebar that appears as you publish each new post, telling you the post has loaded and making posting suggestions. With **Snow** active, the default, you see falling, blowing snow on your screen from about December 1 through January 4. The snow is a bit of whimsy, but if you have a slow Internet connection, you might want to turn it off.

CHAPTER 3

Set Up Your WordPress.org Blog

Your self-hosted WordPress blog requires a little more effort, but the payoff is in total control of the look and function of your blog.

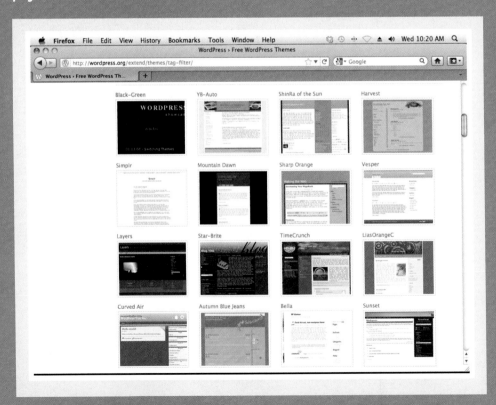

Choose a Host for Your Blog

When you choose a reliable and accessible web host, you can count on your WordPress.org blog staying online and available. You might even get some technical support for WordPress.

What Web Hosts Do

A web host provides a computer server that stores your blog's files and databases and makes them available over the Internet. Web hosts usually offer a control panel to help you manage your files and low-cost domain registration options.

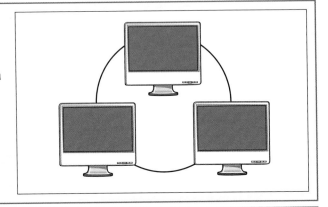

WordPress Requirements

Running WordPress 3.3 requires that the web host provide two basic software packages: PHP version 5.2.4 or greater and MySQL version 5.0 or greater. PHP is a scripting language, and MySQL is database software. WordPress also recommends, but does not require, Apache or Nginx as the server software.

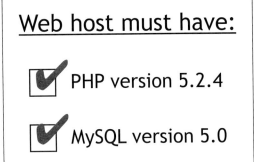

Web host must have:

☑ PHP version 5.2.4

☑ MySQL version 5.0

Your Requirements

You also need to consider your blog's specific requirements, such as the amount of traffic you expect or hope for, and the type and quantity of media you expect to use. When you start from scratch, this information can be hard to determine, so make your best guess and, when contacting potential hosts, find out how they handle a surge in traffic or changing host packages if your needs change.

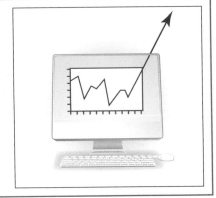

Shared or Dedicated Server?

A *shared server* means that the computer on which your website resides is also home to other websites. A *dedicated server* is reserved for your site alone and is naturally more expensive. A shared server is usually adequate for most small blogs.

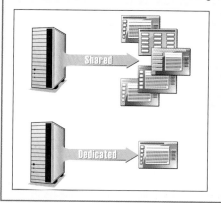

Options to Consider

Among the countless web hosts available are your Internet service provider, or ISP, and WordPress-recommended web hosts. Your own ISP may — or may not — be the least-expensive alternative. Some WordPress-recommended hosts, available at WordPress.org/hosting, provide one-click WordPress installations. For other host recommendations, ask friends and read reviews at www.webhostingsecretrevealed.com.

Checking Them Out

Once you have two or three web hosts to consider, check them out by reading reviews and by calling the host's support line — not the sales line — to see whether you are likely to be able to get help when you need it. Getting someone to talk on the sales line is easy, but a 10-minute wait when you call support may not be acceptable to you.

Take a Tour

Once you have made a decision and signed up for web hosting, get familiar with your host's control panel. It makes managing your blog easier and most likely also provides access to site data that you will find helpful.

Install WordPress via Your Host's Automatic Installation

If you chose a web host with automatic WordPress installation, you can have all the necessary WordPress files installed in the right spot on your directory in a minute or less. If you have trouble, the web host is there to help.

In this example, the host offers Simple Scripts installation. Other hosts may offer installation via Fantastico or another service.

Install WordPress via Your Host's Automatic Installation

1 After you log on to your web host and go to its control panel, click its link for WordPress.

A If a WordPress link is not evident, you can call your web host for help, look on the host's support pages, or click **Simple Scripts** in the control panel to see if they have a WordPress option.

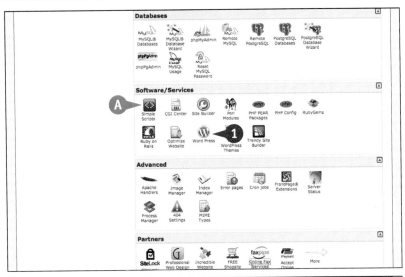

The WordPress installation window opens. In this example, Simple Scripts makes the installation.

2 Click **Install**.

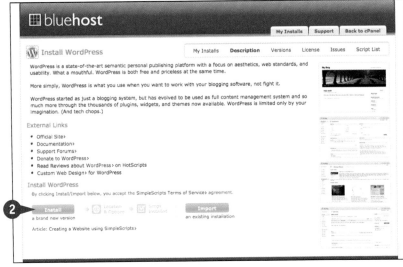

3 Leave the WordPress version at the default setting.

4 Choose where to install WordPress.

5 Click the link to display Advanced Options.

Note: Simple Scripts sets **admin** as your logon name and gives you a random password unless you specify otherwise here.

6 Clear the check box (☑ changes to ☐) unless you want the plugin listed.

7 Review the license agreement.

8 Click the check box to agree (☐ changes to ☑).

9 Click **Complete**.

Ⓑ The Simple Scripts Status window opens and shows the installation progress.

Ⓒ Simple Scripts displays site information including the URL for your new blog and the URL where you go to log on plus your username and password.

10 Click the site URL to see your new blog.

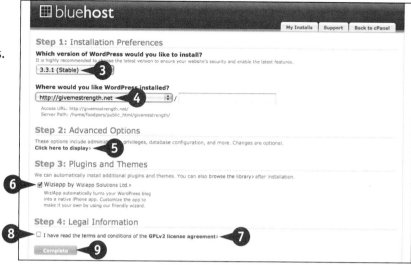

TIPS

How do I know where to install WordPress?
Your web host assigns you a home directory where it stores files for your website. Among them is a root directory, where your WordPress files go. It often is called public_html or web root or something similar. If you are not sure which folder is your root directory, contact your web host and ask.

My web host does not list the domain I bought. How do I get my domain there?
If your host is not your domain registrar, you need to have the registrar point its nameservers to your host. Get the proper nameservers' names from your host and provide them to your registrar. The support pages of each will show you how.

Get an FTP Application for Manual Installation

An *FTP program*, or file transfer protocol program, lets you easily move files from your computer to your web host. You need it to do a manual WordPress installation. Your host may provide an FTP utility through its control panel, but using an FTP program on your computer may be faster.

FileZilla Client is a free, open-source FTP program that works with Windows, Macintosh, and Linux computers.

Get an FTP Application for Manual Installation

1 After starting your web browser, go to http://filezilla-project.org.

2 Click **Download FileZilla Client**.

The FileZilla Client Download window opens.

3 Review the download options to find the version for your computer's operating system.

4 Click the link to the version you need.

A download window opens. Follow the usual steps for your computer for program installation to install FileZilla Client.

Note: You will use your FTP client to upload files to your web host by way of your FTP address. Your FTP address is probably *ftp://yourdomain.com* where *yourdomain.com* stands in place of your regular web address. Check with your web host if you are not sure.

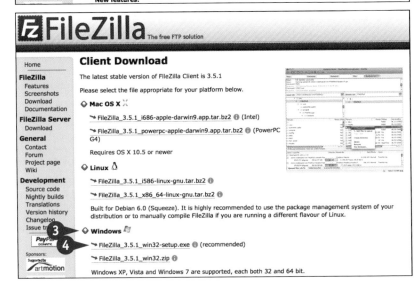

Download WordPress Software

Before you can upload WordPress to your web host for a manual installation, you first must download the software from WordPress.org. After this simple process, you are ready to complete your manual WordPress installation.

Download WordPress Software

1 In your browser, go to http://wordpress.org/download.

2 Click **Download WordPress**. At this writing, the latest version is WordPress 3.3.1.

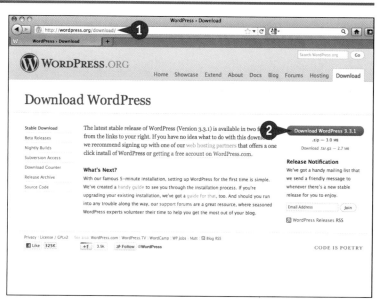

A download window, which varies with your computer's operating system, opens.

Note: Because WordPress software runs on your web host, not on your local computer, it does not matter whether your computer is a PC or a Macintosh.

3 Extract the WordPress files and save them to a location on your hard drive.

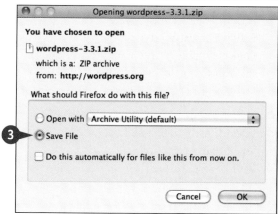

Set Up the MySQL Database

You need a MySQL database to store all the content of your blog or site. No database, no blog, so you need to set up the database before you load your WordPress software for a manual installation.

Go to your web host and log on to its control panel to get started. This example shows the widely used cPanel control panel, but every web host has an equivalent. Check with technical support at your host if you cannot find the appropriate link.

Set Up the MySQL Database

1 In the MySQL Database Wizard, type a name for your database.

You can reach the wizard by clicking **MySQL Database Wizard** after you log in to cPanel.

2 Click **Next Step**.

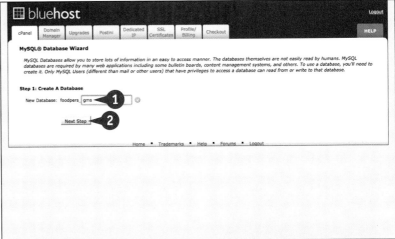

3 Type a username.

4 Type a password.

5 Retype the password.

Note: Be absolutely sure to record the username and password.

6 Click **Create User**.

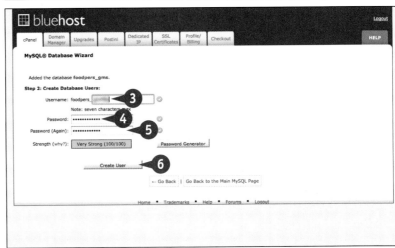

Ⓐ The next window confirms the name and password.

⑦ To give the user you created — that is you, the administrator — all the privileges you require to set up and operate the database, click **All Privileges** (all ☐ change to ☑).

⑧ Click **Next Step**.

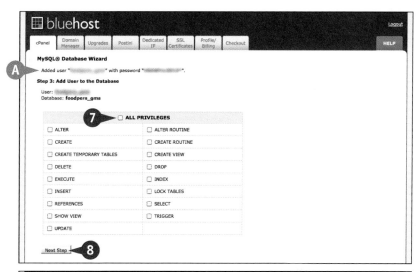

A new screen confirms the action.

⑨ Click **Return Home**.

You are back at the cPanel home.

TIPS

What should I name my database?
Give it a name that you readily associate with your blog so that you will recognize it now and in the future. You may find it helpful if you write it down for the installation process.

Can I use my same username and password?
If you want. The important things are that you can remember them when you want to install your WordPress files.

Upload the WordPress Files

Uploading the WordPress files to your web host gives you all the files you need for your manual WordPress installation. Here is where you put your FTP client to use.

Upload the WordPress Files

① After you open your FTP client, FileZilla in this example, type the host name in the Host box.

Ⓐ The files on your local computer appear in the lower left panel.

Note: The host is your blog's URL, such as *myblog.com* unless you want to install your blog somewhere besides the root folder.

② Type the username for your web host in the Username box.

This is the name that your host requires when you log on to its site or your control panel there.

③ Type your password at your web host into the Password box.

④ Click **Quickconnect**.

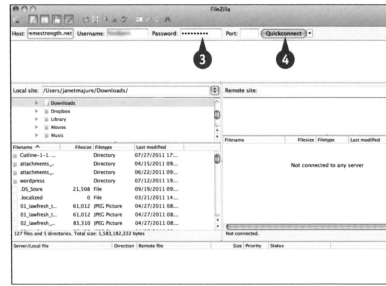

B FileZilla shows the progress of the connection.

C When the connection is made, the files on your web host appear in the lower right panel.

5 Navigate in the left panel until you find the folder containing the WordPress files you downloaded and extracted, and open that folder by double-clicking it.

6 Select all the files and documents within the WordPress folder.

D Those files include the three folders, or *directories*, starting with *wp-* and numerous other files.

7 Drag all files to your blog's root directory, which you can find in the public_html directory on your web host.

FileZilla uploads the files to your web host. You can watch the progress in the bottom pane of the FileZilla window. This process probably will take several minutes.

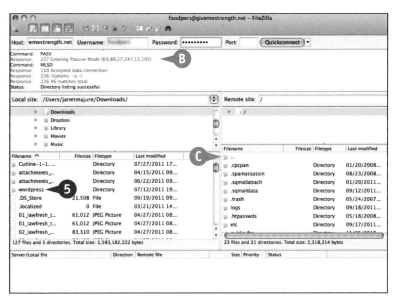

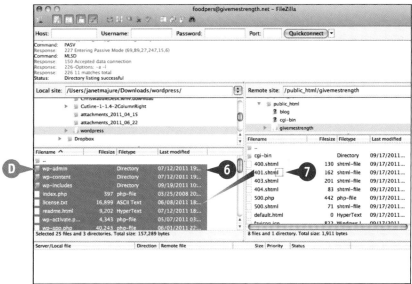

TIPS

Can I just use the FTP utility on my web host's control panel?
Yes. Go to your web host's control panel and look for something referring to FTP, such as a Java applet called Unlimited FTP. In addition, cPanel has a web-based utility called File Manager that serves much the same purpose. Some people think that client FTP programs are easier to use.

How do I know what my blog's root directory is?
If you have purchased your own domain, the root is probably the folder, or directory, with the domain name inside the directory for web files. If you do not know the root directory or cannot figure it out, ask your web host.

Complete the Configuration and Installation

Completing the configuration of your manual WordPress installation allows your MySQL database and WordPress files to communicate with each other.

Complete the Configuration and Installation

1 Type your blog's URL in your web browser address bar, followed by **/wp-admin/install.php**. So, if your site is mysite.com, type **http://mysite.com/wp-admin/install.php**. Press **Enter**.

A A WordPress message appears, telling you that WordPress does not find the necessary wp-config.php file.

2 Click **Create a Configuration File**.

A WordPress window opens and reminds you of the information you need to create your configuration file.

3 Review the list of needed information — which you created when you set up your MySQL database — and make sure you have it all available.

B This example covers an individual blog installation, so you can ignore item 5 on the list.

4 Click **Let's go**.

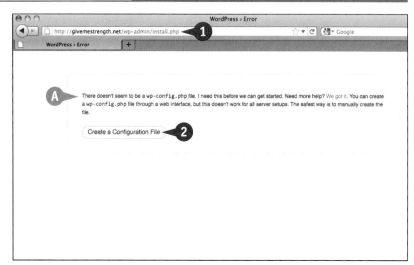

48

The Setup Configuration File window opens.

5 Type your MySQL database name.

6 Type your database username.

7 Type your database user password.

8 Click **Submit**.

9 If all went well, a confirmation screen appears. Click the **Run the install** button.

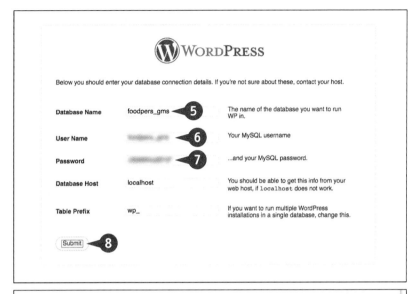

The Welcome window opens.

10 Type your blog title.

11 Type a username for your site.

12 Type and confirm a password.

Note: Record your username and password.

13 Type your e-mail address.

14 If you intend your blog to be private, click the check box to prevent your blog from being visible to search engines (☑ changes to ☐).

15 Click **Install WordPress**.

The Success! window opens and shows your WordPress username. Click **Log In** if you are ready.

Note: WordPress e-mails your username to the e-mail address you provided.

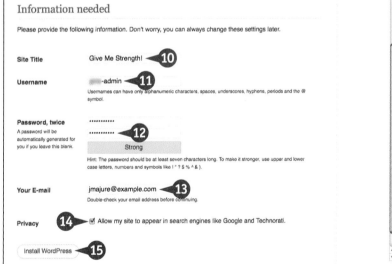

What if my installation did not work?
Although even the manual installation is fairly simple, occasionally things can go wrong. The error message or messages you see will guide you. See the next section of this chapter for troubleshooting.

Troubleshoot Installation Errors

Things do not always go as planned, of course. When this happens, a little troubleshooting can address typical problems with manual installation. You can easily overcome most problems.

Trouble Uploading Files

If your Internet connection is slow, you may have trouble uploading the WordPress files to your host. If so, and your web host uses cPanel, you can upload the WordPress Zip file and then extract it by using the cPanel File Manager. If you do not have cPanel, you can download an inexpensive program called ZipDeploy for Windows and Linux systems, which also lets you extract Zip files at your web host.

Cannot Get to First Base

If you have uploaded your files and typed your site's URL, and you get a window saying the site cannot be found or is under construction, you may have uploaded the WordPress *folder* rather than its *contents*. If so,

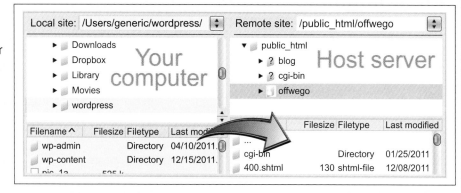

just move the files out of the folder using FileZilla or your host's file management utility.

Error Messages

If you get an error message, the first step is to read it. Really. In its short life, WordPress has become very easy to install, and its error messages are one reason why. They provide brief but explicit information to help you fix the problem.

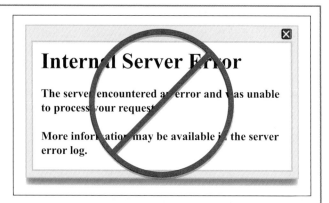

Error Establishing a Database Connection

This error message means you probably made a mistake in typing your database name, username, and user password in the Setup Configuration File window. These names are associated with the MySQL database that you created, as distinct from the username and password you may use to log on to your web host's control panel. Go back and confirm that you entered these correctly. Also, make sure that you have given the database user *all* privileges.

Other Installation Problems

For other problems, start at the beginning: Make sure that your host meets the minimum requirements as described earlier in "Choose a Host for Your Blog." Also, double-check that you do not need to use something other than Localhost in the Hostname box. Check with your host, or you can see a list of some popular hosts' hostnames at codex.wordpress.org/Editing_wp-config.php.

Possible DB_HOST values

Hosting Company	DB_HOST Value Guess
1and1	db12345678
BlueHost	localhost
DreamHost	mysq1.example.com
HostGator	localhost
LaughingSquid	localhost
MediaTemple GridServer	internal-db.s44441.gridserver.com
pair Networks	dbnnnx.pair.com

Try a Fully Manual Installation

A fully manual configuration process involves entering your user information into the configuration file and running the installation script. For details, go to http://codex.wordpress.org/Installing_WordPress.

Forgotten Database Details

You misplaced your database details? The easiest solution is to simply create another empty database and this time keep track of your username and password. The database name is always available via your host control panel.

Username: Myname
Password: *&Kuj19

Log On to Your Blog's Dashboard

Once you are logged onto your WordPress administrative interface, whose main page is called the Dashboard, you can do just about anything you want or need to do with your blog.

You do not need to log on to your web host to log on to your self-hosted WordPress Dashboard.

Log On to Your Blog's Dashboard

From the URL

1 After you start your browser, type your blog's URL, followed by **/wp-admin** into the address bar, and press Enter.

The browser takes you to your WordPress Log In page.

2 Type your WordPress username in the Username box.

3 Type your WordPress password in the Password box.

Ⓐ If you want WordPress to remember your computer so that you do not have to log on again, click the **Remember Me** check box (☐ changes to ☑).

Note: Do not use Remember Me if other people have access to your computer.

4 Click **Log In**.

The Dashboard opens.

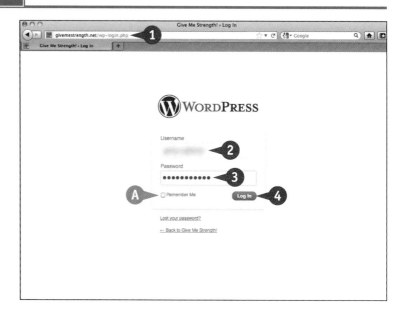

From Your Blog

1 Type your blog's URL in the address bar of your browser, and press **Enter** to open your blog's home page.

2 Click the **Log in** link.

WordPress takes you to the Log In page, where you enter your information as you did in steps **2** and **3**, and then the Dashboard opens.

Note: If you later change the appearance of your blog, you may not necessarily have a Log In link, but you still can log on from the URL.

What do I do if I cannot remember my password?
Click **Lost Your Password?** on the logon screen. The Lost Password window opens, where you type the e-mail address you used when you set up your blog, and then click **Get New Password**. Thus, keeping track of the information you used when creating your blog is important. WordPress sends your password to your e-mail address. Follow the directions in the e-mail.

I thought I typed my password right, but I am still having trouble logging in.
Your password is *case sensitive*, so be sure that you are typing capital or lowercase letters the same when you are logging in as you did when you created the password.

Review the Dashboard

You can get an overview of your blog on the Dashboard and start presenting your blog's public face in the General Settings.

The Dashboard of your self-hosted WordPress blog works a lot like Dashboard at WordPress.com, although some content is different. You can learn more in "Get to Know Your Blog's Dashboard," in Chapter 2.

Review the Dashboard

Ⓐ The default post, pages, theme, and other information appear in the Right Now box.

Ⓑ The Incoming Links box is empty until other sites start linking to yours.

❶ After logging into your self-hosted WordPress Dashboard, review the Dashboard to get familiar with it, and then click **Settings**.

The General Settings window opens. See "Select Your General Settings" in Chapter 2 for settings not mentioned in this section.

❷ Type or review your blog's URL in the WordPress Address (URL) box. Be sure to type the **http://** portion of the address.

Ⓒ You can store your self-hosted WordPress blog's files and WordPress software files on different directories on your server. To do so, click the link after the Site Address (URL) box for instructions.

Ⓓ See Chapter 11 for information on user capabilities and creating member communities.

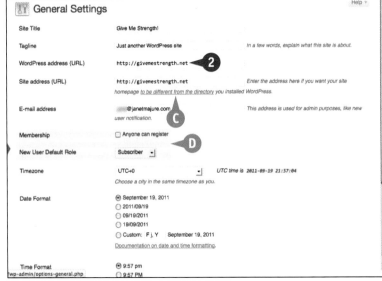

③ Choose a city in your time zone from the drop-down menu.

④ Click **Save Changes**.

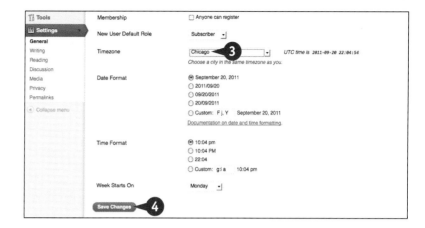

TIP

How do I create a custom time or date format?

Type the following letters in any order you choose in the custom boxes. Other characters, such as hyphens or commas, appear exactly as you type them. Here are the most frequently used date and time codes.

Date codes	
l (lowercase L)	Full name for day, such as *Saturday*.
D	Three-letter abbreviation for day, such as *Mon* — without a period.
d	The number for the day without leading zeroes; use *j* if you want leading zeroes.
S	The ordinal number suffix for the day of the month, such as *st* in 1st or *th* in 5th.
F	Full name for the month, such as *March*.
M	Three-letter abbreviation for month, such as *Mar*.
n	The number of month, such as *4* for April; use *m* if you want leading zeroes, such as *01* for January.
Y	The year in four digits.
y	The year's last two digits.

Time codes	
a	Lowercase am or pm.
A	Uppercase AM or PM.
g	12-hour format for hour, without leading zeros.
h	12-hour format of hours, with leading zeros.
H	24-hour format of hours with leading zeros, 00 through 23.
i	Minutes with leading zeros.
s	Seconds with leading zeros.
T	Time zone, abbreviated.

Therefore, if you wanted the time on posts to appear as *Monday, December 03rd, 2012, 22:14 CST* you would type **l, F jS, Y,** in the custom date field and **H:i T** in the custom time format field.

Get to Know the Dashboard

The Dashboard — the main administration panel for your self-hosted, WordPress.org installation — puts links and tools at your fingertips to manage your blog or site. From the Dashboard, you can get a snapshot of the quantity of content on your site and read about WordPress and more.

A new installation of WordPress shows an orientation module above the Dashboard modules. Try it out, or click **Dismiss** to get rid of the orientation module. You can get it back by clicking **Welcome** in Screen Options.

Note: Most of the Dashboard's modules in this section are shown *collapsed*, meaning only their title bars appear. The default setting has the content *expanded*, as explained in "Customize and Navigate the Dashboard" in Chapter 4.

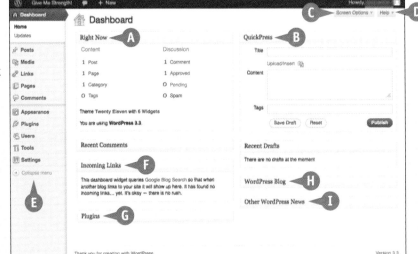

Ⓐ Gives a summary of your site's content, discussions, theme, widgets, and WordPress version.

Ⓑ Lets you make a quick posting.

Ⓒ Provides options for the modules you want to display. Every admin panel has different screen options.

Ⓓ Offers help information. Every admin panel has different help information.

Ⓔ Known as the left menu bar; contains links to the other admin panels.

Ⓕ Lists blogs that have linked to your blog.

Ⓖ Posts news about plugins, which are covered in Chapter 7.

Ⓗ Displays the latest news from the WordPress.org blog.

Ⓘ Displays the Planet WordPress news feed or other news feeds, which are described in Chapter 9.

Understanding the Admin Bar

The Admin Bar for self-hosted blogs, visible at the top of your site when you are logged in, gives you quick access to the administrative functions you most need. You can remove the bar if you want, as explained in the next section.

A Drop-down menu links to information about WordPress.org and to support.

B Links to Dashboard and frequently used administrative modules.

Note: When working in the admin panels, clicking the site name here takes you to your site's home page.

C Shows number of comments awaiting approval, if any, and goes directly to the Comments panel to moderate them.

D Gives quick access to the panels for creating or adding posts, media, links, pages, and users.

E Takes you to panel to edit current page.

Note: This link does not appear when viewing the home page or admin panels. The link says Edit Post when viewing an individual post.

F Shows username of person logged on to site. Drop-down menu links to profile or lets you log out.

Create Your Profile

Your profile lets you select settings for important aspects about how you want to work on your self-hosted WordPress.org blog. These include the color scheme of your administrative interface and whether you want the Admin Bar to be visible.

Create Your Profile

1 Click **Your Profile** under Users.

The Profile page opens.

2 Click an administration pages color scheme (○ changes to ◉).

3 Click the option to view the Admin Bar (☐ changes to ☑).

4 Type your first name in the First Name box.

5 Type your last name in the Last Name box.

6 Type a nickname in the Nickname box.

Note: The nickname defaults to your username. For security reasons, you should not make your username publicly available.

7 Click the arrow to reveal the drop-down menu.

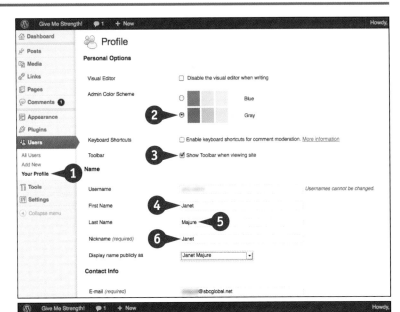

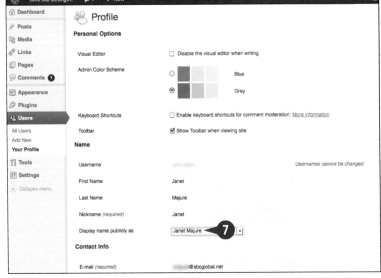

A menu lists options for how you will be identified publicly.

8 Click the public identity you prefer.

9 Scroll to bottom part of panel.

10 Confirm your e-mail address.

11 Add a website address if desired.

12 Type a little about yourself if desired.

13 Click **Update Profile**.

Your profile is saved, and WordPress gives you a confirmation message.

Your public identity appears in the WordPress greeting.

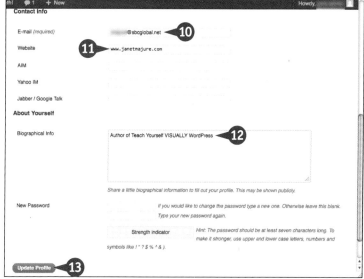

TIPS

Why not change the Visual Editor or Keyboard Shortcuts settings?

You can change the settings if you want by clicking the check box next to each item. First, though, you may want to read "Introducing the HTML Editor and Toolbar" in Chapter 5 and "Moderate Comments" in Chapter 9. Click **More Information** next to Keyboard Shortcuts on the Profile page for details on using those keyboard shortcuts.

Do I have to include contact information?

Only e-mail is required — which is not public and is only for receiving e-mail notices, such as when comments appear on your blog or when you forgot your password. You are free to add other contact information or biographical information if you understand it may become public, usually depending on your theme.

Choose a New Theme

Self-hosted WordPress blogs have nearly limitless options when it comes to *themes*, or visual templates. As a result, you probably can find one that looks and behaves exactly as you want it. The two basic themes that come with your installation are also attractive — and guaranteed to work.

Importance of Appearance

Before anyone reads a word on your blog, a reader first notices its overall appearance. Also, once people associate a certain look with your site, the look helps build the blog's identity. Choosing your theme carefully is worthwhile for these two reasons, keeping in mind what kind of first impression you want your blog to make.

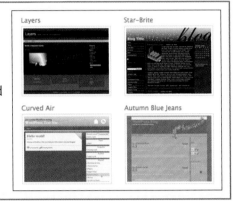

Theme Organization

Consider the purpose and content of your blog. A standard, latest-post-at-the-top blog can use any basic theme that pleases you. If, however, you want to show off artwork, you might search for *portfolio* themes. If you want to highlight multiple posts on your blog's front page, consider *magazine* or *news* themes. Social-network-type blogs need a front-page posting option.

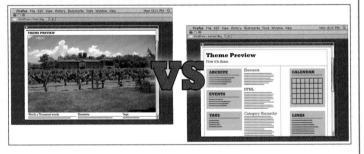

Free Themes

Perhaps the best way to review hundreds of free themes is to go to the Themes Directory at http://wordpress.org/extend/themes. The directory includes users' ratings and comments on free themes, notes about the themes, and theme preview. You can also search from your WordPress installation much as you can in WordPress.com, by clicking **Appearance** in the left menu bar and then the **Install Themes** tab to search. (See also "Choose and Install a New Theme" in Chapter 2.)

Commercial Themes

Commercial or *premium* themes refer to themes you pay for. The expected advantage of premium themes is that, unlike most free themes, they include ongoing support for theme users, and they keep their themes aligned with updated WordPress versions, although there is rarely a guarantee. These themes do not appear on your site's Appearance/ Install Themes search. You can find links to such themes at http://wordpress.org/extend/themes/ commercial or by doing a Google search on *premium themes*.

Customize a Theme

Many, if not most, free and premium themes allow you to make limited adjustments to them simply by making selections in the theme's options panel within the Dashboard's Appearance menu. Those adjustments often include color changes or custom header images. Chapter 10 discusses making additional changes.

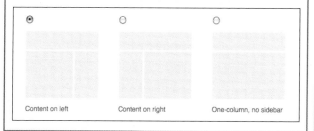

Custom Themes

In addition to free and premium themes, you also can pay someone to design a theme entirely to your specifications. If you want a custom theme, it is a good idea to get a designer experienced with WordPress themes. It also is a good idea to get a clear understanding up front as to what you get and what it costs.

Try Out Your Theme

As exciting as it is to get your site running, you probably will not have a lot of readers at first. That situation lets you try out a theme or two without upsetting your audience. In this initial phase, get a few posts up and ask people whose opinion you value to comment on your blog's theme. Also, try out its options. If your site is established, try a test-drive plugin, as described in Chapter 7.

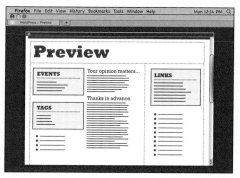

Install Your New Theme

You can install and activate most free themes more easily than you can change your clothes. Installing commercial themes is only slightly more involved. With your new theme, you are ready to make your first impression.

This section assumes you already chose a theme by following the guidance in the preceding section.

Install Your New Theme

Themes Selected through Install Themes on Your Site

Ⓐ After clicking **Appearance** on the Dashboard, the Manage Themes panel opens and displays the two standard WordPress themes.

Ⓑ Twenty Eleven is installed by default.

Ⓒ Twenty Ten is also available in the standard installation.

1 Click **Install Themes**.

The Install Themes panel opens.

2 Type the name of your chosen theme in the search box.

Note: If you have not yet found a theme you like, you can search for a theme by typing terms into the search box.

3 Click **Search**.

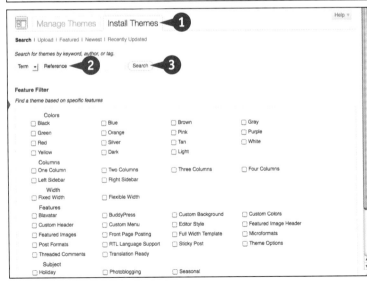

④ The Install Theme panel displays the designated theme; click **Install**.

⑤ A confirmation window opens, and you click **Install Now** to confirm.

WordPress displays installation progress as it installs the theme.

⑥ Click **Activate** to make the theme active.

WordPress activates the theme and returns you to the Manage Themes panel, where your newly active theme appears at the top of the page.

continued ▶

TIPS

My theme does not look the way I expected. Why is that?

You may need to have more content. Or, as themes have gotten more complex, they may require you to select certain theme options to get the expected look. Read the theme's home page for guidance. Find it by going to Wordpress.org/extend/themes for free themes, or to the vendor's home page for premium themes.

What if I have questions about my theme?

The first place to check is the theme designer's website. Designers usually include a link to their site in the footer of their themes, and, if you got the theme at Wordpress.org, you will find a link on the theme's page there. If you have no luck, try the WordPress Codex or the forums at WordPress.org, which Chapter 12 discusses.

Numerous attractive themes are available beyond those listed at WordPress.org. One of them may be closer to the look you want, but they may require manual installation directions, which work for all themes.

Install Your New Theme (continued)

Themes Installed Manually

1 Download the theme you have chosen from the Wordpress.org or the developer's site, and save it to your computer.

A Do not extract it; leave it as a Zip file.

2 Click **OK** in the download window.

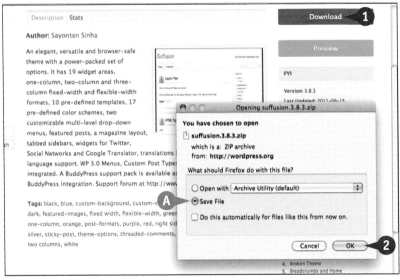

3 On the Install Themes panel — which you reach by clicking **Appearance** in the Dashboard's left menu bar and clicking the **Install Themes** tab — click **Upload**.

A new version of the Install Themes panel opens.

4 Click **Browse**, and find the theme on your computer.

Your computer's File Upload window, or the equivalent, opens. When you locate the theme's Zip file, click **Open**.

The file location appears in the box next to Browse.

5 Click **Install Now**.

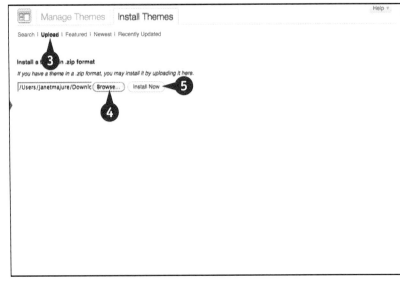

WordPress lists the progress of your installation.

6 When the theme is successfully installed, click **Activate**.

The Manage Themes panel opens with the new theme activated, or it may take you directly to the theme's options panel.

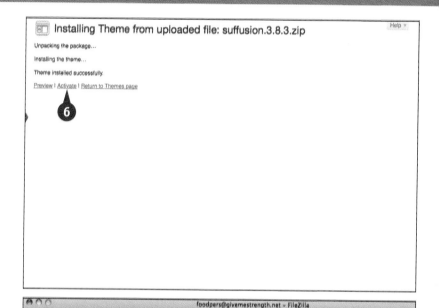

When Uploading from Install Themes Panel Does Not Work

1 After downloading your theme, extract the file, and upload the extracted folder with your FTP software to the themes folder inside the wp-content folder at your web host. Then, go to the Manage Themes panel to activate it.

Note: Check inside the extracted theme folder for a ReadMe.txt file, which may have additional installation instructions.

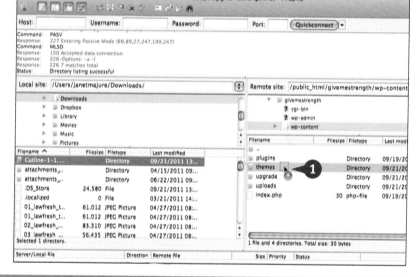

TIPS

I got a bunch of gibberish on my screen when I clicked Activate. What happened?
There is a good chance the theme was activated anyway. Click **Themes** in the left menu bar, and see if your theme appears as the current theme. If not, try clicking **Preview** under the theme image, and then **Activate** in the preview window.

How can I tell if my cost-free theme is also problem-free?
Alas, virtually no theme, including paid ones, guarantees flawless performance. The ratings and comments on the WordPress.org themes pages and forums can help identify potential problem themes. For other themes, review the theme's home page to see whether it provides significant support information or a forum where users can post questions. Try to get a sense of whether the theme developers respond to questions and how quickly.

Choose among Your Theme's Special Settings

Even with a ready-made theme, you can customize the look and function of your theme with its special settings. These may include a wide range of options.

The theme settings vary with each theme, and just two examples appear on these pages. Most theme settings are accessible under Appearance in the left menu bar of the Dashboard or at the bottom of the left menu bar. In Chapter 10 you learn how to change your site's background or header image.

Choose among Your Theme's Special Settings

With the Default Theme

1 Click **Theme Options** under the current theme description.

Note: You can also click **Theme Options** under Appearance in the left menu bar.

The Theme Options window opens.

2 Choose a color scheme (○ changes to ◉).

3 Click **Select a Color** to change the Link Color from the default.

4 A color selector pops up. Choose the hue by clicking in the circle and the intensity by clicking in the square. When you are satisfied, click in the main window.

Ⓐ Click the **Default color** link to restore it.

5 Choose a layout (○ changes to ◉).

6 Click **Save Changes**.

WordPress confirms that the changes have been saved.

7 Click the site name to see your blog in its adjusted theme.

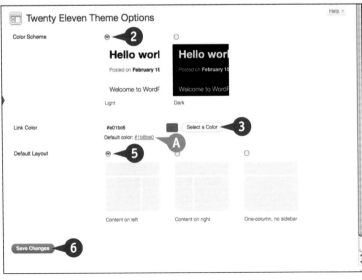

With a Theme with Many Options

1 With a theme such as the Suffusion theme active, click the **Suffusion Options** menu in the left menu bar.

The Suffusion Options window opens and reveals many links — and a *Don't Panic!* message.

B A link to the Support Forum gives you easy access to additional information about using the theme.

C The Quick Search box lets you search for particular Suffusion theme topics.

2 Click the **Skinning** link.

The Suffusion Options Skinning panel opens to the Theme Selection subpanel.

3 Scroll down to see all the preset theme color schemes.

4 Click a color scheme (○ changes to ⊙).

5 Click **Save/Reset** to save the changes.

6 Click the navigation buttons to see more color and type options.

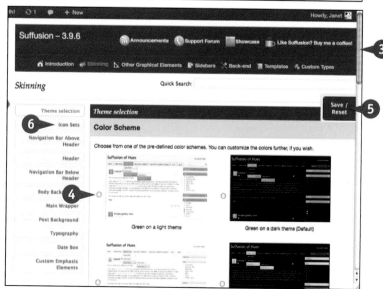

TIPS

The options on my theme are overwhelming. Where do I begin?
One possibility is to stick with the default theme until you feel comfortable with WordPress and its terminology. The other is to get a pencil and paper and crayons — or whatever your preferred tools — and figure out what you are trying to achieve, and then look for those specific theme options, instead of trying to decide yes or no to the plethora of options available to you.

The Dashboard says that my theme supports widgets but that I need to configure them. How do I do that?
You can click the link provided and give it a shot, or read about it in Chapter 7. If you do nothing, the theme presents its default sidebar widgets, which may include content such as a search box or list of recent posts.

CHAPTER 4

Know Your Administration Tools

The WordPress administration panels provide the tools and information you need to manage your website.

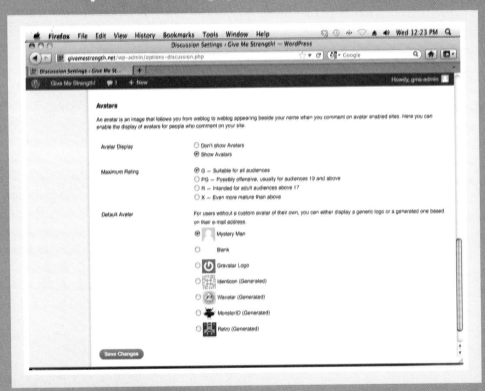

Customize and Navigate the Dashboard

After you log on to your administration pages, which is described in "Log On to Your Blog's Dashboard" in Chapter 3, you can adjust the Dashboard to suit the way you work.

Customize and Navigate the Dashboard

1 Position your mouse pointer over one of the content modules, such as Right Now.

An arrow (▭) appears.

2 Click the arrow to collapse the module.

The module collapses, and only the heading appears.

3 Click the arrow again to expand the module.

Note: This technique works on all the WordPress Dashboard modules.

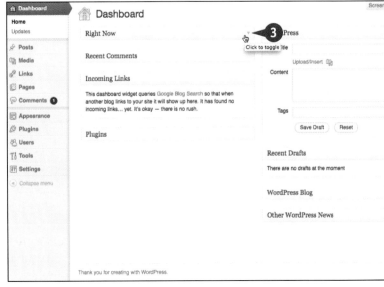

4 Position the mouse pointer over the Recent Comments module (↖ changes to ↜).

The arrow appears, and a link, Configure, also appears.

5 Click **Configure**.

The Recent Comments module reveals a setting for how many comments you want to appear on your Dashboard.

6 Type the number of comments you want in the box.

7 Click **Submit**.

WordPress saves your comments preference and returns to the Recent Comments module.

Note: If you do not want to change the number, you can click **Cancel** to return to the comments list.

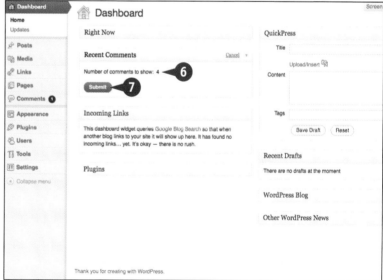

TIPS

How can I hide the left menu bar?
A left-pointing arrow appears next to the words Collapse Menu at the bottom of the menu. Click it, and the menu changes to a narrow band that lists icons with a right-pointing arrow at the bottom. Click it to expand the menu.

My site is at WordPress.com, and it shows modules not discussed here. What are they about?
The Your Stuff module shows your latest WordPress.com activity, including comments you have made on other WordPress.com blogs. What's Hot highlights activity at WordPress.com, including the host and other blogs, and the Stats module reveals data about your site's traffic.

Review the Writing Settings

The writing settings you choose affect the mechanics of how you write your blog posts, whether you write directly into your WordPress interface or post by e-mail or other means. Your writing settings also set your default blog post category.

The Writing Settings page is accessible by clicking **Writing** under the Settings menu in the left menu bar.

Review the Writing Settings

Ⓐ Size of the Post Box

Sets the number of lines of text visible on the New Post page, where you probably write most of your blog posts. 20 is the default number; many people increase or decrease the number according to their typical post length.

Ⓑ Formatting

Lets you select whether WordPress automatically inserts graphic emoticons as you type, such as replacing :) with 😊. Also lets you decide whether WordPress automatically corrects certain XHTML errors. XHTML is a web page programming language. Selecting this is a good idea, although the occasional plugin will not work well with this option selected.

Ⓒ Default Post Category

Lets you choose what category to assign your posts to when you do not specify at the time you write the post. Until you create your own categories, as explained in Chapter 8, the only option is Uncategorized.

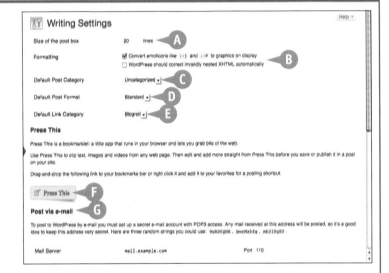

Ⓓ Default Post Format

Lets you choose the default format for posts. Click the arrow (🔽) to see the options, which may vary by theme.

Note: Many themes have only one post format and therefore do not offer this option.

Ⓔ Default Link Category

Lets you choose what link category your favorite links go to. The default and only option is Blogroll until you create more on the Link Categories page.

Ⓕ Press This

Lets you instantly open a writing window with a link to the web page you are viewing. Just drag the Press This icon to your browser's bookmark or favorites bar.

Ⓖ Post via E-Mail (or Post by E-Mail at WordPress.com)

Sets you up to be able to post straight to your blog from e-mail.

Set Up to Post by E-Mail

Posting to your blog by e-mail lets you use your familiar e-mail program to create and publish new blog posts, which can be handy especially when you have a smartphone for sending e-mail. You can set up to do so on the Writing Settings page.

For a self-hosted blog, first create a special, hard-to-guess e-mail address with your web host or Internet service provider to use exclusively for blog posts — because everything sent to that address will be published to your blog.

Set Up to Post by E-Mail

On a Self-Hosted Blog

1 After you set up a special e-mail account, type the mail server information for that account next to Mail Server under Post Via E-Mail.

Note: You can get server information from the provider of your special blog-posting e-mail address.

2 Type your special e-mail address in the Login Name box.

3 Type the e-mail account's password in the Password box.

4 If you have set up post categories, select the default category for your e-mailed posts.

5 Click **Save Changes**.

When you send an e-mail to your special address, WordPress publishes it to your blog, with the e-mail subject line as the post's title.

On WordPress.com

1 After clicking **My Blogs** on the Writing Settings page or Dashboard menu, click **Enable** under Post by Email.

An e-mail address replaces the Enable button. Use that address to post to blog via e-mail.

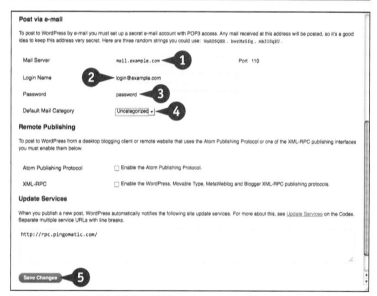

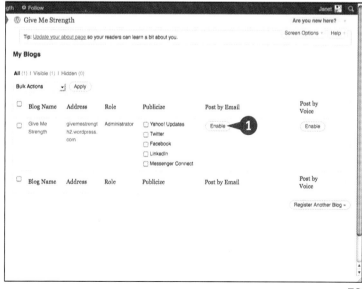

Choose the Discussion Settings

A great thing about blogs is the opportunity to interact with readers. The Discussion Settings let you decide how that interaction operates. Approving, or *moderating*, comments lets you avoid comment spam and block inflammatory comments.

Ⓐ Default Article Settings

Lets you make the default choice as to whether WordPress notifies blogs you link to, accepts notice of links to your site from other blogs, and allows readers to comment.

Ⓑ Other Comment Settings

Sets rules for conditions under which you allow comments.

Ⓒ Threaded Comments

Allows readers and you to respond directly to other comments.

Ⓓ Comment Display Order

Lets you choose whether readers see the newest comment first — or last.

Ⓔ E-Mail Me Whenever

Specifies whether you receive e-mail notification of comments posted or held for moderation. WordPress.com also offers e-mail notifications when someone "likes" a post or subscribes to the blog.

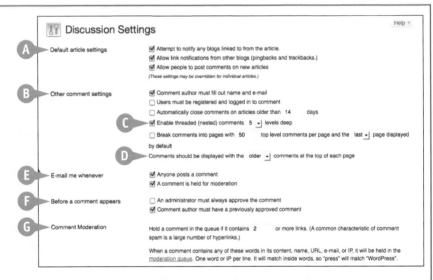

Ⓕ Before a Comment Appears

Lets you choose to review all comments or automatically accept comments from a previously approved commenter.

Ⓖ Comment Moderation

Sets parameters under which comments are held for your review before posting. Options include a box to specify the minimum number of links that provoke moderation and a box in which you can list terms that may be signs of spam comments. A second box, Comment Blacklist, lets you list terms that automatically identify comments as spam. WordPress.com also lets you choose to respond to comments via e-mail and whether to allow visitors to *subscribe to comments*, a feature that notifies them when a comment is added to a particular blog post.

Ⓐ Avatar Display

Indicates whether or not to show *avatars*, which are like personal logos associated with comment writers.

Note: WordPress.com sites also have a setting on this panel for Gravatar hovercards. The setting lets you chose whether to allow hovercards to pop up when you mouse pointer over a person's Gravatar. See "Create Your WordPress.com Profile" in Chapter 2 for more information.

Ⓑ Maximum Rating

Lets you choose which avatar ratings you allow, using the ratings that users provide when they create avatars at Gravatar.com, the avatar service that WordPress uses.

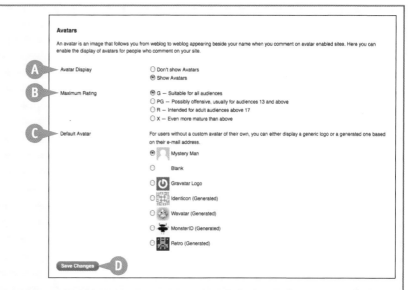

Ⓒ Default Avatar

Allows you to pick a default image for commenters who do not have an avatar. The *generated* options change slightly from one person to the next.

Ⓓ Save Changes

Must be clicked to retain choices on the Comment Settings page.

About Privacy Settings

The Internet may not be the place for you if you want to keep your thoughts secret. Still, you can limit what and where your blog posts are broadcast, and the WordPress privacy settings let you decide.

Self-Hosted Blog Privacy

On self-hosted WordPress blogs, only two settings are available, to allow or disallow search engines such as Google to find your blog. Whichever setting you choose, anyone with the right URL can find your blog. If you do not link to other websites and do not give out your URL, however, your blog is not easily found.

TYV blog 🔍

TYV blog not found; showing *TV* blogs instead

What I'm watching
whatimwatching.blogspot.com/
12 hours ago - Whoa - I just discovered the 'RetroKids' channel! It's every single show I ever watched as a kid! I can't tell you how happy I am - I just curl up on the couch with some hot chocolate and I'm perfectly content. Now where's my teddy bear...?

WordPress.com Blog Privacy

WordPress.com offers the same privacy settings as self-hosted blogs as well as a third option, letting you specify a select group of people who can see your blog. The users must be registered at WordPress.com. WordPress.com employees can read your blog regardless of the settings, and you can add more users for a fee.

○ Allow search engines to index this site.
○ Ask search engines not to index this site.
Note: Neither of these options blocks access to your site — it is up to

◉ I would like my site to be private, visible only to users I choose

Users allowed to access site:

(Invite viewers to your blog)

If you don't add anyone to your site, only you will have access.

Other Kinds of Privacy

If you are concerned about being identified as the writer of your blog, be sure to read the privacy policy of your web host (or of WordPress.com if it hosts your blog). Additional privacy settings called *Visibility* are available on a per-post basis. These are discussed in the next section.

AUT⊙MATTIC

Privacy Policy

Your privacy is critically important to us. At Aut

- We don't ask you for personal information unless we truly gender or income level for no apparent reason.)

Select Your Privacy Settings

You get to choose whether you want the world beating a path to your blog, or whether you would rather keep it to a select few viewers. Once you decide, you can select the appropriate privacy setting. This setting can be changed later, but if your site has been open to search engines, cached pages still may show up in search results.

Select Your Privacy Settings

At WordPress.org

1 Click **Privacy** under the Settings menu in the left menu bar.

2 Choose to ask search engines to index your site, or to ask them not index your site (○ changes to ◉).

3 Click **Save Changes**.

At WordPress.com

1 Click **Privacy** under the Settings menu in the left menu bar.

2 Choose to ask search engines to index your site, to ask them not index your site, or to make your site private (○ changes to ◉).

Note: The last option is not available on self-hosted blogs.

3 Click **Save Changes**.

WordPress saves changes. If you chose to make your site private, the panel adds more options.

4 Click **Invite viewers to your blog**.

5 WordPress.com opens the Invite New panel, where you can invite viewers to your private blog. Friends who are not WordPress. com members will have to sign up.

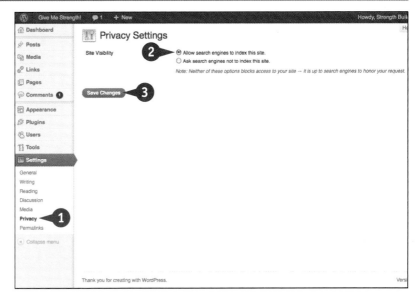

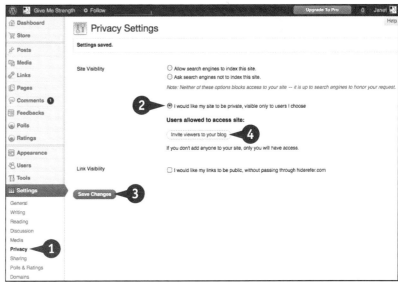

Set the Permalinks Structure

For the self-hosted site owner, the Permalinks setting lets you choose your posts' web addresses pattern. They can be taken from posts' headlines, typically requiring many characters but search-engine friendly, or they can be a relatively short ID that WordPress assigns. Choose a setting that works best for you, and plan to stick with it for best site function. WordPress.com sets the Permalink structure for sites it hosts.

Set the Permalinks Structure

1 Expand the Settings menu, and click **Permalinks**.

2 Click your preferred permalink structure (○ changes to ◉).

Ⓐ The code for your selection appears in the code box.

Note: It is a good idea to select one structure and stick with it as long as you operate your site.

3 Click **Save Changes**.

WordPress saves your selection.

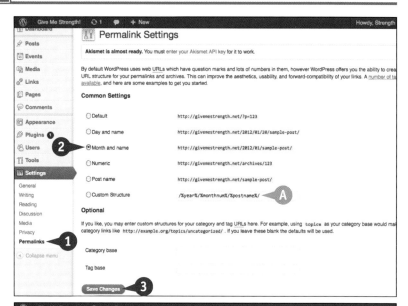

Ⓑ WordPress confirms your Permalink structure change.

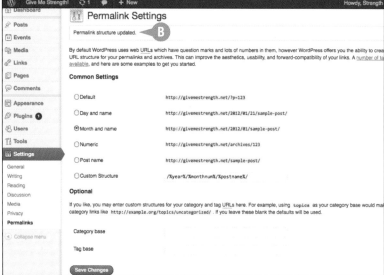

Consider Other Settings

hen you are just starting, you can ignore many of the setting panels. Still, knowing what they are about is helpful so you do not worry. Some of the settings will come into play later as you develop your site. You may never find a use for others.

WordPress.org versus WordPress.com

The settings panels in the two versions of WordPress are among the bigger differences. If you are self-hosting a WordPress.org installation, you choose from a vast array of functions, due primarily to plugins, as discussed in Chapter 7, but the initial basic setup shows just seven items under Settings. That number may grow as you add plugins. WordPress.com comes with a standard set of functions and thirteen items under Settings. They may change from time to time at the discretion of WordPress.com administrators.

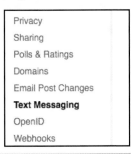

Sharing and More

Sharing, Polls & Ratings, Email Post Changes, Text Messaging, and Open ID settings are available by default only at WordPress.com. They are especially important for building traffic to your blog. See Chapter 9. WordPress.org users can get these same options using plugins.

Reading and Media

These settings affect how your blog content appears. These are discussed in later chapters. The default settings are fine to start.

Webhooks

Webhooks are tools for advanced users. They let you set up WordPress.com to send out notices when particular actions occur on your site. When you are ready to try them out — which may be never! — WordPress.com provides instructions on their use.

CHAPTER 5

Create Written Blog Content

With your blog set up, you can now get in there and produce content! For most blogs, that means writing, and WordPress offers multiple ways to produce written content. One of them will be ideal for you.

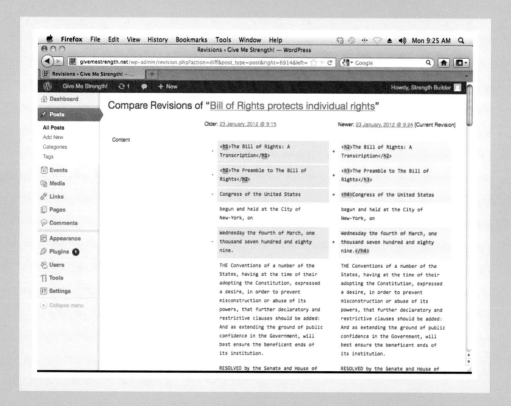

Get to Know the New Post Page

The Add New Post page provides the primary location for creating new posts. You can find everything you need to write, edit, and format your written content on the Add New Post page.

Find the Add New Post page by clicking **Add New** under Posts in the left menu bar. Note that the Add New Post page changes to Edit Post after you have saved or published your post, but the modules stay the same.

Ⓐ Headline Box

Where you type your post's headline.

Ⓑ Media Tools

Let you upload or insert photos (🖻), videos (🎞), and music files (♫). The last icon, 🔆, lets you upload and add links to PDFs, text files, and other documents. WordPress.com has another icon (🎙) for adding a poll.

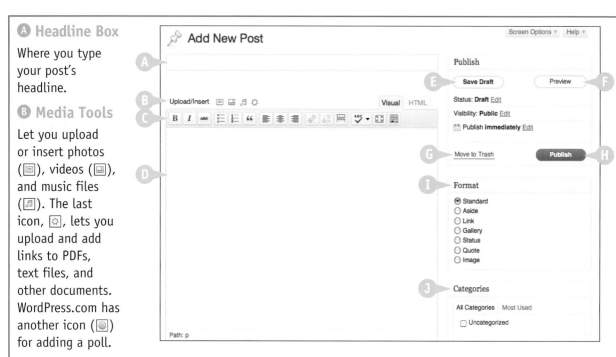

Ⓒ Toolbar

Provides tools to use as you write, edit, and format your post.

Ⓓ Post Box

Gives you room to type your prose.

Ⓔ Save Draft Button

Saves your post.

Ⓕ Preview Button

Prompts browser to display how your draft post would look if published.

Ⓖ Move to Trash Link

Puts an unwanted post into the Trash — to hold or to eliminate later.

Ⓗ Publish Button

Publishes your post to the Internet.

Ⓘ Format Box

Lets you choose post format options. Options — and even the format box — may vary by theme.

Ⓙ Categories Box

Lets you assign your post to a category of your blog.

Ⓐ Writing Helper

Offers two tools to make writing easier, available at WordPress.com but not on self-hosted installations. A copy post plugin is available for WordPress.org users.

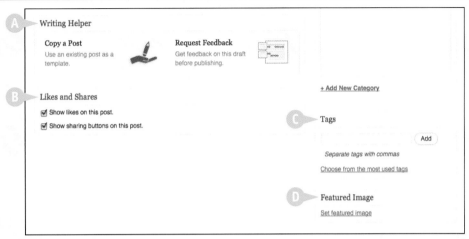

Ⓑ Likes and Shares

Lets you choose whether to show *likes* on a WordPress.com post and to show buttons that make sharing your post easy via social media or e-mail.

Ⓒ Tag Box

Lets you assign tags, which are like keywords, to your posts.

Ⓓ Featured Image

If your theme uses this option, lets you choose images to be featured on particular posts.

Ⓐ Screen Options

Reveals modules that WordPress displays on the Add New Post — and Edit Post — panel.

Ⓑ Discussion

Lets you choose whether to allow comments on an individual post. Overrides default selection under Discussion Settings.

Ⓒ Slug

Specifies the words portion of the post's permalink but generally is not needed for most users.

Ⓓ Author

Presents a drop-down list of authors, which is helpful for multiauthor sites.

Ⓔ Excerpt

Provides a space to write abstracts or teasers for your post that may appear in search results, RSS feeds, and on the front page of some themes.

Ⓕ Send Trackbacks

Lets you notify non-WordPress blogs when your post has linked to them.

Ⓖ Custom Fields

Allows you to add extra information to your post. That information may be data to help search engines find your post or to make a special feature of your theme work. Not available at WordPress.com.

Introducing the WYSIWYG Editor and Toolbar

Y ou can write your blog posts almost as though you were using a word processor when you use the WordPress WYSIWYG — *what you see is what you get* — editor.

The official name of the WYSIWYG editor, or visual editor blog post interface, is TinyMCE, which was created by Moxiecode Systems AB.

A Visual Tab

Is dark gray when active, which means you can use the WYSIWYG editor to write or edit your post.

B Text Formats

Change text you select in the post box to bold, italic, or strikeout, as shown on the formatting buttons.

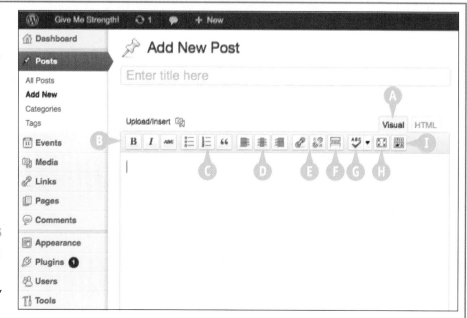

C Paragraph Formats

Assigns special paragraph formats as indicated on the buttons: bulleted list, numbered list, and *block quote*, a style format intended for use when quoting others.

D Text Alignment

Aligns selected text to the left, center, or right.

E Links

Lets you insert or remove links to other web locations.

F Post Break

Inserts a *More* tag in a spot you choose within your blog post so that only part of the post appears on the front page of your blog.

G Spell-Checker

Checks the spelling on the post.

H Full Screen

Toggles your post box to and from a full screen to make it easy to see more or less of your post.

I Extra Buttons

Shows or hides an additional row of buttons.

Ⓐ Styles Menu

Lets you assign an HTML tag to selected text. Read more about HTML in the next section, "Introducing the HTML Editor and Toolbar".

Ⓑ More Formats

Adds underlined text and justified alignment as WYSIWYG formats.

Ⓒ Text Color

Provides the option to add color to text you select.

Ⓓ Pasting Tools

Lets you paste text from browsers or other applications without formatting errors.

Ⓔ Format Eraser

Removes formatting from selected text.

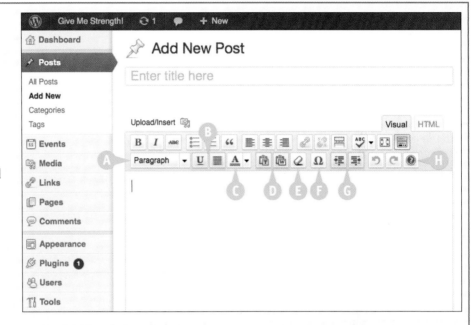

Ⓕ Special Characters

Opens a pop-up window in which you can choose special characters such as mathematical operators, bullets, letters with accents, or *diacritics*, and dashes.

Ⓖ More Indentions

Changes the indention on paragraphs you select but does not add bullets or block quote formats.

Ⓗ Help

Provides added information about the visual editor, including keyboard shortcuts.

I f you are a veteran HTML user, you may prefer to write in the HTML editor window of the post box. Even if you are not an HTML vet, you need to know about it when things do not go as expected with the WYSIWYG editor.

You can find the HTML editor on the New Post Page by clicking the **HTML** tab at the top of the post box.

What Is HTML?

HTML, which is short for *Hypertext Markup Language*, is the publishing language for web pages. HTML, using instructions called *tags*, tells browsers how to display text and other content on a web page.

Benefit of the HTML Editor

As handy as the WordPress WYSIWYG editor is, it sometimes makes mistakes, particularly when you make a lot of formatting changes or paste text from other applications. The HTML editor helps you to clean up the

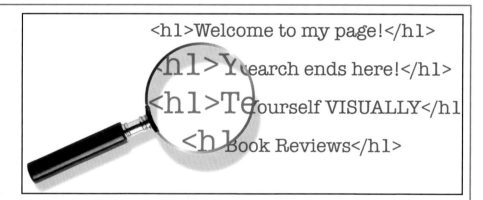

problems. Also, at some stage you may need the HTML editor to insert special advertising links, or *shortcodes*, which are a sort of coding shortcut.

The HTML Editor

Ⓐ HTML Editor Tab

Tells you that you are in the HTML editor.

Ⓑ Quicktag Buttons

Inserts HTML tags individually or as opening and closing HTML tags if you select text before clicking a button.

Ⓒ Post Box

Displays post text with its HTML tags instead of as it appears in a web browser. Shows most HTML tags, as indicated by angle brackets, with a starting tag and an ending tag for each instruction.

Getting the Hang of the Editor

You do not have to be an HTML pro to use the HTML editor, but take a moment to get a little familiar with HTML conventions. When you write your first few blog posts, compare the WYSIWYG versions and the HTML versions simply by clicking the Visual and the HTML tabs at the top of the post box.

Advanced HTML

If, on the other hand, you *are* an HTML whiz, you may love the HTML editor because you can use any HTML tags that you want and thereby do more with your posts than what the visual editor allows. If you want to, you can even disable the visual editor with your Personal Options.

Write and Publish Your First Blog Post

Time to put your words of wisdom on the web! When you write and publish your first blog post, you are a real blogger; no better time to start than now. You can do it in more than one way, but this section covers the most basic method.

Write and Publish Your First Blog Post

Write a Blog Post

1 Click in the headline box and start typing.

Ⓐ WordPress displays your post's permalink. If your permalink structure uses the blog post headline (as all WordPress.com blogs do), WordPress inserts hyphens between the words.

Ⓑ WordPress saves your post as a draft and displays the time saved.

2 Press **Tab** to move to the post box, and start typing.

3 Click **Save Draft** periodically as you work and when you are done.

4 Click **Preview** to see how your post will look when published.

5 Return to the Add New Post window, and review the permalink. To change it, click **Edit**.

A box opens that displays the part of your permalink that you can change.

6 Make any changes you want.

7 Click **OK**.

WordPress saves the permalink and closes the edit permalink box.

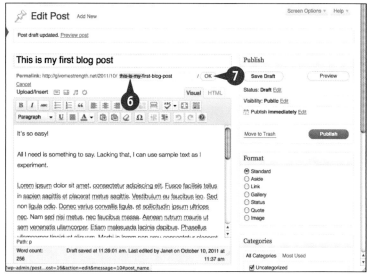

Publish Now

1 If you are satisfied with your post and are ready to publish to the Internet, click **Publish**.

WordPress publishes your post, and notifies you of that fact. You can click **View Post** next to the notice to see your newly published blog post.

Publish Later

2 To schedule your post to publish at a different time, click **Edit**.

The current date and time appear.

3 Change the date and time to when you want the post to publish to the web.

4 Click **OK**.

WordPress displays the Publish box showing the scheduled time. The Publish button now reads Schedule, which you click to confirm that you want the post to be published at the specified time.

What is the Get Shortlink button that appears next to the permalink in the New Post window?

Clicking that button opens a little window that displays a short, alternate link that you may copy for use in places such as Twitter, where a long link might not work well. It does not change the actual permalink.

Can you explain the Visibility settings that appear when you click Edit next to Visibility in the Publish box?

The settings determine who can see a particular post. The default is *Public*, so the reader can see the post. You also may make Public posts *sticky,* which means that post always appears at the top of your home page. *Password Protected* lets you assign a password to the post so only people with the password can read its content. *Private* posts are visible only to you and anyone else you have made an editor or administrator on your site. (More on user capabilities in Chapter 11.)

Add Formatting to Your Text

When you add formatting to your text, you transform your post from one with a rather monotonous appearance to one that looks more inviting and may be easier to skim.

If you previously saved your post as a draft or published it, you can find it by clicking Edit under the Posts menu in the left menu bar.

Add Formatting to Your Text

Add Subheads in the Visual Editor

1 Select the text whose format you want to change.

2 Click the drop-down menu next to Paragraph to reveal formatting options.

3 Click the format you want to apply.

WordPress applies the formatting to the selected text.

Note: In default HTML, the smaller the heading number, the bigger the type.

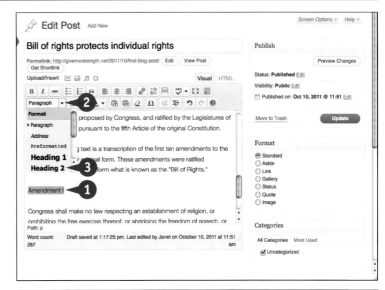

Change the Appearance of Type

1 Select the text whose format you want to change.

2 Click the toolbar button that corresponds to the change you want to make.

WordPress changes the text as you directed.

Note: **B** (B) is for bold, *I* (I) for italic, ~~ABC~~ (ABC) for strikethrough, and U̲ (U) for underline.

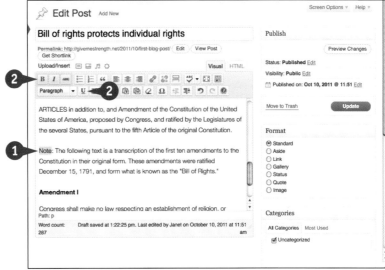

Change Paragraph Formatting

1 Click anywhere within the paragraph you want to change.

Note: Click and drag to select multiple paragraphs.

2 Click a paragraph formatting button to apply.

WordPress changes the paragraph format as you specified. In this example, it indented a paragraph.

3 Click **Update** to save changes.

4 Click **View Post** to see how your changes look.

WordPress opens the blog post.

View Your Changes

A An example of boldface.

B An example of a Heading 2.

C An example of an indented paragraph.

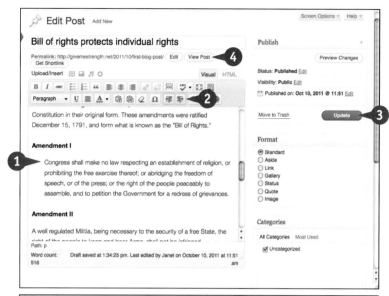

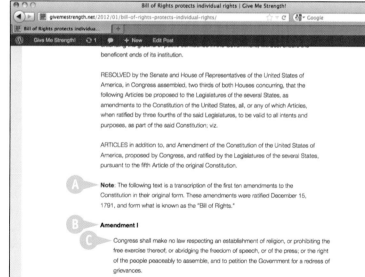

TIPS

How do I change the text color?

Select the text you want to change, click the color formatting button (🔲), and then click the color of your choice.

Is there any quicker way to change the formatting?

Yes. Pressing **Ctrl** on a PC (**⌘** on a Mac) plus the following letters changes the text using keystrokes only:

B	Bold	**1**	Heading 1
I	Italic	**2**	Heading 2
U	Underline	**3**	Heading 3
		4	Heading 4

Recall an Earlier Version of Your Blog Post

U h-oh. You have writer's remorse and wish you could change your post back to the way you wrote it earlier. Post Revisions to the rescue! This revision-saving feature of WordPress lets you view and restore earlier versions of a post. What a relief.

Once you have saved your post, even if you have not published it, a simple *undo* command does not undo the changes.

Recall an Earlier Version of Your Blog Post

1 Click **Screen Options** to expand the Show on Screen options.

2 Click **Revisions** (☐ changes to ☑).

3 Click **Screen Options** to collapse the options.

4 Scroll to the bottom of your Edit Post page. A list of post revisions appears.

5 Click the version that you think you would like to restore.

WordPress opens a new page that displays that version, in the HTML format and, at the bottom of that page, the list of revisions that you can compare.

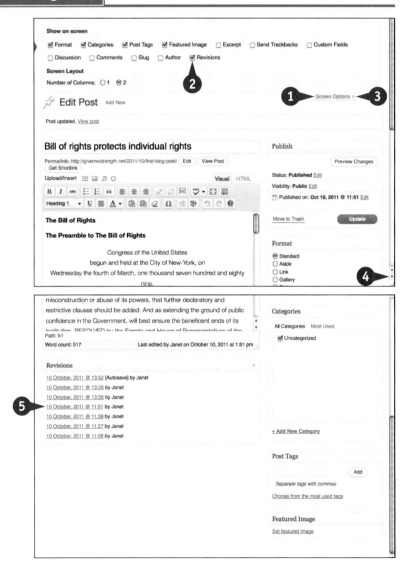

6 Click the revisions that you want to compare (○ changes to ◉).

Note: One button must be in the left column of buttons, and the other must be in the right column.

7 Click **Compare Revisions**.

WordPress displays the two versions side by side, and it highlights places in which the two versions are different.

Ⓐ Older version appears on left.

Ⓑ Newer version appears on right.

Ⓒ Specific changes show darker highlighting.

8 When you have identified the desired previous version, click **Restore**.

WordPress restores the desired version and returns you to the Edit Post page.

9 Make any changes you want, and then click **Update** if the post already has been published (or **Save Draft** if the post has not been published).

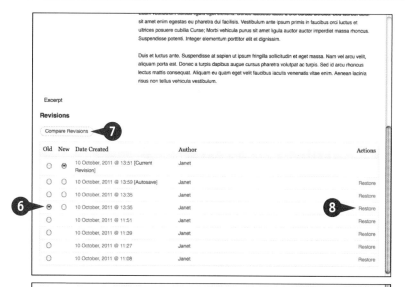

TIPS

Can I compare one old version with another old version?
Yes. Just click the radio buttons beside the versions you want to compare.

I relied on WordPress automatically saving my post as I worked, but I see only one Autosave version in the list. How can I get an earlier Autosave version?
You cannot. WordPress keeps only the most recently automatically saved version. Hence, you need to click **Save Draft** (or **Update Post**) as you work if you want to have access to older versions.

Write and Publish a Page

U nlike many blog platforms, WordPress allows you to write and publish *pages*. Pages are *static*, meaning they do not change as you add posts. Most themes make pages always accessible from your blog's home page.

The initial installation of the WordPress software (or blog registration at WordPress.com) by default includes one page. WordPress also lets you make *child* or *subpages* of pages.

Write and Publish a Page

1 Under Pages in the left menu bar, click **Add New**.

The Add New Page panel opens.

2 Type a headline or label in the headline box.

Note: If your theme displays your pages as tabs on your home page, use a short label.

3 Type your text in the page text box.

Note: If desired, add formatting as described in "Add Formatting to Your Text."

4 Click **Save Draft**.

A WordPress saves your work.

Note: Click **Save Draft** periodically as you work and when you are done.

B A permalink appears, which you can edit if desired.

Note: Unlike post permalinks, page default permalinks have no reference to dates or numbers.

C The panel title changes to Edit Page.

5 Click the drop-down menu under Parent, next to *(no parent)*.

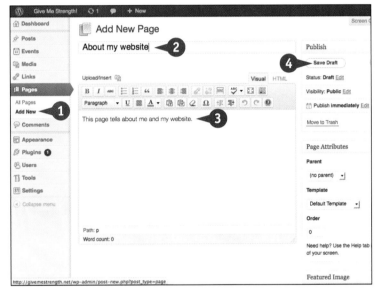

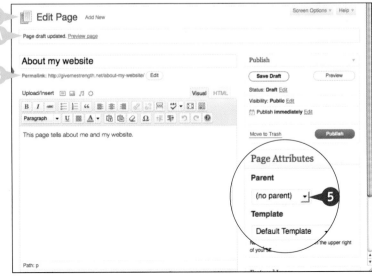

6 Click **Sample Page** (or **About** at WordPress.com) to make that page the *parent* of the new page you just made. If you prefer to keep your page as a main page rather than a subpage, simply collapse the menu and proceed.

D Pages usually appear in alphabetical order, but you can assign each page a number to specify the order in which your home page lists your other pages.

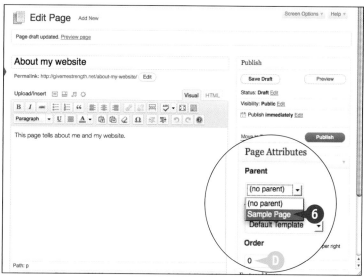

E Some themes include more than one page template, or standard page layout. Those themes have a Template section in the Page Attributes module, and you can choose a template from this list.

7 When you are done, click **Save Draft**.

8 When you are ready to publish your page to your website, click **Publish**.

Note: The Publish module works the same for pages as it does for posts. See "Write and Publish Your First Blog Post" for more.

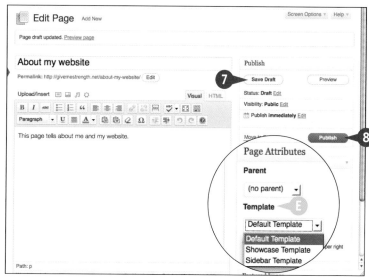

TIPS

What can I use pages for?
You can use one as the home page for your blog by selecting it in the Reading Settings. You can use a page or pages to display products or family photos or link lists or *FAQs*, frequently asked questions. Essentially, you can use them for just about anything you would use a web page for. See Chapter 11 for more ideas.

I do not understand the parent and child pages.
Parent pages are main pages and their names generally appear on your home page's menu bar. *Child* pages are like subpages; that is, they are secondary to the parent pages, which can be helpful to avoid cluttering your main page menus.

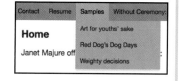

Edit or Delete a Post or Page

Knowing how to edit or delete a post or a page after you have published it or saved it as a draft lets you keep your content current. It also lets you write and edit at your convenience and then return to finish later. The Quick Edit feature lets you edit just about everything but the text in a post or page — all without leaving the main Posts or Pages panel.

The editing process is the same for posts and pages. This section uses a post as an example.

Edit or Delete a Post or Page

Basic Editing

1 Click **Posts** (or **Pages**).

The Posts (or Pages) panel opens and lists all your posts. You can:

A Filter posts by date or category or both.

B Search posts.

C View posts in a list, as shown, or with the headline and *excerpt*, which is either a summary you wrote on the Edit Post page or the first 55 words of your post if you did not write an excerpt.

D Browse the Posts list.

2 Click the title on the post (or page) you want to edit.

The Edit Post (or Edit Page) window opens. You can edit and update as you did when you first wrote a new post or page.

Basic Deletion of Post or Page

1 Position the mouse pointer over the post (or page) you want to delete.

2 Click **Trash**.

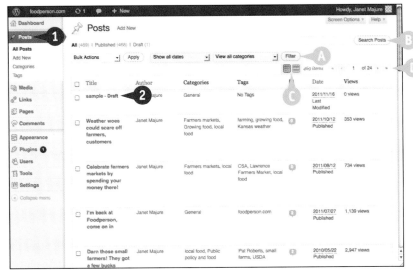

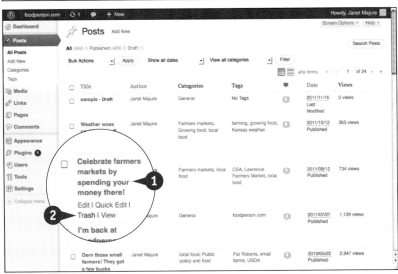

Quick Edit Posts or Pages

1 Position the mouse pointer over the post (or page) you want to edit.

2 Click **Quick Edit**.

The Quick Edit panel opens.

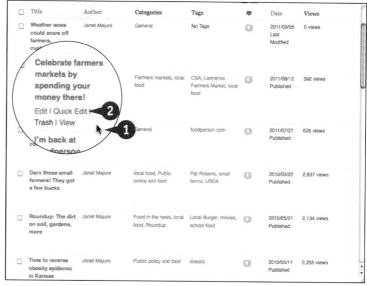

E The Quick Edit panel lets you edit the post or page title, slug — the editable part of the URL — categories, and more. Options are slightly different on the Quick Edit page screen.

3 After you make your changes, click **Update** to save.

WordPress collapses the Quick Edit panel and returns you to the list of posts or pages.

Can I recover a post or page I sent to Trash?

Yes, for up to 30 days. At the top of the Posts or Pages panel is a count of your current posts or pages. If you have any items in Trash, a Trash link appears. Click it to find your trashed items. Position your mouse pointer over the item you want to keep until you see the Recover link, and click it.

Is the Edit link that appears under the post or page title different from clicking on the title?

No, it is just another way to arrive at the same destination, the Edit Post (or Edit Page) panel.

Add Text Hyperlinks to Your Post or Page

When you add hyperlinks, you can give others credit for ideas you mention or quote, lead readers to additional pertinent information, and reach out to fellow bloggers, who love it when you link to them.

A hyperlink is a reference to another location on the web — including elsewhere on your site.

Add Text Hyperlinks to Your Post or Page

1 Select the URL on the page you want to link to and copy it.

Note: With most browsers, you can copy the URL by pressing `Ctrl`+`C` (`⌘`+`C` on a Mac). Or, you can select **Copy** from the Edit menu.

2 Click the text that you want to make into a hyperlink within your post or page.

3 Click the link icon on the toolbar (🔗).

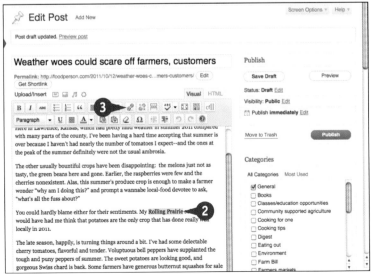

④ In the Insert/edit link window, paste the URL in the URL box.

Note: The URL needs to include the *protocol*, or http:// portion, of the web address, and WordPress automatically includes it.

⑤ Type the name of the page.

Note: The Title text is optional. Readers see it when they position their mouse pointer over a link. If you do not type anything in the Title box, readers see the URL.

⑥ Click **Add Link**.

WordPress returns to the Edit Post page.

Ⓐ The text you selected appears as a hyper link, and the Title text appears when you position your mouse pointer over the link. The link is active when you preview the page or publish it.

⑦ Click **Save Draft**.

The link is saved to your site.

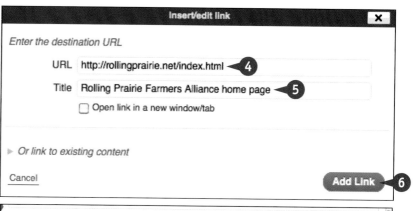

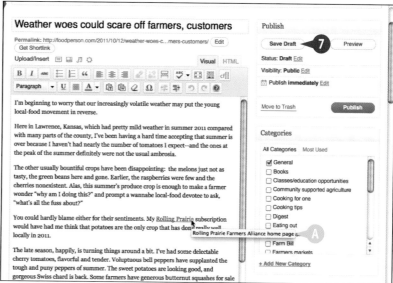

TIPS

How do I link to another page on my site?
Click **Or link to existing content** and then scroll through your site's posts and pages or search to find what you are looking for. When you type a search term in the Search box, WordPress automatically filters your site's content for that word. When you click the content you want, WordPress enters the URL and the post or page title for you, and all you need to do is click **Add Link**.

Can I get the link to open in a new window rather than the same window as my blog?
Yes. Simply click **Open link in a new window** (☐ changes to ☑). If not specified, WordPress sends readers to the linked page in the same window where they were reading your blog.

Paste Text from Other Sources

You can write blog posts in Microsoft Word — even do considerable formatting — and then paste them into your WordPress post (or page text) box and keep the formatting, as long as you know how. Doing so eliminates extra coding that can mess up web pages. You also can remove unwanted formatting from word processors or web pages with WordPress's special pasting tools.

Paste Text from Other Sources

Paste from Word Documents

1. After copying the text in a Word document that you want to use in your blog, go to the New Post or Edit Post page where you want to paste the text in WordPress. Click the **Word Paste** button (▤).

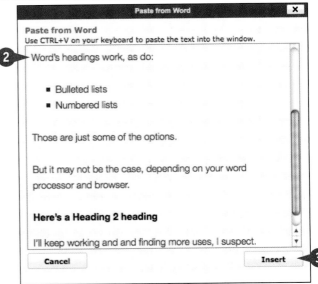

The Paste from Word window opens.

2. Press **Ctrl**+**V** (**⌘**+**V** on a Mac) to insert the copied Word text.

WordPress pastes the text without extraneous coding.

3. Click **Insert**.

Your copy, as written in Word, appears in the post (or page text) box.

Paste Formatted Type as Text

1 After copying the text, such as from another web page, that you want to put in your post or page, click the **Paste Text** button (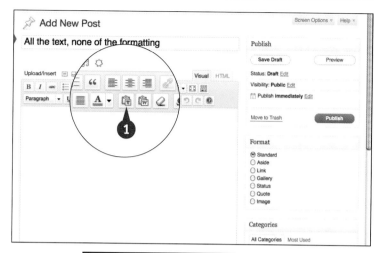).

The Paste as Plain Text window opens.

2 Press `Ctrl`+`V` (`⌘`+`V` on a Mac) to insert the copied text.

WordPress pastes the text without formatting.

Ⓐ You may choose not to retain line breaks by clicking **Keep linebreaks** (☑ changes to ☐).

3 Click **Insert**.

Your copy appears as plain text in the post (or page text) box.

TIPS

Why would I want to paste text without formatting?

Pasting copied material from other websites as plain text and then adding whatever formatting you want is often easier than removing and reformatting text that you copied. If you are skeptical, paste something from another web page straight into the Visual blog post window. Then, click the **HTML** tab to see the coding. Chances are you will see a *lot* of code, even though it may not appear to change things much in the Visual editor.

I pasted a table from Word, which looks fine, but I cannot seem to type anything below it. What should I do?

Click the **HTML** tab at the top of the post or page text entry window. You will see `</table>` at the end of the table. Click after that HTML tag and start typing. Then, return to the Visual editor and proceed as usual. The same remedy — switching to the HTML editor — can solve similar problems whenever you are having trouble adding or formatting text.

Post from Your Mobile Device

E ven if your main computer is in your pocket, you can still post updates to your WordPress website or blog. Exactly how you do it will vary according to the device, but no matter what device you use, you probably can do it. Once you are set up, most apps also let you moderate comments.

Apps for Self-Hosted Sites

WordPress.org apps are available for iOS, Android, Blackberry, Windows Phone 7, Nokia, and webOS. Go to http://wordpress.org/extend/mobile for links to downloads and more information.

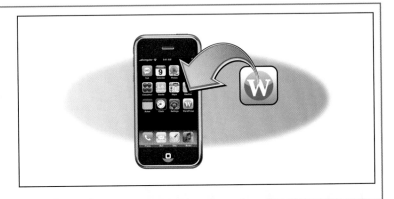

Apps for WordPress.com Sites

The same operating systems — for iOS, Android, Blackberry, Windows Phone 7, Nokia, and webOS — that have apps for WordPress.org sites also have apps for WordPress.com. Get more information or downloads at http://en.support. wordpress.com/apps.

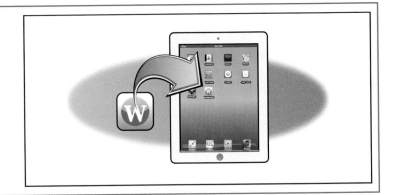

Options for Other Mobile Devices

If you are a WordPress.com user, you can go to m.wordpress.com on your mobile device, log in using your Wordpress.com login information, click the **Post** tab, and start writing. Self-hosted site owners can use a plugin for other mobile devices. Chapter 7 discusses plugins.

102

Create a Post with QuickPress

The QuickPress module on your Dashboard lets you write and publish posts or save drafts in a hurry. See something on the Dashboard that inspires you — maybe a recent comment or news item? You can type up your thoughts without so much as going to another page.

Create a Post with QuickPress

1 Type a headline or title in the Title box.

2 Type your post in the Content box.

Note: You can add simple HTML tags such as <b> for bold and </b> for end bold.

Ⓐ The media buttons are available.

Ⓑ A Tags box lets you assign tags.

3 Click **Save Draft**.

WordPress saves your draft and clears the QuickPress entry boxes.

Note: You can publish immediately if you prefer by clicking **Publish**.

4 Click **Edit post** in the confirmation box.

WordPress opens the post in the Edit Post panel.

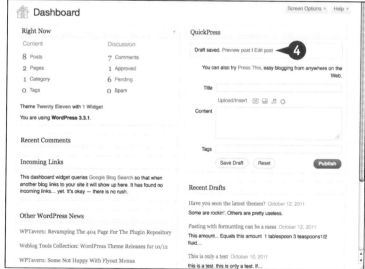

Create a Post with PressThis

T he Press This *bookmarklet,* a bit of JavaScript stored as a bookmark, grabs web page information and lets you see it immediately in a post-writing box. It does not get much simpler when you want to write about something you see on the web.

Create a Post with PressThis

1 On the Tools panel, accessible by clicking Tools in the left menu bar, click the **Press This** bookmarklet and drag it to your bookmarks or *favorites* menu bar of your browser.

Press This appears as a bookmark on your browser.

Note: You only need to install the bookmarklet the first time you use it.

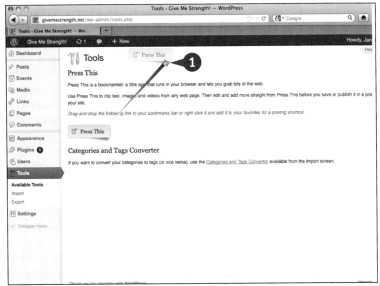

2 Select the text you are interested in quoting or commenting on.

3 Click **Press This**.

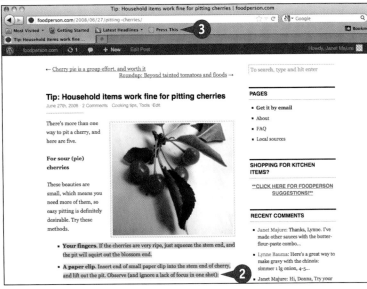

A Press This window opens.

Ⓐ The web page's title appears in the Title box

Ⓑ Your selected text appears in the content box.

Ⓒ A link to the page appears at the bottom.

④ Edit the title and content.

⑤ Click **Publish**.

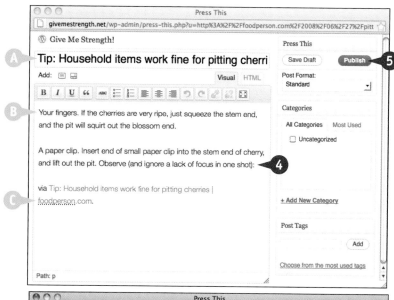

WordPress publishes your post and gives you a confirmation message.

Note: You can save a draft if you prefer by clicking **Save Draft**.

⑥ Click **Close Window** to return to the web page you were browsing.

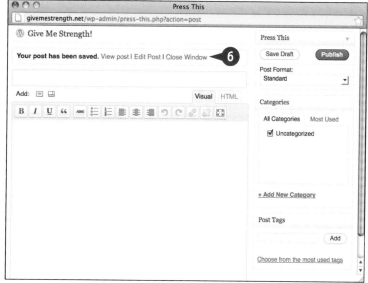

I am using Internet Explorer, and I cannot get the bookmarklet to work. What do I do?

Unfortunately, Press This and IE do not play well together. If you want to use it, try a different browser, such as Firefox, Google Chrome, or Safari.

I dragged the bookmarklet to the toolbar, but I do not see it. Where is it?

Check to make sure your bookmarks toolbar is visible. Click **Help** in your browser if you are not sure where that option is.

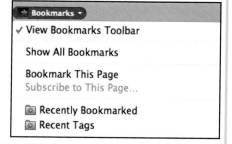

Consider Using a Blogging Client

You can download programs, called *clients*, that let you write your blog post offline. These programs mean you do not have to be connected to the Internet to write your posts, and you may like the interface more than you like the WordPress Write/Edit Post panels.

Advantages of Blogging Clients

Advantages vary, but a couple are fairly consistent among blog clients. One is that you can write posts without having to go online, and then you can post your creations, formatted and with images if you want, in fewer steps. Also, many clients allow you to use more keyboard shortcuts when typing and provide easy ways to do fancier formatting, including inserting tables.

Available Blogging Clients

Windows Live Writer, which is for PCs, is among the most popular clients, but several others are available, including clients for Macintosh and Linux. You can find lists at http://codex.wordpress.org/Weblog_Client or http://en.support.wordpress.com/xml-rpc for WordPress.com blogs.

Windows Live Writer 2011

How Blog Clients Work

When you use a blog client, you write in the interface provided and you supply the logon information that you use for your blog. You then create your blog posts, and when you are ready to publish, the client publishes your post. Some clients can publish to multiple blogs.

Other Writing Interfaces

In addition to blogging clients, which are on your computer, some third-party online blog-writing and browser extensions are available. They offer features such as seeking additional content for you from the web as you write or complex formatting options. They are listed at the same URLs as the clients.

Create a Post with Windows Live Writer

A popular blogging client, Windows Live Writer, is free, and you will recognize many functions if you are familiar with Microsoft Word. Windows Live Writer is an excellent blog client for PC users but is not available for Mac.

To start, download the client from http://explore.live.com/windows-live-writer and install it. Then, start the program and provide the configuration information requested. You can get help at http://explore.live.com/windows-live-writer-help-center.

Create a Post with Windows Live Writer

1 While logged into your blog, go to the Writing Settings page and click **XML-RPC** (☐ changes to ☑).

2 Click **Save Changes**.

Note: WordPress.com blogs always have this setting enabled.

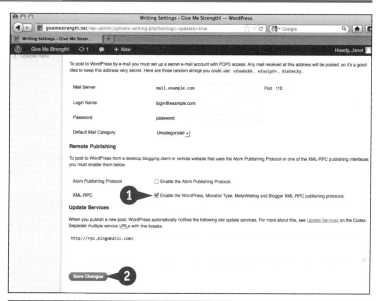

3 In Windows Live Writer, type a headline in the box provided.

Note: The headline box outline disappears after you click outside the box.

4 Type your message in the space below the headline.

5 Click the **Preview** tab to see how your post will look on your site.

6 Click **Save** under the File menu, or press `Ctrl`+`S` to save your work.

7 When you are finished with your post, click **Publish**.

Windows Live Writer uploads your post to your blog and publishes it.

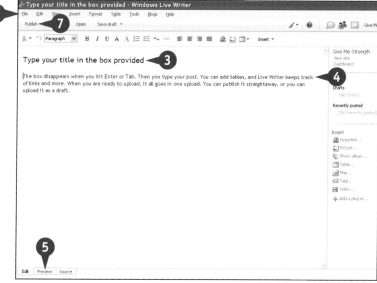

Import Posts from Another Blogging Platform

I f you have come to WordPress from a different blogging platform, you probably can import your old posts to WordPress. WordPress provides tools to help you make the transition.

This example imports from Blogger, the widely used blogging platform from Google.

Import Posts from Another Blogging Platform

1 Click **Tools**.

The Tools menu expands.

2 Click **Import**.

The Import panel appears.

3 Click **Blogger**.

4 An Install Importer window opens. Click **Install Now**, and then click **Activate Plugin & Run Importer** in the next screen.

The Import Blogger panel opens.

5 Click **Authorize** to allow Google to send your Blogger data.

6 The Google Accounts window opens, where you click **Grant access**.

A Blogger Blogs panel opens that displays all Blogger blogs associated with your Google account.

7 Click **Import** next to the blog you want to import.

Ⓐ The Posts and Comments columns indicate the progress of your import. If your previous blog was large, the import process may take a while. WordPress allows you to go to other pages and check back periodically if you want.

8 When the import is finished, your Blogger posts and comments appear on your WordPress blog, and the Import button changes to Set Authors. Click **Set Authors**.

The Author Mapping panel opens.

9 Click the drop-down menu under WordPress Login to associate the Blogger username with the WordPress user.

Note: You will have only one choice if there is only one author on your WordPress blog.

10 Click **Save Changes**.

Your former Blogger entries now are published and listed with the author you selected.

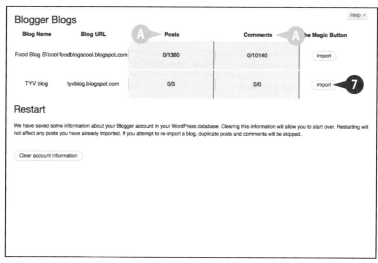

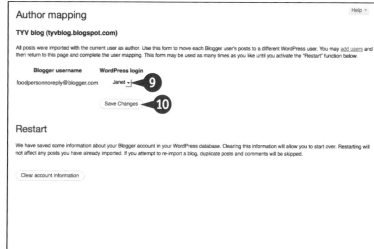

TIPS

I got a message saying the importer cannot authenticate my Blogger blog at Google. Is there anything to do?
You can go to www.google.com/support/blogger/bin/answer.py?hl=en&answer=97416. It explains how to export your blog, which creates a file you can save to your hard drive and then import to your WordPress blog.

My import was going okay and then stopped. What do I do?
Click **Clear account information**. It takes you back to the import panel. You can repeat the steps you took before, and WordPress will resume your import without duplicating posts.

CHAPTER 6

Create Visual and Audio Content

Just because the program is called *Word*Press does not mean pictures and sounds are not welcome. In fact, WordPress provides all the tools you need to use images, audio, and video files with your blog.

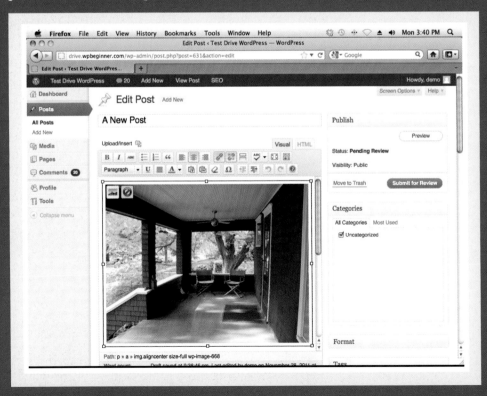

Consider Media Issues

A blog rarely includes words and only words. You, too, can enrich your readers' blog experience by including images, sounds, and even video on your blog. For best results, it helps to understand a bit about how the Internet handles your media.

Images and Dimensions

Web browsers display images according to the number of pixels specified for them. If you upload an image 1600 pixels wide, but you have room only for a 500-pixel image, the browser reduces the image to display it. The large image causes the page to load more slowly than a 500-pixel image would have.

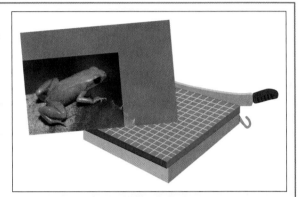

Media Selection

Well-chosen media enhances a blog, but too much or poorly chosen media can be a distraction. Well-chosen media includes a map that shows a location you recommend, a photograph that illustrates a point you have made, or a video clip that demonstrates a process you describe. A poor choice might include a fuzzy photo that fails to make the desired point.

Media and Memory

One picture may be worth *more* than a thousand words in terms of computer memory. Sound and video files use even more memory. In fact, WordPress.com requires you to pay for increased memory if you want to upload sound and video. If your blog is self-hosted, make sure to you have enough space with your host to accumulate sound and video files.

Review Media Settings

The default settings may be fine for you, but you need to review them to make sure they provide the best options for your needs. They let you set standard image sizes for a consistent look and keep track of where you store media files online. These settings can save you time and trouble in the long run.

Review Media Settings

At WordPress.org

1 Click **Media** under the Settings menu in the left menu bar.

The Media Settings window opens.

2 Review the thumbnail, medium and large dimensions to make sure they are appropriate for your blog and theme.

Note: You can use Information button in the Web Developer Toolbar introduced in Chapter 10 to determine your blog theme's dimensions.

3 Click **Crop thumbnail** (☑ changes to ☐) unless you want thumbnails to display to an exact size that you specify. (This option is unavailable at WordPress.com.)

4 Click **Save Changes**.

At WordPress.com

1 Review settings as for WordPress.org above.

2 Ignore the Video Player setting for now.

Note: This setting is applicable only if you purchase the VideoPress add-on discussed later in this chapter.

3 Click **Save Changes**.

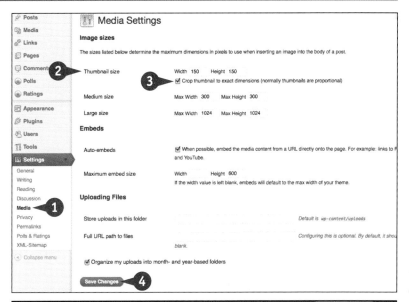

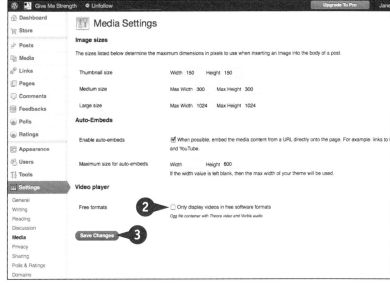

Prepare Images for Uploading

When you take the time to edit and resize images before you post them on your blog, you assure that your images look their best and do not slow down your site.

Although WordPress provides some online editing tools, you will do better with an image editor to prepare your photos and other images. It can be a simple and free program, such as GIMP or Picasa, or the do-it-all Adobe Photoshop. If you have a digital camera, it may provide a basic editing program, too.

Crop to Focus Interest

Crop is the term that editors use for trimming images. Use your editor's cropping tool to eliminate distracting activity, objects, or blank areas or to zero in on the item of particular interest. Save an unedited version of the photo, although your editor may do so automatically, in case you change your mind.

Adjust the Image

Take advantage of the editor's tools to eliminate "red eye" in flash photos, to straighten out sloping horizons, and to correct poorly rendered color, contrast, and other image flaws. You want people to see the image, not be put off by its shortcomings.

Annotate the Image

Add arrows, labels, and other notations to your image if they would help readers. For example, a simple "start here" and an arrow can make a map much more meaningful to your readers than a large amount of text. Similarly, clear labels on graphs aid in understanding.

Save the Image

After you have finished editing, you need to save your image in a file format that web browsers can display properly. The acceptable formats are JPEG, which stands for Joint Photographic Experts Group; GIF, or Graphics Interchange Format; and PNG, for Portable Network Graphics.

Choose a File Format

GIF is best for images with few colors because it retains quality and creates a small file. GIF often is good for logos. JPEG supports millions of colors and thus is good for photographs, but it creates bigger files unless you increase compression, which reduces JPEG image quality. PNG is the newest format and shares many GIF advantages, but a few old browsers may not support it.

Resize the Image

Chances are reasonably good that your image is bigger than you want on your blog, especially if you downloaded it full size from a digital camera. View the image at 100 percent size in your image editor to see how big the image *really* is. Use your editor's resizing tools to reduce it to the largest size you would want it to appear on your site.

Upload and Insert an Image While Posting

By using the tools that WordPress provides, you can upload your images from your computer in a batch or one at a time. Then, you can insert them into your blog posts to add some visual pizzazz to your site.

You can upload and insert images as part of your post-writing process or as a separate operation.

Upload and Insert an Image While Posting

① From the Add New Post or Edit Post page, click in your post at the location where you want to insert your image.

② Click the **Add Media** button (🖼).

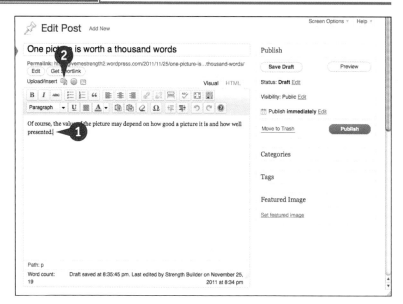

Ⓐ The Add Media window opens.

③ Drag an image from a folder on your computer to the upload window, and release the mouse button when the border of the drop-files area changes color.

A bar appears, showing the upload progress. When the item is done uploading, a thumbnail of the image and details about it appear at the bottom of the window.

Note: You can drag multiple files if you want. Also, if you do not like drag and drop, you can click **Select Files** instead to choose your file or files.

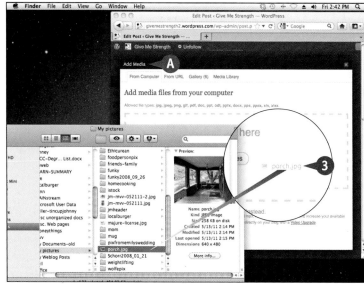

116

④ In the Title box, type the words that you want to appear on the web page when a viewer positions the mouse pointer over the picture.

Note: The default title is the image's filename.

⑤ Type alternate text to describe the image.

⑥ Click **Insert into Post**.

Ⓑ The Add Media window disappears, and the Edit Post window displays the image at the cursor location.

⑦ Click **Save Draft/ Update Post**, depending on whether the post is a new draft or an existing post, to save the change.

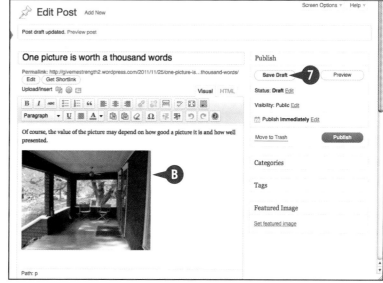

TIPS

I followed the directions, but my image did not upload. What should I do?
The first thing to do is to click the *browser uploader* link under the area for dragging and dropping files. After the window changes, click **Browse** to find the file on your computer, and upload it. This way allows you to upload only one file at a time.

My image took forever to upload, and I have a high-speed connection. What is going on?
First, Internet upload speeds typically are slower than download speeds. The bigger issue, however, probably is that your image file is too large. Try to keep it less than 150 kilobytes or so for fast uploads and space conservation.

Insert Images into the Media Library

Depending on how you work, you may find it more convenient to upload your images without worrying about where they go in your blog posts. You can do that by adding them to the Media Library with the multi-file uploader. The Media Library also provides a searchable repository for your images and other media.

Insert Images into the Media Library

1 Click **Media** in the left menu bar.

The Media menu expands, and the Media Library window opens.

2 Click **Add New**.

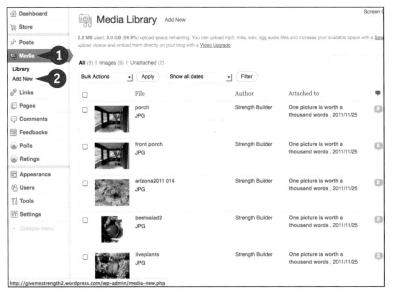

The Upload New Media panel opens.

3 Click **Select Files**.

Note: You also can drag and drop images as described in the previous section.

A file selection window opens.

④ Select the file or files you want to upload.

Note: Press **Ctrl** (⌘ on a Mac) to select multiple files.

⑤ Click **Open**.

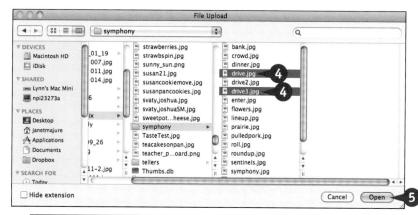

WordPress uploads the files to your server and stores them in your Media Library.

⑥ When finished, click **Save all changes**.

WordPress returns to the Media Library, which shows the new additions.

Can I just upload images with my FTP client?
Yes, if you have a self-hosted blog. Simply upload the images from your computer to the correct folder, or directory, or your server. See your Miscellaneous Settings if you are unsure where to upload your files.

How do I insert images from the Media Library into my posts or pages?
When writing a post or page, click the **Add Media** button (⊞), and then click the **Media Library** tab in the Add Media window. Click **Show** to the right of the image you want to use, which reveals its settings, and click **Insert into Post** to close the dialog box and add the image to the post or page.

Add Media

From Computer From URL Media Library

Add media files from your computer

Allowed file types: jpg, jpeg, png, gif, pdf, doc, ppt, odt, pptx, docx,

Insert Images from Web Sources

You can save storage space on your web host when you insert images based on other websites. You do not have to download or upload the image files; you embed, or *link*, them with a URL. Sometimes, though, this can slow your page loading time or set the stage for a future broken link.

Get permission from the image owner to use the image, unless the image is in the public domain or the website gives copyright permission.

Insert Images from Web Sources

1 Right-click the image you want to link to (or ⌘+click on a Mac).

2 Click **Copy Image Location**.

The link is saved to your computer's clipboard.

3 Click the **Add Media** button (🖼) at the top of a post- or page-writing window where you want the image to appear.

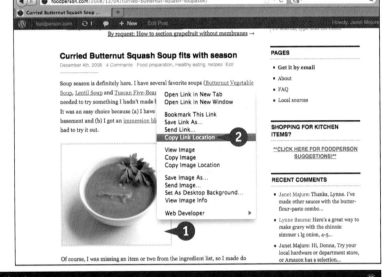

The Add Media window opens.

4 Click **From URL**.

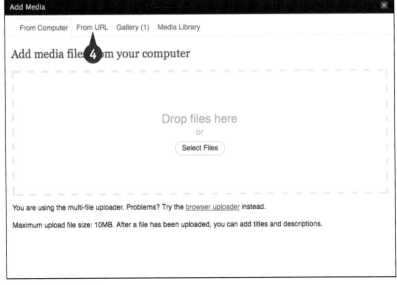

The Insert Media from Another Website window opens.

5 Type or paste a copied image URL in the URL box.

A WordPress checks the URL and displays a green check mark for a valid URL and a red X for an invalid one.

6 Type a title, which a reader sees when positioning the mouse pointer over the image, in the Title box.

7 Type alternate text describing the image.

8 Click **Insert into Post**.

B The Add Media window disappears, and the Add New Post/Edit Post window displays the image where your cursor was.

9 Click **Save Draft**.

10 Click **Publish** to publish the post on your website.

Note: Media embedded into your blog via other websites' URLs are not saved to your Media Library.

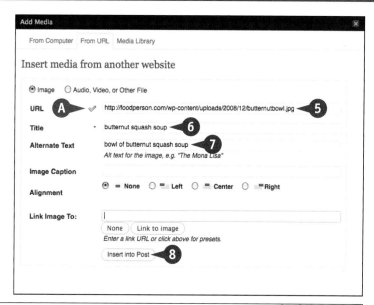

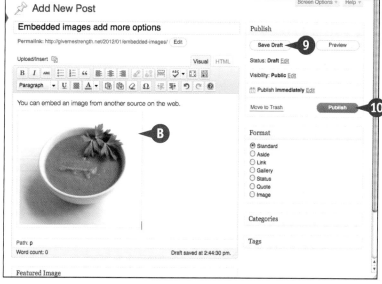

TIPS

Where can I find images in the public domain?

A favorite location for finding images is Wikimedia Commons, at http://commons.wikimedia.org. Click the public domain category. Also, images on U.S. government websites almost always are available copyright-free.

I found photos that say they are subject to the Creative Commons Share Alike license. What does that mean?

Numerous licensing and copyright options exist. The most common seem to be standard copyrights, which means you must get permission before using the photo, and Creative Commons licenses, of which there are several versions. For more information about the Creative Commons licenses, go to http://creativecommons.org/licenses.

Understanding Featured Images

Some themes allow you to highlight content by using featured images or to incorporate thumbnails of posts' images on the front page or with widgets. The featured images, a relatively new WordPress element, behave differently depending on your particular theme, and documentation for using them is not always the best.

Featured Header Images

Some themes that have an image header allow you to display an image specific to your post. The default theme, Twenty Eleven, is one such theme. For it (and most) to work properly, the image has to be as big or bigger than the header image specifications.

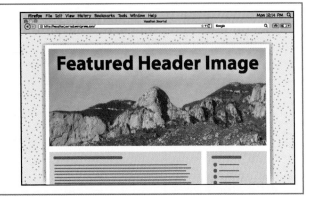

Featured Images as Thumbnails

Some themes use featured images as thumbnails or as a slide show; others combine multiple image sizes and display locations. Thumbnails can be especially useful when your front page shows only a few lines of your post, such as with magazine-style themes, and slider or slide shows are a great option for image-heavy sites.

Getting Help with Featured Images

Because featured-image behavior is theme-dependent, your best bet for getting help is with your theme developer. You can find a link to the theme developer by clicking **Appearance** in the left menu bar to reveal the Themes panel.

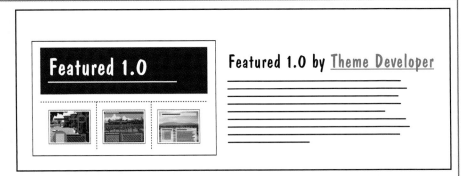

Add a Featured Image

When you designate a featured image, you can call attention to the post associated with it. Doing so is a simple variation on uploading an image to your site's Media Library.

Add a Featured Image

1 While writing or editing a post or page, click **Set featured image** in the Featured Image module.

The Set Featured Image window opens.

A If you do not see the Featured Image module, click **Screen Options** and click **Featured Image** (☐ changes to ☑) to reveal the module.

2 Choose a file as you did in one of the "Insert an Image" sections earlier in this chapter.

B The selected image appears in the Set Featured Image window.

3 Type a title in the Title box.

4 Type alternate text for screen readers.

5 Click **Use as featured image**.

6 Scroll to the bottom of the window and click **Save all changes**.

The featured image is set. When you return to the associated post, be sure to click **Update** (or **Save Draft**). The image appears in the Featured Image module and on the site.

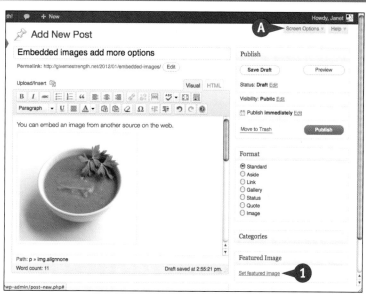

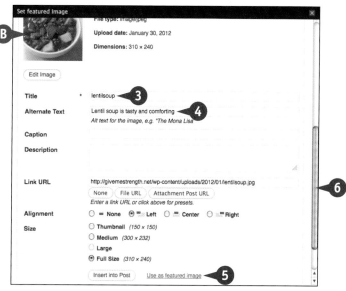

123

Format an Image from the Add Media Window

The Add Media window provides formatting options that allow you to present images with text wrapped around them, in various sizes, and with additional information attached.

These options appear when you upload images or view them in the Media Library. More formatting options are available after your images are in your blog post.

Ⓐ Edit Image

Expands an editing panel that allows you to crop, rotate, or resize your image.

Ⓑ Title

Text that appears when a viewer positions the mouse pointer over an image in a published blog post.

Ⓒ Alternate Text

A short description to be read aloud by a screen reader or other assistive device, or when a browser has images turned off. Also helps search engines.

Ⓓ Caption

Typically provides information for readers about the photo, which may appear in the post with the photo depending on your theme's style sheet and may aid screen readers.

Ⓔ Description

Optional information that some themes may display.

Ⓕ Link URL

Associates the image with a URL that displays when someone clicks the image. Click **File URL** for the browser to display the image in a plain browser window, or click **Attachment Post URL** for the browser to display the image as if it is a blog post. You also can click **None** for no link, or type some other URL.

G Alignment

Provides the options of None, meaning the image aligns according to surrounding formatting tags; or Left, Right, or Center alignment, which provide text wrapping around the image in addition to aligning the image to the specified location. Note that the alignment setting defaults to whatever alignment you used last.

H Size

Lets you display the image in one of the default sizes — Thumbnail, Medium, or Large as determined on your Media Settings page — or Full Size, the size you uploaded. Note that the size setting defaults to whatever size you used last. The exact dimensions appear beneath the size name. If no dimension appears, as with Large in the figure here, the uploaded image is smaller the standard size listed.

I Insert into Post

Places image into post at the cursor's last location.

J Use as Featured Image

Lets you set as featured image; see the preceding section.

K Delete

Starts process to delete an image from your Media Library. A confirmation message appears when you click **Delete**.

L Save All Changes

Saves changes and stores the image in the Media Library but does not insert the image in post if it is not already there.

Format an Image from the Edit Image Window

Once an image is inserted into a post, you can move it around, adjust its size, alter or add borders, and more. In other words, you can make it exactly the way you want it. It all starts by clicking the image in the Edit Post window.

A Image Handles

Resizes image proportionally when you click and drag corner handle — and stretches or squeezes image when you click and drag a side handle, although not at WordPress.com. You can click anywhere within the image and drag it to a new location in the post.

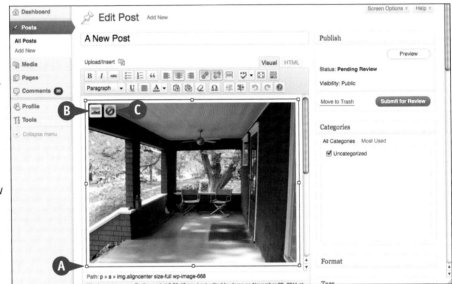

B Edit Image

Opens the Edit Image window, to edit size, link, caption, and alignment settings and Advanced Settings, as explained in the next section.

C Delete Image

Deletes image from location in post, but not from Media Library.

Ⓐ Size Scale

Resizes image display to a percentage of the inserted size.

Ⓑ Alignment

Specifies whether image is in line with text via the None setting, or whether the image aligns to the left, right, or center relative to the text.

Ⓒ Edit Options

Let you enter or change the information you provided when you uploaded your image.

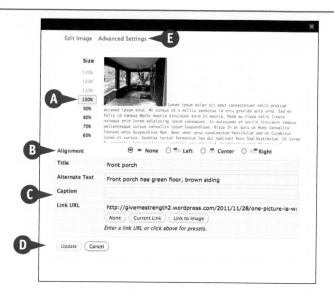

Ⓓ Update/Cancel

Saves or cancels changes you made in Edit Image window and returns to Edit Post window.

Ⓔ Advanced Settings Tab

Opens Advanced Settings window.

Ⓐ Original Size

Resets image to uploaded size.

Ⓑ Image Properties

Add or alter borders and spacing around the image.

Ⓒ Advanced Link Settings

Edit characteristics of links associated with the image. These are useful if you are familiar with HTML and CSS.

Ⓓ Update/Cancel

Saves or cancels changes you made in Advanced Image Settings window and returns to Edit Post window.

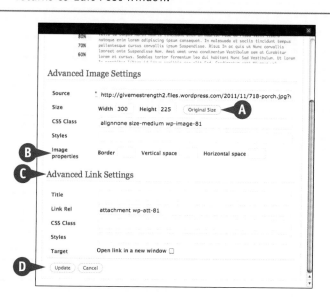

Insert an Image Gallery

The WordPress Image Gallery gives you a quick and easy way to display a set of photos or other images on your website. The gallery displays thumbnails of the images, and then you can click the individual images to view larger versions.

To get started, upload images to your post while you are in the Edit Post window. After you have uploaded the images, click **Save All Changes**, rather than **Insert into Post**. The Add Media window changes to the Gallery tab.

Insert an Image Gallery

Insert an Image Gallery

1 From the Gallery tab, expand the Order Images By drop-down menu, and select the order in which you want your images to appear. For now, choose the **Menu order** option.

2 Type a number in each box to specify the order in which you want the images to appear.

3 Click **Save all changes**.

The images reappear in numerical order according to the number you assigned them.

4 Click **Insert gallery**.

The settings are saved, the Add Media window closes, and the post box appears.

A The gallery placeholder image appears in the Edit Post window.

5 Click **Preview** to see how the gallery will appear.

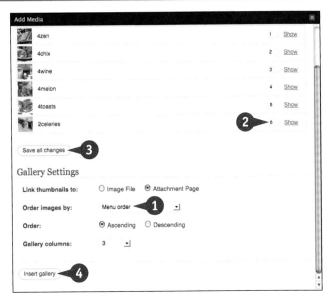

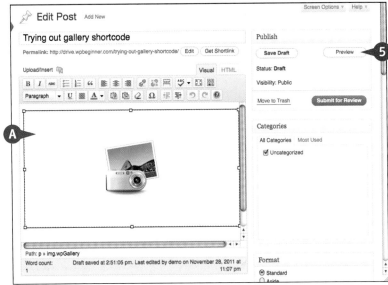

The post preview page opens, showing image thumbnails.

6 Click any image to see it individually.

Trying out gallery shortcode

Change Gallery Settings

1 Click the placeholder box to reveal the Edit Gallery and Delete Gallery buttons.

2 Click the **Edit Gallery** button (🖼).

A window to change gallery settings appears.

Note: You also can change the settings, such as size, for individual images from this window.

3 After changing any settings, click **Update Gallery Settings**, and then click **Update** in the post panel.

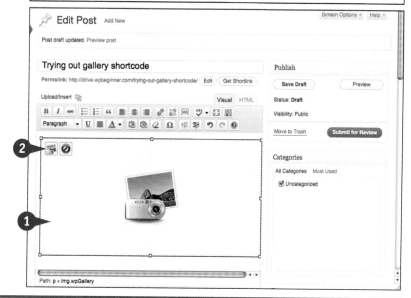

TIPS

I notice that on the HTML tab of the post panel, the text [gallery] appears instead of the gallery placeholder. Why is that?

WordPress allows use of some *shortcodes*, indicated by the opening and closing square brackets, and the gallery shortcode is one of them. If you want, you can type the gallery shortcode into either the WYSIWYG or HTML box, and doing so inserts a gallery of images associated with or attached to the post.

What is the difference in the two Link Thumbnails To gallery settings?

This setting determines how individual images appear when you click them in the gallery. The Attachment Page option opens the image in a separate page using your theme's image attachment template. The Image File option opens the image alone on a blank browser page. At this writing WordPress.com has changed galleries to automatically appear as slide shows, although this feature continues to be refined.

Add a Slide Show to Your Posts

Why limit yourself to an image or two, or even a gallery, if you can have a slide show simply and easily? If you use Picasa or Flickr to host or store your photos, you can make a Flash slide show for free with PictoBrowser, and you do not even have to sign up for anything new.

WordPress.com does not support PictoBrowser slide shows, but it has other options as described in the tips at the end of this section.

Add a Slide Show to Your Posts

Note: This example adds a slideshow to a self-hosted blog.

1. In your web browser, go to www.pictobrowser.com and click **PictoBuilder**.

2. In the screen that appears, click to indicate whether you are using photos from Flickr or Picasa (☐ changes to ☑).

3. Type the username for your Flickr or Picasa account.

4. Click **Continue**.

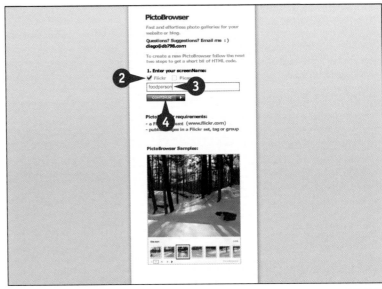

The Step 2 window opens.

5. Click a tab to choose whether to view images according to sets, tags, or groups.

Ⓐ A list lets you scroll through pages of sets, tags, or groups. In this case, the list displays tags.

6. Click your choice from the list.

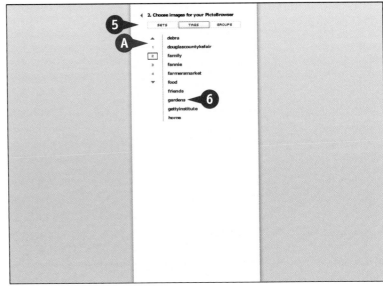

7 In the PictoBrowser settings page, change settings for the size or alignment of your slide show.

8 Change settings for the size or title settings for the slide show window.

9 Change settings for the background color and transparency of the player.

B Adjustments appear in the preview.

10 Test your settings by clicking the play button (▶).

11 Click the **Get HTML Code** tab.

The left pane changes to reveal HTML code, which you need to select and copy.

12 On the New Post or Edit Post panel, click the **HTML** editor tab.

The post box opens in the HTML editor.

13 Paste the copied HTML in the post box.

14 Click **Save Draft**.

The slide show now is embedded in your post.

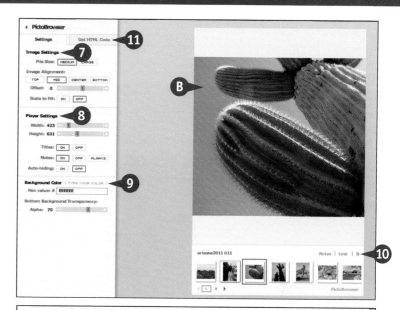

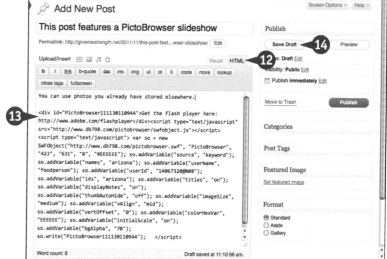

TIPS

What slide show options are available for WordPress.com blogs?

Slide shows compatible with WordPress.com are available at RockYou.com and SlideShare.net, and galleries at WordPress.com appear as slide shows, although they cannot be customized at this writing. WordPress.com also has a Flickr widget.

Are there other slide show options for self-hosted blogs?

You can use the services in the first tip with self-hosted blogs, but, as with PictoBrowser, you have to post the HTML in your post box on the New Post or Edit Post page. Self-hosted blogs also can use plugins. Possibilities include NextGEN Gallery and Smooth Slider.

Link to YouTube (and Other) Videos

Videos are a little more trouble to deal with than images, but they add a lot of visual energy to your blog posts. Using embedded videos through links may be the easiest way to get them up and running, and you do not have to use your own host space to store the videos.

You can link to most videos hosted at YouTube.com, and you can upload your own videos there, too.

Link to YouTube (and Other) Videos

1 After you find the video you want to post on your blog at YouTube.com, click **Share**.

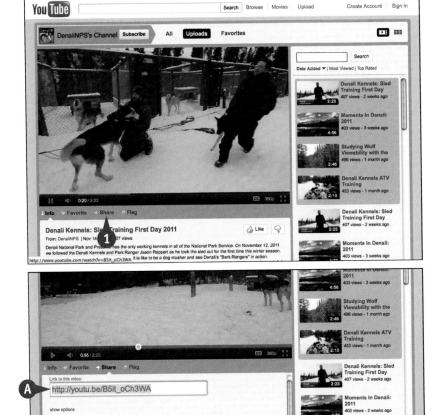

The linking box appears.

2 Click **Embed**.

A Embed code appears.

3 Scroll down to see embed options, and make any selections you want.

4 Scroll back up and copy the code.

5 Back at your WordPress Dashboard, start a new post, and click the **HTML** tab.

6 Click in the post where you want the video to appear, and paste the code you copied from YouTube.com.

7 Click **Save Draft** for a new post or **Update** for an existing post.

WordPress saves the post and inserts a placeholder for the video in the visual editor.

8 Click **Preview** to see how the video appears on your site.

A preview of your post appears in a new window, where you can click a play button to view the video.

9 Click **Publish** to publish the post on your site.

Note: Use the same process to embed a video on a page or an existing post.

TIPS

Do I have to pay for the video add-in to post YouTube videos with WordPress.com?
No, because you are posting a *link* to the video rather than hosting the video on your WordPress.com account.

Is there any other way to link to videos?
You can simply put the video's URL in a separate line in the HTML editor and save it. To customize it at WordPress.com, see the instructions at http://en.support. wordpress.com/videos/youtube, or check for YouTube plugins, explained in Chapter 7, at WordPress.org. Also, you can link to videos, often just by pasting the URL, at other video hosts such as Vimeo.com and Viddler.com.

Upload Video Files to Your Host

You have more control over the look and performance of your videos when you host them yourself. Doing so takes a few more steps than when you link to videos posted elsewhere.

If your blog is hosted on WordPress.com, your first step is to buy the VideoPress upgrade.

Upload Video Files to Your Host

Basic Installation on a Self-Hosted Blog

1 On the New Post or Edit Post page, click the **Add Media** button (🖼).

The Add Media window opens.

2 Click **Select Files**.

3 A file selection window opens, from which you select the video you want to upload and then click **Open**.

Ⓐ The Add Media window returns and shows the progress of the upload.

When the upload is complete, the Add Media window shows details about the video.

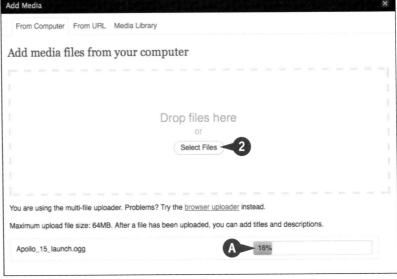

4 Type a title, which is the text that appears for a link to the video.

5 Add caption information.

6 Click **Save all changes**.

7 Click **Insert into Post**.

A *link* to the video file — but no image — appears in your post box.

Full-Featured Installation on WordPress.com

1 After clicking **Store** in the left menu panel and then buying the VideoPress upgrade, go to a New Post or Edit Post page, and upload as described in steps **1** to **3** for installing video on a self-hosted blog.

A message appears, informing you that your video is being processed and will be ready in a few minutes.

Note: If you use many videos you may also need to purchase a space upgrade.

2 While you wait for the video to be processed, go to http://en.support. wordpress.com/videopress to read detailed instructions on setting up your video.

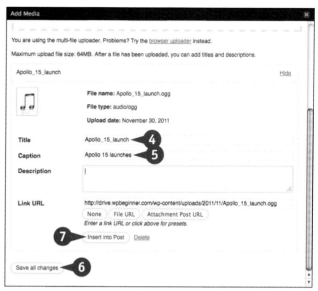

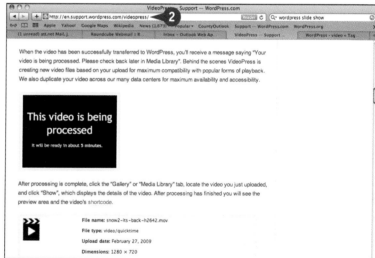

TIPS

Is a link the best I can do for video on my self-hosted blog?

You can do much better, actually, but it requires use of a plugin. See Chapter 7 for information about plugins, and then search for a video plugin that suits your needs.

I get a message saying that my upload is too big on most videos. On other videos, they take forever to upload. What can I do?

With your self-hosted blog, you can speed things up and avoid that upload limit by uploading files directly to your uploads folder on your web host via FTP as described in Chapter 3. Unless you have customized your upload folder in your Miscellaneous settings panel, the default uploads folder is wp-content/uploads.

Link to a Podcast or Sound File from Your Blog

With audio files, you can give your readers the sound of your voice, of bird calls, of music. Linking to such files is much like linking to videos, and you also can host them on your site if you do not want to embed or link to audio files.

First, you need to find the audio file that you want to link to.

Link to a Podcast or Sound File from Your Blog

1 From the New Post or Edit Post window, click the **Add Media** button (🖼).

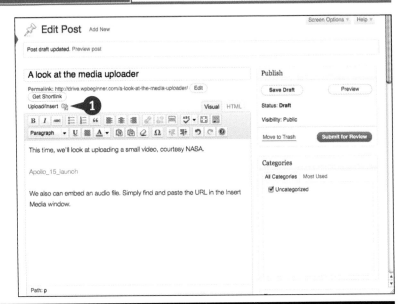

2 The Add Media window opens, where you click **From URL**.

The Insert Media from Another Website window appears.

3 Click **Audio, Video, or Other File** (⚪ changes to ⚫).

4 Type or paste the URL of your chosen audio file into the URL box.

5 Type a title for the audio file into the Title box. The title provides the link text.

6 Click **Insert into Post**.

The Add Media window closes, and a link to the audio file appears in the post box.

7 Click **Save Draft**.

8 Click **Preview**.

WordPress displays the post in your browser, where you can click the link to hear the sound file.

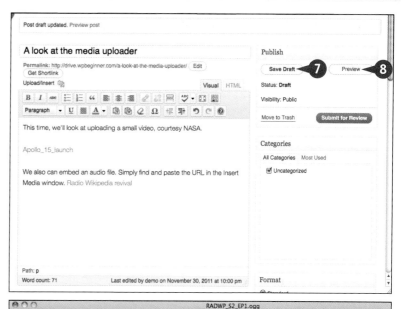

The sound file opens at its URL and begins playing.

A You can click the pause button (⏸) if you want to pause the file.

Can I host files on my blog so that people do not get transferred to another location?

If your blog is self-hosted, the steps are the same as for uploading a video file described in "Upload Video Files to Your Host" earlier in this chapter. Again, you may want to get a plugin, as explained in Chapter 7, so that the player appears on your site. On a WordPress.com blog, you need to buy an upgrade if you want to upload an audio file. See http://en.support.wordpress.com/audio for the options.

Can I make music automatically play in the background?

It is not a good idea; many people object to that audio intrusion. Much better to make the file available and let people choose to listen or not.

Create and Install a Favicon for a Self-Hosted Blog

Y ou can add to your "brand" by displaying a favicon, the tiny icon that appears next to a web address in many browsers. The favicon also may appear in a browser's Favorites or Bookmarks list. See Chapter 2 for icons related to your WordPress.com blog.

Do not worry about pronouncing favicon correctly. There is no definitive pronunciation. Options include FAVE-icon, from the word's root as *favorite icon*, and FAVV-uh-con, with a short *a*, as in hat.

Create and Install a Favicon for a Self-Hosted Blog

1 Go to www.degraeve.com/favicon and click **Browse**.

2 A file selection window opens, where you browse for an image that you want to convert to a favicon and then click **Open**.

3 When the path to your image appears in the Upload this Image box, click **upload image**.

Note: Alternatively, you can click **Clear All**, click a color in the palette, and then move your mouse pointer to the square editing area at the left to draw a favicon.

The image appears in a new window.

4 Click and drag, even stretch, the selection box until it surrounds the part of your image that you want to make into your icon.

5 Click **Crop picture**.

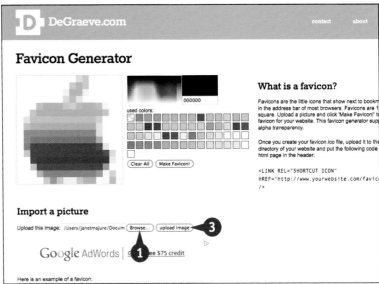

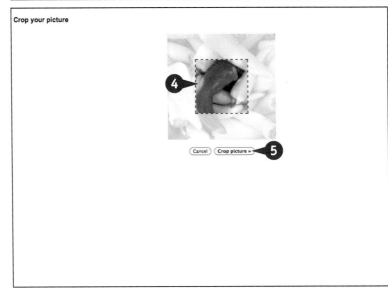

Note: The DeGraeve icon generator lets you crop from a larger image. Many icon generators, such as the one at Dynamicdrive.com, simply reduce an entire image to create a favicon.

The browser returns to the Favicon Generator window and shows your pixilated favicon.

⑥ Click **Make Favicon!**.

The favicon appears on the screen. Follow the directions for saving the favicon, named favicon.ico, to your hard drive.

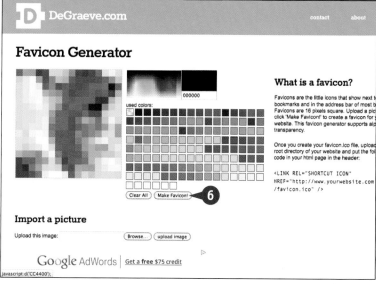

⑦ Using your FTP client, such as FileZilla, upload favicon.ico to the root of your blog site, as in /public_html.

Ⓐ The file appears in the directory listing.

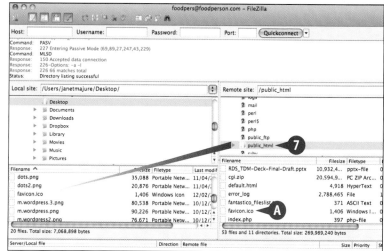

Is there some other way to make a favicon?

You can make your own custom favicon with a paint or image-editing program. Just make sure the favicon is 16 x 16 pixels (although some browsers support 32 x 32 pixels) and then name it favicon.ico.

I followed the directions, but the favicon is not appearing. Why not?

Most likely, it will not appear until your browser's cache has been cleared; go to your browser's Help menu to learn how. Or, it should appear in a couple of hours. If you have waited two days or so and it still does not appear, your theme may need to be modified to support favicons. Search the WordPress.org forums for help.

CHAPTER 7

Explore Widgets and Plugins

Although WordPress software gets your blog up and running, WordPress widgets and plugins make your blog do cartwheels. These miniprograms add functions, ease effort, and do just about anything else you may want your blogging software to do.

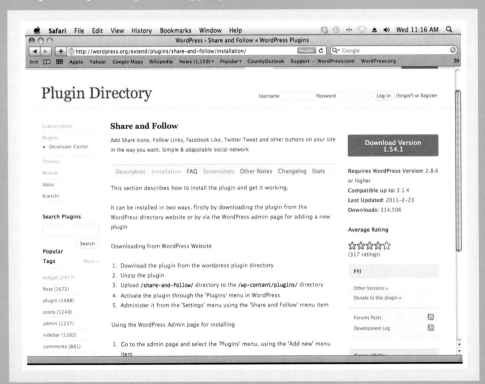

Introducing Widgets and Plugins

Widgets and plugins may sound like games, but they are seriously useful bits of code that extend your WordPress blog beyond the basics of writing and posting information on a regular basis.

Widgets for Sidebars

Widget is the term that WordPress uses for items that appear in the sidebars of your blog — and sometimes in other locations such as the footer. Both hosted and self-hosted blogs come with a few standard widgets. If your theme supports widgets, your Dashboard prompts you to configure the widgets when you activate the theme.

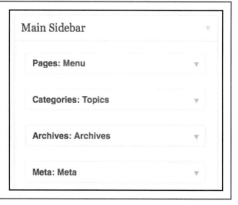

Plugins for Everything

Plugins, available only on self-hosted blogs, are like miniprograms that do lots of things, from adding buttons to your post box interface to installing a media player so that you can play your own photo gallery, podcasts, and videos. Plugins can serve ads, increase your search-engine visibility, point out frequent commenters, and do lots, lots more.

Standard Widgets at Self-Hosted Blogs

At this writing, self-hosted blogs generally have widgets to display a monthly archive of posts, a calendar, blog categories, your links list, a *meta* section for logging in and other tasks, a list of static pages, a display of recent comments, a list of recent posts, the RSS feed of your choice, a search box, a tag cloud, a custom menu, and text widgets, which give lots of options, such as for images and HTML.

Standard Widgets for WordPress.com Blogs

WordPress.com does not allow users to upload and install plugins, but the host makes up for it in large part by having numerous widgets in addition to most of those included on self-hosted blogs. You can add any of the widgets to your sidebar just by following some simple directions.

Related

Akismet Widget
Archives Widget
Author Grid Widget
Authors Widget
Blog Stats Widget
Box.net Widget
Calendar Widget
Categories Widget
Custom Menu Widget
Custom Theme Widgets
Delicious Widget
Flickr Widget

WordPress.com Widgets and What They Do

The following WordPress.com widgets are in addition to those standard on self-hosted blog installations.

WordPress.com Added Widgets	
Widget	**What It Does**
Akismet	Displays the number of spam comments caught by Akismet spam catcher.
Author Grid	Shows a grid filled with author avatars.
Authors	Shows capsule information about all authors on your blog.
Blog Stats	Displays number of hits to your blog.
Box.net File Sharing	Provides way to share files by way of the Box.net service.
Delicious	Displays your Delicious bookmarks according to your settings.
Flickr	Displays photos based at Flickr.com.
Follow Blog	Lets readers sign up to get your posts by e-mail.
Gravatar	Shows your Gravatar image.
Image	Lets you easily display an image in a sidebar.
Meebo	Connects to the Meebo service to allow live chat.
RSS Links	Provides links for readers to sign up for your RSS feed or feeds.
SocialVibe	Connects with commercial sponsors to earn donations to charities.
Top Clicks	Lists blog links that get the most clicks.
Top Posts	Lists posts that get the most views.
Top Rated	Lists posts or pages that have the highest reader ratings.
Twitter	Displays your tweets.
Vodpod Videos	Inserts a Vodpod video player in your sidebar where readers can view videos you have selected through your Vodpod account.

Choose and Insert Widgets

You can add or remove widgets any time you want after you have your blog running. Widgets make it easy to add sidebar features on your blog. Take advantage of them!

When you first install a theme, it may remind you to visit the widgets settings panel to configure them. If you do not, the theme displays a standard set of widgets, which may vary by theme.

Choose and Insert Widgets

1 In the left menu bar, click **Appearance** to expand the Appearance menu.

2 Click **Widgets** to open the Widget panel, which lists available widgets in alphabetical order.

Ⓐ Active widgets appear in the sidebar list.

Ⓑ If your theme has more than one widget area, a list appears for each available sidebar or other widget area.

3 Use the scroll bar or page-down until you see a widget you want to add, such as the Search widget.

4 Click and hold on the **Search** widget until ▶ changes to ✋.

5 Drag the Search widget to the sidebar list.

When the widget reaches the list, a dotted line appears under the sidebar label indicating that you can release the mouse button.

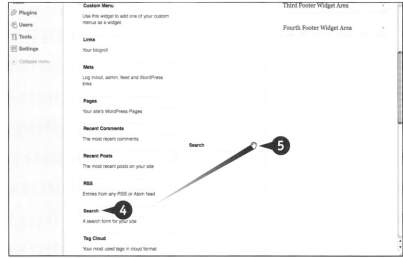

Note: The sidebar area needs to be expanded, not collapsed, to accept the widget. Click the arrow (▼) to expand the sidebar area.

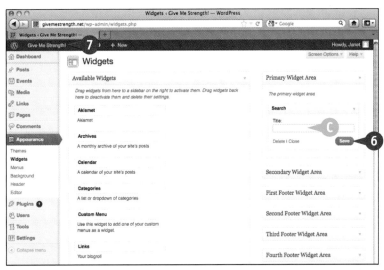

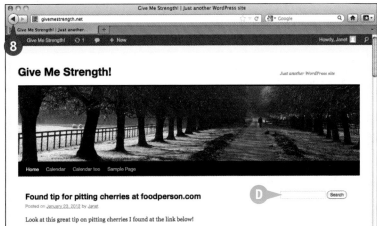

C You can type a title for your Search widget in the title box.

Note: Widget titles are usually optional.

6 Click **Save**.

Note: Options for each widget may vary from one theme to the next. If your widget has no options, simply dragging it to the sidebar is all you need to do.

7 Click your blog's name to see your widget in action.

D The Search widget appears in the sidebar.

8 Click the **Back** button (◀) to return to the Widgets panel, where you can add more widgets to your sidebars.

TIPS

After I installed my first widget and looked at it on the site, all the other widgets that appeared with my theme were no longer there. When I clicked the browser's Back button, even the widget I added did not appear in the sidebar on the Widgets panel. What did I do wrong?
Not a thing. Themes include numerous widgets as part of their installation. Once you configure your first widget, the default widgets go away in self-hosted blogs. If the widget does not appear on the Widgets panel, click your browser's **Refresh** button or click **Widgets** in the left menu bar, and your newly activated widget reappears. Then, click and drag any other widgets you want to the sidebar or sidebars.

I have a self-hosted WordPress blog, but I have more widgets than the standard ones previously mentioned.
Virtually every self-hosted WordPress blog has the standard widgets mentioned in "Introducing Widgets and Plugins." Some themes have additional widgets. It just means your theme's developer automated more functions for you. Try them out. If you installed plugins that add widgets, those will be available as well.

Rearrange and Remove Widgets

Another great thing about widgets is that they are as easy to remove as they are to add, which makes experimenting with different arrangements a simple task. You can rearrange and remove widgets — and even retain your settings if you want.

If you scroll down the Widgets panel, you can see an Inactive Widgets box below the Available Widgets.

Rearrange and Remove Widgets

Rearrange Widgets

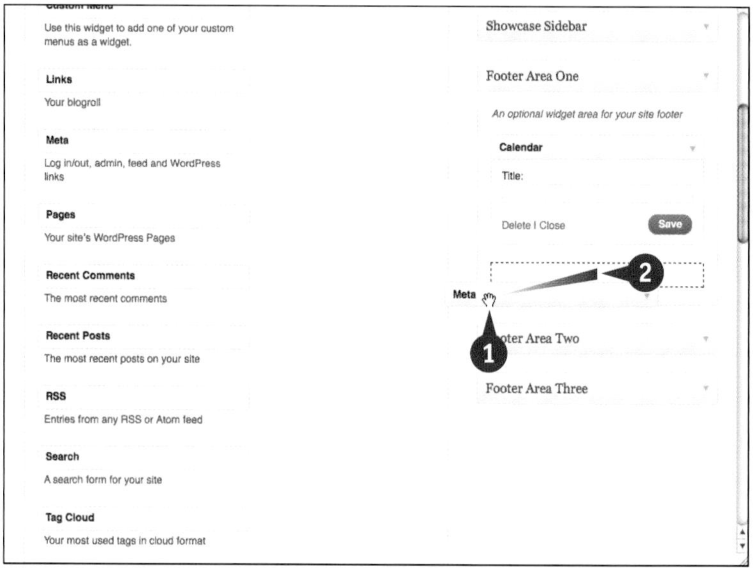

1. Click and hold on the widget that you want to move in your sidebar (↖ changes to ✋), and then drag the widget to the position you want it to have in your sidebar.

2. When a rectangle with a dotted line appears at the desired location, release the mouse button.

   The widget appears in its new position in the sidebar.

Remove a Widget and Retain Its Settings

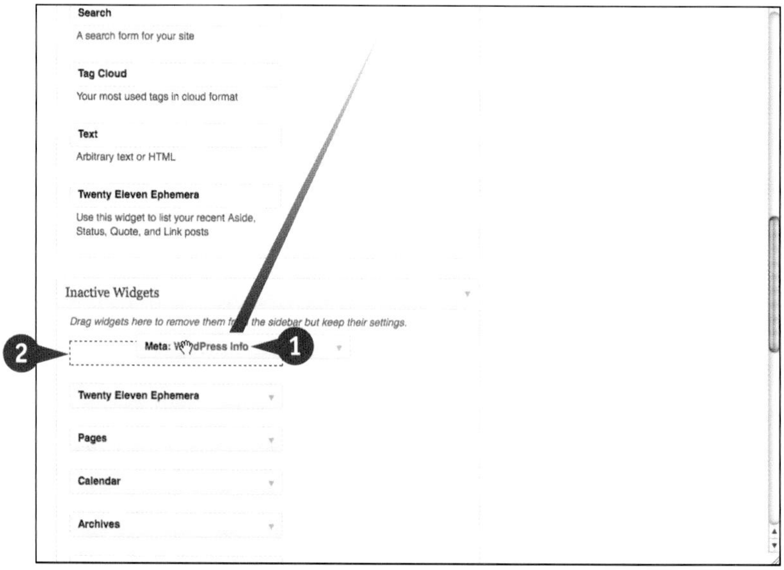

1. Click the widget you want to deactivate, and drag it to the Inactive Widgets box in the lower portion of the Widgets panel.

2. Release the mouse button when the dotted box appears. WordPress keeps the title you assigned to the widget.

Remove a Widget without Retaining Its Settings

1 Click and hold the widget you want to remove (⬉ changes to 🖑). Drag the widget to the Available Widgets box of the Widgets panel and release the mouse button.

A A deactivate message appears at the top of the Available Widgets box, and the widget disappears from the Sidebar box.

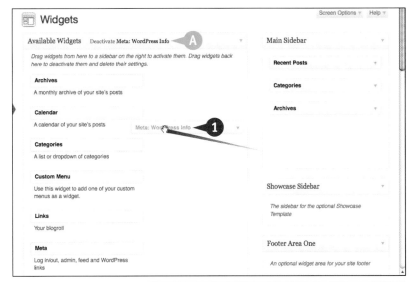

Reactivate a Saved Widget

1 Click and hold the mouse button on the widget you want to reactivate (⬉ changes to 🖑).

2 Drag the widget to the Sidebar box, and then release the mouse button when a dotted-line rectangle appears in the location where you want the widget.

The widget reappears in the Sidebar widget list.

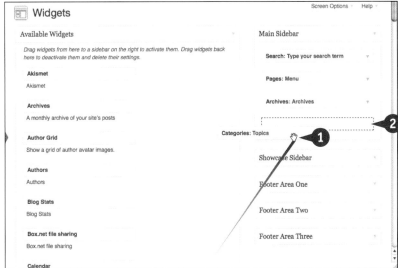

TIPS

I am having trouble dragging the widgets around. Any suggestions?
Yes. Expand the Screen Options on the Widgets panel, and click the **Enable accessibility mode** link. Each Available widget then has an Add link, and each Active and Inactive widget has an Edit link. Click those links to open subpanels to add, configure, edit, or reorganize your widgets.

Why do my widgets appear only on my front page?
Different themes vary in their widget displays. Some limit them to the front page or static pages. Others have some, but not all, widgets appear on individual post pages. If you want them to appear on every screen of your blog, you may need to search for a theme that uses widgets in that way. Note, though, that you lose your widget settings when you change themes.

Add Sidebar Items Using HTML in a Text Widget

Among the many widgets WordPress themes offer is one innocuously titled Text. And, yes, you can use it to show, say, a favorite quote or a bio about yourself in a sidebar. But you also can use it to insert more complex additions that use HTML.

Like most other widgets, the Text widget can be used multiple times simultaneously in your sidebars.

Add Sidebar Items Using HTML in a Text Widget

Add a Basic Text Widget

Ⓐ After you click and drag a Text widget to a sidebar, a large configuration box appears.

1 Type a title in the Title box.

2 Type text in the text box.

3 Click **Save**.

The text appears in the sidebar location you selected, using the formatting specified in your theme's style sheet.

4 Click **Close** to collapse the configuration box.

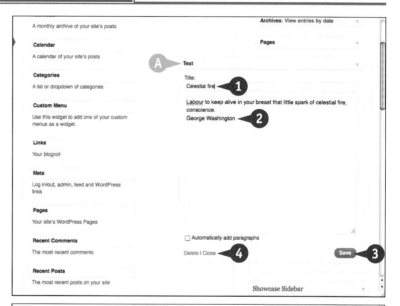

Change Text Widget Format

1 Type simple HTML tags around text you want to format, in this case `<em>` and `</em>` around the text to put it in italics and `<p style="text-align: right;">` to align the last line right.

2 Click **Automatically add paragraphs** (☐ changes to ☑) to have WordPress start a new paragraph when you press `Enter`.

3 Click **Save**.

Your formatting is saved and appears on the blog's sidebar.

Note: Your theme's style sheet may override some HTML styling.

148

Add Functional Content via Text Widgets

1 Go to http://yowindow.com/ weatherwidget.php in your web browser.

2 Provide the information requested.

Note: If you do not know the desired window size, use the default and change it later.

3 Scroll or page-down to complete all the requested information.

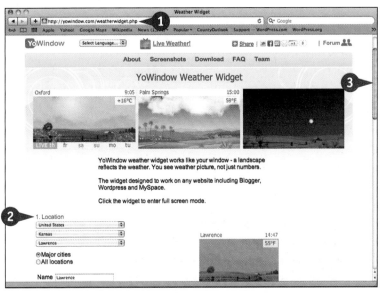

4 Choose a publishing option (○ changes to ◉), using **Any website or blog** for self-hosted sites, or **WordPress** if your site is at WordPress.com.

B YoWindow supplies code that fits your information.

5 Click in the code box, which selects the code, and copy the code using your browser's Edit menu or by pressing Ctrl+C (⌘+C on a Mac).

Paste that code into your Text widget and save. The Weather widget for your blog appears in your sidebar.

TIPS

How can I put an image in a sidebar?
WordPress.com has an Image widget just for that purpose. If your blog is self-hosted, you use a Text widget, odd as that sounds. Simply drag a Text widget to the sidebar, and in the large box, type the HTML to call the image, such as `<img src="http://foodperson.com/wp-content/uploads/2009/10/mkt102409.jpg">`.

What else can I do in a Text widget?
You can find a list of other content you can add via a Text widget, including maps and translators, at http://codex.wordpress.org/ WordPress_Widgets#Using_Text_Widgets. Note that WordPress.com does not allow JavaScript and PHP.

Get a Key and Activate Akismet

Sadly, junk producers have created junk comments just like junk e-mail. Happily, WordPress comes with the Akismet spam-capturing and spam-identification feature built in. WordPress.com bloggers have the service running by default. Users of self-hosted WordPress blogs have to take a couple of extra steps for Akismet to work for them.

Get a Key and Activate Akismet

1 Go to http://Akismet.com/wordpress in your browser.

2 Click **Get an Akismet API** key.

3 A new window opens listing Akismet plan options. Click **Sign Up** under Personal, which opens a new window.

Note: Click one of the other Sign Up buttons if you have a commercial site.

4 Type your first name and last name in the First Name and Last Name boxes.

5 Type your e-mail address in the two e-mail boxes.

6 Move the slider to show how much you want to pay for the service; zero is an option for personal sites.

A Links take you to the service's terms and conditions and privacy policy.

7 Click **Continue**.

A confirmation screen appears if you made a contribution of zero. Otherwise, you first see and complete a payment screen before getting confirmation.

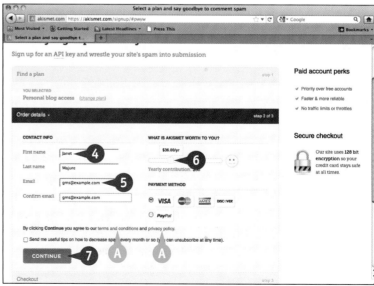

8 After getting your API key from your e-mail, log on to your blog's Dashboard, and click **Plugins**.

The Plugins menu expands, and the Manage Plugins panel opens to reveal installed plugins.

9 Click **Activate** in the Akismet section.

The Plugins panel alerts you that the plugin is activated and prompts you to enter your API key.

10 Click **enter your Akismet API key**.

The Akismet Configuration panel opens.

B The Akismet Configuration panel includes instructions on how Akismet works.

11 Paste or type your API key in the API Key box.

12 If desired, click here to discard spam comments after a month (☐ changes to ☑).

13 Click **Update options**.

WordPress confirms that your options are saved.

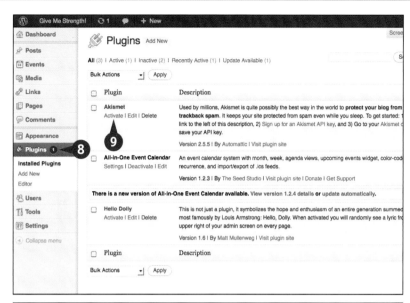

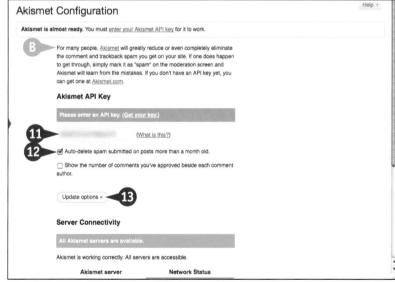

How will I know if Akismet has caught any spam comments?
A count of comments in the spam comment queue appears at the top of the Edit Comments panel, which you reach by clicking **Comments** in the left menu bar of the Dashboard. You can see the comments by clicking the **Spam** link there. If your site is at WordPress.com, you also can activate the Akismet widget to show how many spam comments the tool captured.

Does Akismet ever catch comments that are not spam?
Rarely, but it does happen, which is why checking the junk comments listing periodically is a good practice.

Find Plugins

Plugins provide all sorts of functions for your self-hosted WordPress blog besides those that are built in, from media players you can embed in your blog to post and comment rating systems and lots more. You can investigate plugins from the Plugins panel, accessible via Plugins in the left menu bar of the Dashboard, or at WordPress.org.

Find Plugins

Find Plugins via the Plugins Panel

1 Click **Plugins**.

2 Click **Add New**.

A In the Install Plugins panel, you can find plugins that are featured, popular, new, or recently updated at WordPress.org.

B Search for plugins here.

C A tag cloud reveals popular plugin tags.

3 Click a link or do a search.

A list of the plugins that fit your selection appears.

D The Details option links to the plugin's information page.

E The rating from plugin users appears here.

F The list includes a brief description of the plugin.

G A link to the plugin developer's home page appears here.

4 Click **Details.**

5 An information window opens. Read the information about the plugin by clicking each tab, and then click the **WordPress.org Plugin Page** link.

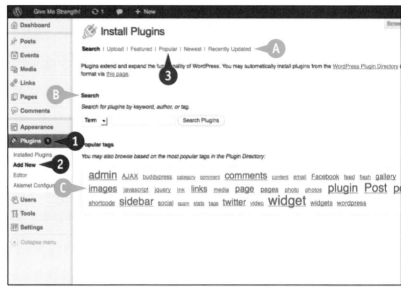

The WordPress.org Plugin Directory opens in a new tab to the plugin page you selected.

⑥ Scroll down past the Compatibility box.

⑦ Click what **others are saying** in the right sidebar to see what problems and praise others have made about the plugin.

⑧ Click to close the tab and return to the information window.

⑨ Click the Close box to close the information window.

Find Plugins via the WordPress. org Directory

① In your browser, go to http:// wordpress.org/extend/plugins.

The Plugin Directory lets you search by keyword and sort the results by relevance or other options listed below the search box. Click the plugin title to read more information.

Ⓗ The plugin tag cloud is accessible by clicking **More** next to Popular Tags in the Plugin Directory.

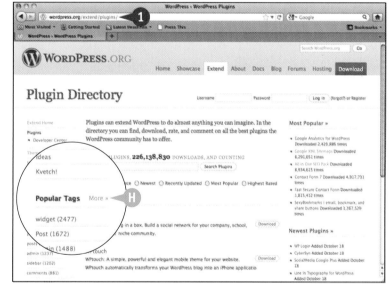

Why do I need to read plugin details before I install a plugin?

As helpful as plugins are, they also can cause problems. Some plugins may conflict with other plugins, for example, or a plugin may not work on the version of WordPress that you are running. By doing a little research first, you can avoid headaches.

Is it any better to search from the Install Plugins panel rather than WordPress.org?

Not really. The two search and present the search results somewhat differently, but the plugins are the same.

Consider These Popular Plugins

E ven with thousands of plugins available, a few are consistently popular due to their success in helping blogs address certain ongoing needs, such as attracting search engine traffic and helping your blog to work efficiently. Some of them are sure to address your needs, and most are free, although premium plugins may offer more support.

Spread the Word

Blogging is all about communicating, and some plugins add to the buzz. Among them are the Share and Follow, Slick Social Share, Social Sharing Toolkit, and SexyBookmarks plugins. With one of these plugins active, your blog posts automatically include buttons that let your readers add the post to their favorite networking site or send a link via e-mail.

Hello world!

Posted on September 30, 2010 by andyk

Welcome to WordPress. This is your first post. Edit or delete it, then start blogging!

Posted in Uncategorized | 1 Comment | Edit

Save the Data

Keeping your WordPress data backed up saves you from disaster should your web host lose or corrupt your blog. It *can* happen! The WP-DB-Backup plugin makes it easy for you to regularly back up your WordPress database, which stores your posts, pictures, and other media, and WordPress Backup backs up site customizations like theme and plugin settings. EZPZ One Click Backup does it all.

Home » **My WordPress Plugins** » WordPress Database Backup

WordPress Database Backup

WordPress database backup creates backups of your core WordPress tables of your choice in the same database.

Speed Blog Performance

The bigger your blog and the more photos and other content it has, the slower it can run. The WP Super-cache plugin speeds things up by automatically converting your dynamic blog pages to static pages for most visitors. Also popular is W3 Total Cache.

Pretty Galleries

The standard WordPress image gallery is fairly limited, and the plugins NextGEN Gallery and WordPress Gallery are just two of the plugins that give you more control over how images are shown on your blog. You can style the gallery, create and manage slide shows, and have a simple interface.

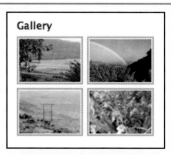

Search Engine Optimization

Search engine optimization, or SEO, makes your site more attractive to search engines. All-in-One SEO allows you to add keywords and to create a special keyword-rich post title and post summary in the Edit Post panel. Google XML Sitemaps helps search engines index — and refer to — your site.

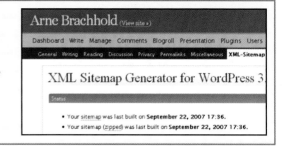

Statistics Trackers

The Google Analytics for WordPress and Google Analyticator plugins take advantage of Google Analytics' data to show what is happening on your blog, such as traffic numbers and sources.

E-Commerce

If you want to sell products through your site, you need an e-commerce solution. The popular WP e-Commerce plugin is an excellent free option, as is eShop. Premium plugin options include Cart66 and ShopperPress.

Plugin Package

Automattic, the company behind WordPress, offers a set of plugins that replicate many WordPress.com features. That set is Jetpack, and it includes the WordPress.com statistics, Twitter, sharing, editing, and other features. Read the forums at WordPress.org to see if this package is right for you.

Install and Activate a Plugin

Once you have identified the plugins that you need — or simply want — installing them is easy. Most plugins can be installed with a few clicks from the Add Plugins panel, but even manual installations are easy.

Once installed and activated, each plugin may have other settings and operations that you configure according to the instructions on the plugin's information screens.

Install and Activate a Plugin

Install and Activate a Plugin from the Add Plugins Panel

1 After you have found your chosen plugin in the Add Plugins panel and clicked **Install** to get that plugin's details, click **Install Now**.

A progress indicator appears on the screen, and then the Installing Plugin panel, which gives further progress information.

2 After *Successfully installed* appears in the Installing Plugin panel, click **Activate Plugin**.

The Plugins panel appears, which confirms the activation and lists the new plugin. You now can use or configure the plugin according to the instructions provided on the plugin information pages.

Manual Plugin Installation

1 After you find the plugin's page in the WordPress Plugin Directory, click **Download**.

Your browser downloads the Zip file, which you save to your computer and extract.

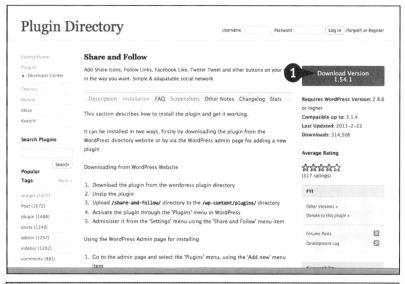

2 After extracting the Zip file, connect to your site using your FTP client or web host FTP panel, and click the extracted plugin folder on your computer.

3 Drag or copy that folder to the plugins directory in your blog's wp-content directory.

The plugin is installed. Activate it from the Plugins panel. If you had the panel open during the upload, refresh the page for the plugin to appear.

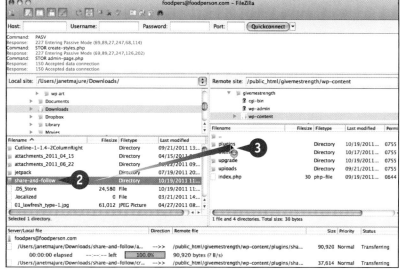

TIPS

I installed my plugin, but it does not seem to be working. What do I do?

First, make sure you activated it on the Plugins panel. If you have, then click **Visit plugin site** in the plugin's listing on the Manage Plugins panel for more information.

> A simple plugin to manage sharing and following. CDN -ultra~fast~stuff-, why not tell us what you w going on. Soon to come, mobile device support, s devices. Options & configuration I Documentation know what icon set to add next to the CDN
>
> Version 1.54.1 I By Andy Killen I Visit plugin site

The plugin I installed has a notice and link about donating money for the plugin. What is that about?

Individuals develop plugins and make them available for free to WordPress users, and many developers ask for donations. Giving money is optional, but it is a good way to assure that developers maintain their plugins and develop new ones as the need arises.

CHAPTER 8

Make Your Blog Content Appealing

A good-looking blog is all well and good, but in the end the content is king. You can improve your content's appeal with careful editing and attention to typography and organization.

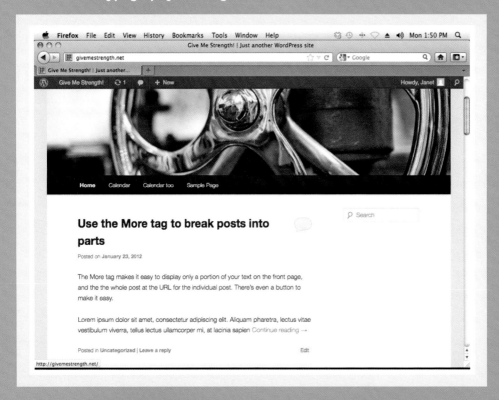

Edit What You Write

etting your message online is good, but getting it out there in an appealing and readable way is even better. By editing your posts you give your blog greater credibility and make reading it easier for your readers. Yes, spelling does matter!

Edit What You Write

Find a Post to Edit

1 Click **Posts** in the left menu bar, or in the Right Now module of the Dashboard.

The Posts panel opens, listing all posts you have written, whether published or not.

2 Click the name of the post you want to edit.

The Edit Post panel opens, where you can edit and save changes.

Note: You also can click **Edit** under the post name, which appears when you position your mouse pointer in that post's row in the list.

Spell-Check on Self-Hosted Blogs

1 In the Visual editor, click the drop-down menu next to the Spell-Checker button to choose the language to check.

2 Click the **Spell-Checker** button (☺).

Red dotted lines appear under misspellings.

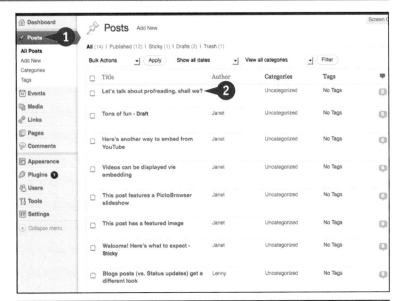

③ Right-click a misspelled word.

A list of options appears.

④ Select a suggested spelling or ignore the spelling.

⑤ Click **Save Draft**.

Note: If you have already published the post, click **Update Post** instead.

Proofread at WordPress.com

① Click the **Spellchecker** button (🔲).

The built-in spelling and grammar checker underlines misspelled words in red, grammar errors in green, and questionable style use in blue.

Note: From the HTML tab, click the **proofread** button instead.

② Right-click an underlined word.

A list of possible corrections appears.

③ Click a correction to replace the questioned word, click **Explain** for more information, or select an Ignore option.

④ When you are finished editing, click **Save Draft**.

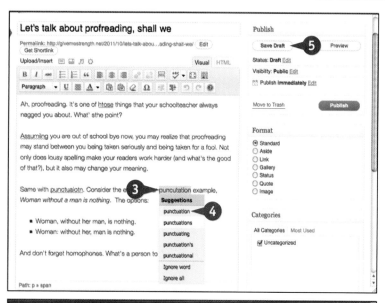

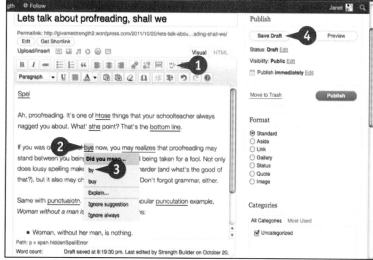

Can I check spelling only — not the grammar and style issues — at my WordPress.com blog?

Yes. You can choose what gets checked on your Personal Settings panel, as described in Chapter 2.

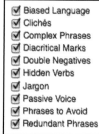

☑ Biased Language
☑ Clichés
☑ Complex Phrases
☑ Diacritical Marks
☑ Double Negatives
☑ Hidden Verbs
☑ Jargon
☑ Passive Voice
☑ Phrases to Avoid
☑ Redundant Phrases

Can I get the proofreading tools for my self-hosted blog?

Yes. They are available as the After the Deadline plugin via the WordPress.org plugin directory. Its settings allow you to choose among several style-checking options, such as whether to check for clichés, on the Profile panel of your blog. Remember, though, these tools are highly imperfect and are no substitute for carefully reading what you wrote.

Use Typography to Enhance Posts

You can make your blog posts easier to read by using headings, subheadings, bulleted lists, numbered lists, and other typographical tools. Knowing when and when not to use these tools makes the most of them.

Chapter 5 covered how to format type. Now you can find out the best way to use your formats.

Choose Your Visual Style

Try to make decisions early in your blogging experience as to when you will use headings, lists, and other style options, because presenting a consistent look is a key part of your blog's identity. You can experiment with draft posts to see how various features look in your theme. Consider also whether to capitalize headings or not.

Headings for Hierarchy

Headings do more than change the size, and perhaps other characteristics, of type. Headings also create a hierarchy for your web posts, and search engines use headings to index your pages and their content. Use heading formats accordingly, with Heading 1 formats for the most important headings, Heading 2 for the next most important, and so on, with Heading 6 the least important heading.

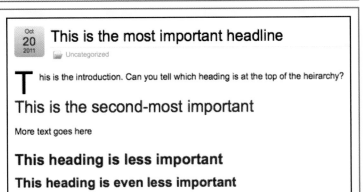

Use Restraint

With all the easy-to-use tools to modify type, you may be tempted to brighten up your text with all manner of colors and type styles. Resist the urge. Too much style variation creates a confusing and often hard-to-read body of text.

Use Bullets for Unordered Lists

An *unordered* list is one in which the order of the items does not matter, such as a list of groceries to buy or a list of WordPress features. When you use bullets for such a list, a reader does not assume that the first item on the list must come first.

- Conversions
- Glossary for beginning cooks
- Grain-cooking guide
- Menu planning grid
- Substitutions

Use Numbers for Ordered Lists

Reserve numbered lists for when you want to communicate that the order of the listed items matters, such as a sequence of steps or items listed in order of importance.

1. Wash and trim tomatoes of anything you wouldn't scars. Halve small tomatoes (such as plums) or cut chunks. Let's say 1-inch cubes, but larger is fine.

2. Distribute tomatoes in large ovenproof pans with a Tomatoes don't have to be in a single layer, but dor above the height of the pan's lip, as the tomatoes w

Use Blockquote for Quotes

The Blockquote format was created particularly for when you insert text quoted from another source. You can use it for another purpose if you want, but be consistent in how you apply it so as not to confuse readers.

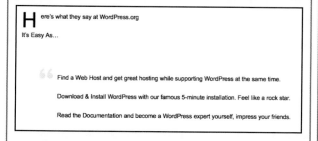

H ere's what they say at WordPress.org

It's Easy As...

" Find a Web Host and get great hosting while supporting WordPress at the same time.

Download & Install WordPress with our famous 5-minute installation. Feel like a rock star.

Read the Documentation and become a WordPress expert yourself, impress your friends.

Formats for Computer Code

The Address and Preformatted paragraph formats and the Code format in the HTML editor are formats especially useful for computer or web developers' blogs. Anyone may be interested in Preformatted because it is the only standard format that retains extra spaces that you insert.

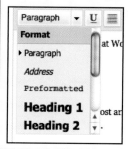

Use Images to Enhance Posts

If one picture is worth a thousand words, one picture *plus* a thousand words must be worth five thousand words, as long as the words and pictures complement each other. A consistent pattern again improves your blog's visual identity.

Chapter 6 identified your image formatting options, and now you can see how and when to use them.

Art for Interest

As with headings, you can use images to break up a large block of uninterrupted text. If you do not have a suitable image, you can consider microstock images in addition to the public domain images mentioned in Chapter 6. Two popular microstock sites are iStockPhoto.com and Shutterstock.com.

Take Advantage of Images' Words

Besides providing information for visitors using screen readers or other assistive devices, the alternate text for your images also leads search engines to your photos. The image title, which defaults to the filename, appears in some browsers when the mouse pointer rests over the image. The filename also can lead searchers your way. So, name it autumnleaves.jpg rather than img0235.jpg.

Captions Not Required

Just because your WordPress image-inserting window allows you to type a caption does not mean you must use that option (Ⓐ). The caption feature generally puts a border around the image with the caption included. You may not like that look. If not, consider putting captions on a separate line under photos, preferably identified with the `<caption>` HTML tag for screen readers. Another option is to provide caption information at the end of your post. And some images require no captions at all.

Consider Wrapping Text

You may want a powerful image to stand alone on a line using the None or Center formats. An image that mainly illustrates your words, however, might work better with text wrapping around it, using the left or right alignment. Make sure the photo is small enough to allow at least three or so words to fit on every line beside it.

Get yer farm-fresh produce here. The Kansas City Star provides a detailed list of farmers markets in the Kansas City region, both in Kansas and Missouri. (KC Star) Of course, other market lists are available that capture most markets in the United States. They include Local Harvest, and the USDA's Agricultural Marketing Service lists. The AMS list currently shows 81 markets in Kansas. For fellow Kansans, don't forget the KS Farmers Markets site.

Offer Two Display Options

You can upload a large photo, say one that is 800 by 1200 pixels, but insert it in your post using the Thumbnail option or a percentage display. That represents the size that the image appears in the post, but readers can click the small image and see its larger version in another window (Ⓐ).

quilt patterns, a vineyard, fruit tree plazas and the children's Fun Food Farm. It is a feast for the eyes as well as th... r. (Click below for larger images of, from left, a portion of parterre, vineyard and Fun Food Farm sign.)

Give Credit

Crediting the source of your images (Ⓐ) is useful to readers — as well as to artists and photographers, perhaps including you. You can do it in alternate text, but doing it on-screen is nicer. Some people recommend doing it both places. Also, if you do not want others to use your photos, declare your copyrights with each image.

Hot beans! Read a profile of Alan Townsend, head of the J. Hawkens Bean Co. in Goodland, Kansas. Growing edible dry beans makes sense in western Kansas. Maybe more growers will follow his lead and quit depleting the Ogallala Aquifer. (Profile by Ron Wilson, at Kansas State University.) Did I mention I love beans? You can read about the aquifer at Scientific American, among other places. (*Map: U.S. Geological Survey*) ◄ Ⓐ

Use the More Option to Break Your Posts in Two

If you would rather your readers see more headlines and less text on your blog's front page, the More option is just the thing for you. When you increase the number of posts that appear on your front page, you get an entirely different look.

Use the More Option to Break Your Posts in Two

Insert the More Tag

1 On the New Post or Edit Post panel, click the location in your post where you want to split the post.

2 Click the **Insert More Tag** button (⊞).

Ⓐ The More marker appears in the post.

3 Click **Save Draft**.

4 Click **Publish**.

The post is published to your blog.

Note: Clicking **Preview** or **View Post** does not reveal the More tag.

5 Click your site name to go to your front page.

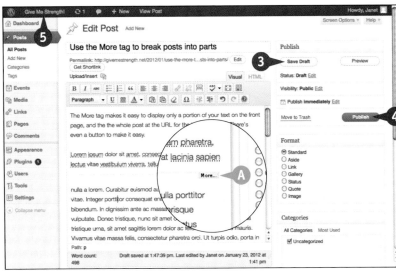

The home page of the blog opens, with only part of the divided post showing.

⑥ Click **Continue reading**, which appears at the location where you inserted the More tag.

The post page opens, revealing the full text of the post.

Note: The wording that refers readers to the full post varies from theme to theme.

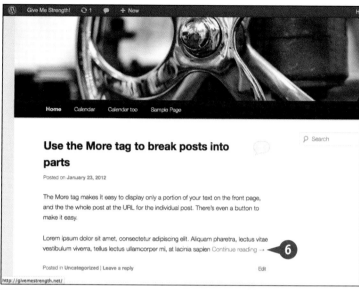

Remove the More Tag

① In the Visual text editor of the Edit Post panel, click the line or tag where More appears.

A box with handlebars appears around the More tag.

② Press Delete or Backspace, and the More tag disappears.

Note: You also can click the More tag and drag the box that appears to another location in the post.

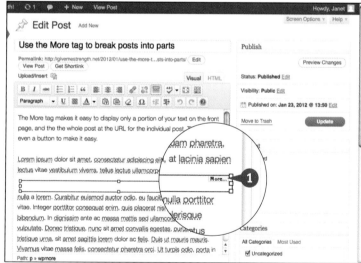

TIPS

I added More tags but still show only four posts on my front page. How can I change that?
Click the **Settings** menu in the left menu bar, and then click **Reading**. On the Reading Settings panel, change the number next to **Blog pages show at most** to the number of posts that you want on the front page.

Is it possible to change the text that the More tag displays?
On an individual post, go to the HTML editor and find the More tag, which reads `<!--more-->`. Click after `more`, type a space, and then type the text you want, such as `<!--more Please keep reading-->`, which inserts the text *Please keep reading*. To change your theme's standard More text at self-hosted blogs, use a plugin such as More Link Modifier, or do it yourself with detailed instructions at http://codex.wordpress.org/Customizing_the_Read_More.

Understanding Categories and Tags

Well-thought-out categories and tags make a convenient way for readers to navigate through your blog. Although you can add them as you go along in your blog, doing a little planning will likely make them more useful.

Categories versus Tags

If you think of your blog as a book, think of categories as chapters and tags as index items. In other words, categories work best for bigger concepts, and tags work best for details. Also, every blog post must be assigned to at least one category, but tags are optional.

Default Category

If you do not specify a category when you create a post, WordPress assigns it to the default category, which initially is *Uncategorized*. You can name and choose your default category, and probably come up with something more pertinent to your topic than *Uncategorized*.

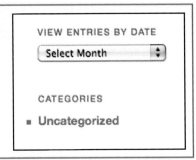

Category Display

Most blog themes include an option for displaying a category list in a sidebar, and the category of a post also may appear at the end or beginning of each post. Sidebar display options include a simple list and a drop-down list. These links take readers to an archive-type page that shows post headlines and, often, excerpts in the selected category (Ⓐ).

Categories and Subcategories

You have the option of creating subcategories, or *child* categories, as well as categories. For example, if you have a gardening blog, you might have *Flowers* as a category with *Annuals*, *Perennials*, and *Biennials* as subcategories. You might also want a *Vegetables* category and *From the Garden* as your default category's name. Tags have no hierarchy.

- Food in the news
- Food preparation
  - Cooking for one
  - Cooking tips
  - recipes
  - Tools

Why Use Tags

Although tags are optional, tags are useful because they provide another means to help and encourage readers to view more of your blog, and because they provide another means for search engines to find your blog posts.

Popular Tags

apples baking beef cherries chicken CSA desserts eggs family Farmers markets Food for change challenge foodperson.com food politics food preservation food safety foraging free food freezing fruits gardening herbs Kansas Lawrence Farmers Market Local Burger local food meat movies mushrooms Nina Planck pasta potlucks raspberries rBGH Real Food recipes restaurants Rolling Prairie Farmers Alliance Roundup salads soup spring spring produce summer produce tomatoes wheat

Best Practices

Your blog will look more professional and be easier to understand if you decide on and apply some rules to provide consistency for category and tag names. For example, you may want to

☐	**farmers market**	farmers-market	2
☐	**Farmers markets**	farmers-markets	13

make your categories nouns and capitalize them and your tags verbs and lowercase. Doing so also reduces odds that you will accidentally create both *Seeds* and *seeds* tags.

Create Categories

The Categories panel lets you create multiple categories, but you also can create categories on the fly, if you will, on the posting panel. Either way, you end up with categories to help organize your blog posts.

Create Categories

Create a Category in the Categories Panel

1 After clicking **Posts** in the left menu bar, click **Categories**.

The Categories panel opens.

2 Type a category name.

3 Type a category slug.

Note: The Slug box does not appear in WordPress.com blogs.

4 Type a description.

5 Click **Add New Category**.

The category appears in the list at right on the Categories panel.

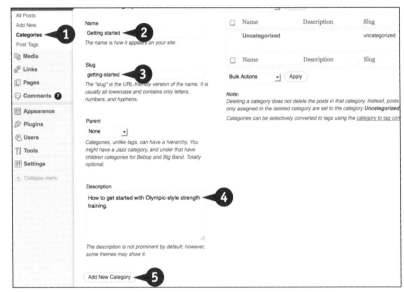

Create a Subcategory

1 Type a subcategory name.

2 Type a slug.

3 Click the drop-down menu under Parent.

4 Click the category that you want as the parent of your subcategory.

5 Type a description.

6 Click **Add New Category**.

The subcategory, preceded by a dash, appears under the parent category in the list at right on the Categories panel.

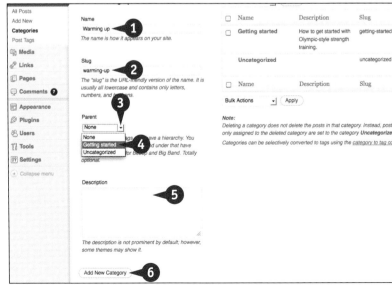

Create a Category in the Post Panel

① On the New Post or Edit Post panel, click **Add New Category** at the bottom of the Categories module.

Ⓐ Two boxes appear under Add New Category.

② Type the new category in the first box.

③ If the new category is a subcategory, click the Parent Category drop-down menu, and click a category.

④ Click **Add New Category**.

The new category appears in the Categories box as checked, meaning the post is assigned to that category.

Edit Categories

Ⓑ After clicking the name of a category in the Categories panel list, the Edit Category subpanel opens.

① Add or change information for the category.

② When you are finished, click **Update**.

The changes are saved, and WordPress returns you to the Categories panel.

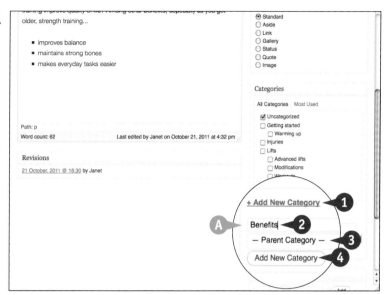

TIPS

How do I change the default category?
You can click **Uncategorized** in the list on the Categories panel to open the Edit Category panel. Then, change *Uncategorized* to the name you prefer. Another option is to click **Writing** under Settings in the left menu bar and then choose the default category from the Default Post Category drop-down menu on the Writing Settings panel.

What is a category slug?
The slug appears in the URL for a page that lists posts by category. If you do not enter a slug, WordPress converts the category name to a slug by making it all lowercase, stripping it of punctuation, and inserting hyphens where you had spaces. WordPress.com does this by default. Thus, the Getting Started category page's URL becomes www.givemestrength.net/category/getting-started.

Create Tags

T ags are like keywords attached to individual blog posts. Tags provide a convenient way for readers to search for information. Or, if they click a tag next to your post, they can get a list of posts that use that tag. Unlike categories, tags are not hierarchical, so you cannot have child and parent tags, but like categories they may improve search engine ranking.

Create Tags

Create a Tag in the Tags Panel

1 After clicking **Posts** in the left menu bar, click **Tags**.

The Post Tags panel opens.

2 Type a tag name.

3 Type a slug.

Note: If you leave the Slug box blank, WordPress creates an all lowercase slug based on the tag name. The Slug box does not appear in WordPress.com blogs.

4 Type a description.

5 Click **Add New Tag**.

The tag appears in the list on the right side of the Tags panel.

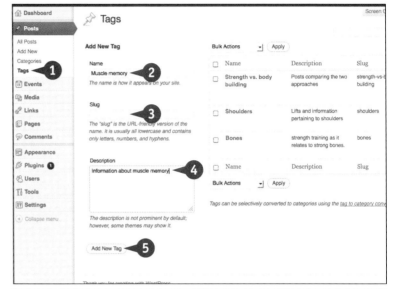

Create a Tag in the Post Panel

1 On the New Post or Edit Post panel, click in the **Add** box in the Post Tags module, and type the desired tag or tags, using a comma between tags.

A As you type, a box pops up revealing existing tags using the same letters. You can click in the box to select an existing tag.

2 Click **Add**.

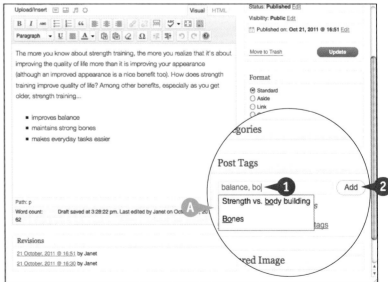

B The new tags appear below the Add New Tags box. The tags also are added to your blog's Tags panel and attached to the post you are editing.

Note: You must go to the Tags panel to edit a tag or add a description.

3 Click **Update** (or **Save Draft** if saving an unpublished post).

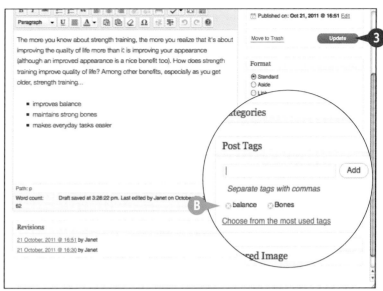

Remove Tags in the Edit Post Panel

1 Position your mouse pointer over the **Cut Tag** button (⊠) until it turns pink. Click the button.

The tag disappears from the Edit Post panel.

2 Click **Update** (or **Save Draft** if saving an unpublished post).

Note: If you do not save the post before you remove a new tag, the tag is not added to the Tags panel.

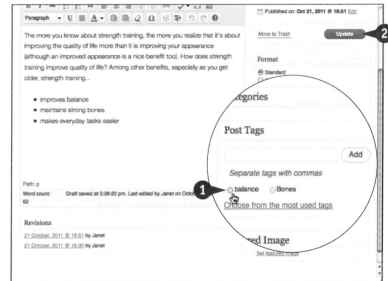

TIPS

What are global tags?

Global tags are a feature of WordPress.com, which collects tags from all the blogs it hosts to let you easily view a large number of posts that used a particular tag. You can see the most popular global tags by clicking **Topics** (ⓐ) under the WordPress button in the Admin Bar of your WordPress.com blog.

Do I need both categories and tags?

Using both is a personal choice, based on what you think works best for your site, but most experts recommend using both if you want search engine traffic.

Apply Categories and Tags to Posts

You can apply categories and tags as you create or edit your posts, or you can add them after the fact, including in bulk, from the Categories and Tags panels. You can use whichever technique fits best into your workflow.

You can use these techniques after you already have created some categories and tags.

Apply Categories and Tags to Posts

From the Post Panel

1 In the Post panel of a new or existing post, click **Choose from the most used tags** in the Post Tags module.

A tag cloud opens.

2 Click the tag you want to add to your post.

The tag appears above the tag cloud.

3 In the Categories module, click the category you want to assign the post to (☐ changes to ☑).

4 Click **Update**.

The post is now assigned to the categories and tags you specified.

From the Edit Posts Panel

1 Click **Posts** in the left menu bar.

The Posts list opens.

2 Click the posts you want to edit (☐ changes to ☑).

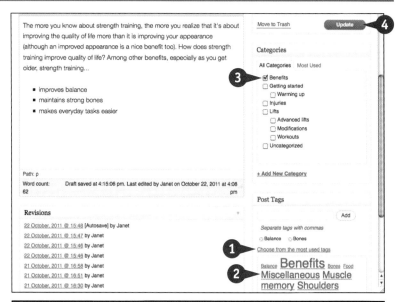

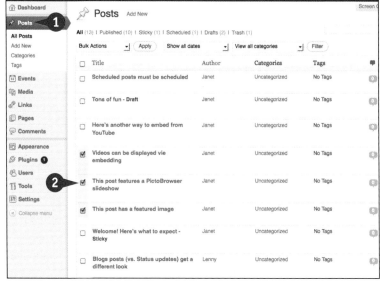

3 Click the drop-down menu next to Bulk Actions.

4 Click **Edit**.

5 Click **Apply**.

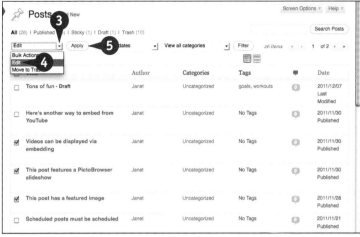

The Bulk Edit Posts pane opens with the posts you are changing listed.

6 Click the categories you want to assign to the posts (☐ changes to ☑).

7 Type tag names you want to apply to selected posts, separated by commas.

8 Click **Update**.

The categories and tags you selected are added to the posts.

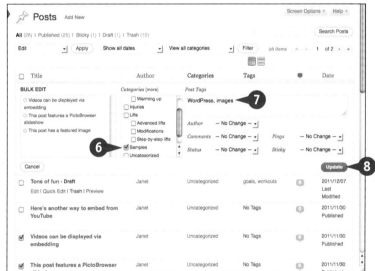

Is there a limit to the number of tags or categories I can have?

No, but it is good practice not to attach too many to a single post. A large number may confuse readers and search engines. Go for three or four of each at most. Also, your chances of getting featured in the WordPress.com global tags listing go down if you have too many tags and categories. WordPress.com suggests five to ten total on a post.

Can I use the Bulk Edit box to remove a category from a group of posts?

Not without a plugin. You must individually edit or QuickEdit each post to remove it from a category or delete the entire category on the Categories panel. If you do the latter and a post is assigned to other categories, those category assignments remain. If the post does not have another category assignment, it goes to the default category. However, a plugin, Bulk Delete, lets you delete groups of posts from selected categories or tags, and another, Bulk Move, lets you move posts from one category to another.

Convert Categories and Tags

If you imported your blog to WordPress from another blogging platform, you may find that all your old tags are now categories. Or maybe you just changed your mind on how you want to classify your posts. Fortunately, WordPress has a tool that lets you convert categories to tags and vice versa.

Convert Categories and Tags

1 Click **Tools** to expand the Tools menu in the left menu bar.

2 Click **Import**, which opens the Import page.

3 Click **Categories and Tags Converter**.

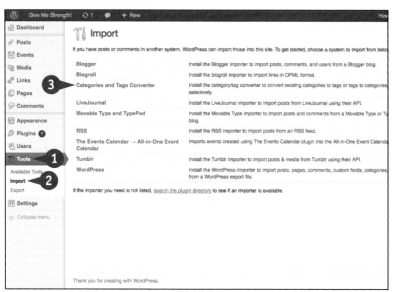

At WordPress.com, the Convert Categories to Tags panel opens. At self-hosted blogs, a plugin screen opens.

4 Click **Install Now**.

Note: WordPress.com users skip step **4**.

5 WordPress installs the plugin, and you click **Activate Plugin & Run Importer** on the installation screen.

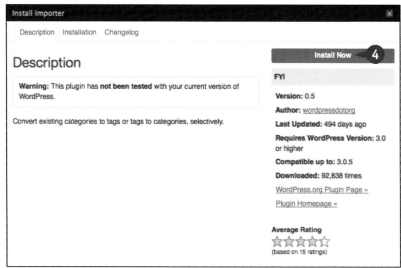

The Convert Categories (*n*) to Tags panel opens, where *n* represents the number of categories available to convert.

6 Click each category that you want to convert to a tag (☐ changes to ☑), or click **Check All** to convert all categories.

7 Click **Convert Categories to Tags**.

WordPress displays the progress and confirms the conversions.

🍴 Convert Categories (14) to Tags.

Hey there. Here you can selectively convert existing categories to tags. To get started, check the categories you wish to be converted, then click the Convert button.

Keep in mind that if you convert a category with child categories, the children become top-level orphans.

Check All

☐ Benefits (4) *
☑ Cleans (0)
☑ Dead lift (0)
☐ Getting started (0)
☐ Warming up (0)
☐ Injuries (0)
☐ Lifts (0)
☐ Modifications (0)
☐ Advanced lifts (0)
☐ Workouts (0)
☑ Presses (0)
☐ Samples (1)
☑ Squats (0)
☐ Uncategorized (14)

* This category is also a tag. Converting it will add that tag to all posts that are currently in the category.

Convert Categories to Tags

8 Click **Tags to Categories** from the progress screen or the category conversion screen, which opens the Convert Tags (*n*) to Categories panel, with *n* as the available tags.

9 Click the tag you want to convert to a category (☐ changes to ☑).

10 Click **Convert Tags to Categories**.

WordPress displays the conversion progress and converts the selected tags to categories.

Categories to Tags   Tags to Categories

🍴 Convert Tags (14) to Categories.

Here you can selectively convert existing tags to categories. To get started, check the tags you wish to be converted, then click the Convert button.

The newly created categories will still be associated with the same posts.

Check All

☐ Balance (1)
☐ Benefits (3) *
☑ Blogging (1)
☐ Bones (1)
☐ Cleans (0)
☐ Dead lift (0)
☐ Food (1)
☐ Miscellaneous (2)
☐ Muscle memory (2)
☐ Presses (0)
☐ Shoulders (2)
☐ Squats (0)
☐ Strength vs. body building (0)
☑ WordPress (1)

* This tag is also a category. When converted, all posts associated with the tag will also be in the category.

Convert Tags to Categories

TIPS

What happens to the posts when I convert categories and tags?
The names are still attached to the posts to which they were previously assigned, but as categories instead of tags, or vice versa. Because categories are required, though, if you changed all categories assigned to a particular post, the post automatically is assigned to the default category.

What happens if I convert a parent category to a tag but do not convert its child, or subcategory?
The subcategory becomes a top-level category.

Create Custom Menus

Y ou can choose what appears on your site's menus to help readers navigate the site. Custom menus give you lots of flexibility to do so, either in the main menu or as a menu widget. You can use them to call attention to the portions of your site that you want to highlight, rather than have the menu point, as it does by default, to your site's pages.

Create Custom Menus

1 Click **Menus** under Appearance in the left menu bar.

The Menus panel opens.

Note: If your theme does not support custom menus, the Menus panel allows you to create a custom menu for a widget.

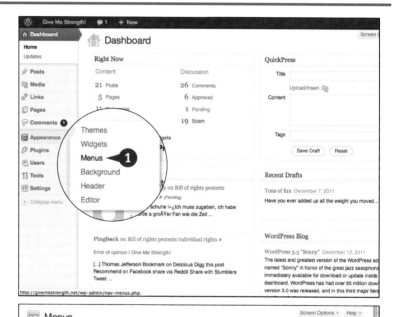

2 Type a menu name.

3 Click **Create Menu**.

A WordPress creates the menu for you and activates the content modules on the left portion of the panel.

④ Click the items you want to appear on your custom menu (☐ changes to ☑).

Note: You also may choose from tags, posts, and more. Reveal their selection modules by selecting them from Screen Options at the top of the Menus panel.

⑤ Click **Add to Menu**.

WordPress adds the items to your custom menu.

Note: If desired, you can drag the items within the module to rearrange their order.

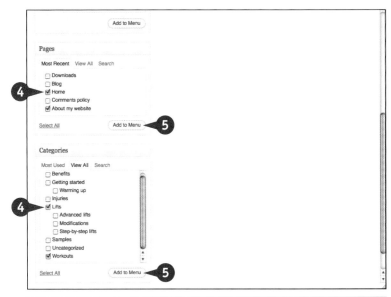

⑥ Click the Primary Navigation drop-down menu, and select your new custom menu.

⑦ Click **Save**.

Your custom menu replaces the default navigation menu on your site.

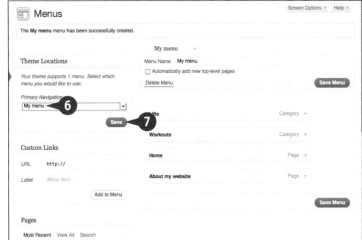

TIPS

What else can I do with custom menus?

Instead of choosing your custom menu as your primary navigation as in step **6**, you can simply save the menu, and then use the Custom Menu widget to place a custom menu in your sidebar. You can do that even if your theme does not give you the option to customize the main navigation menu. Some themes have multiple navigation menus, and you can customize each of them.

There seem to be a lot of options for these menus. What do I do with them all?

You can add a link to a menu, create submenus, edit menu item titles, and more. For details, check out the support for custom menus at http://codex.wordpress.org/Appearance_Menus_Screen for self-hosted blogs, or at http://en.support.wordpress.com/menus for blogs hosted at WordPress.com.

CHAPTER 9

Build Traffic to Your Blog

Unless you are among the minority of blog publishers who want to keep their blogs private, you probably are publishing a blog because you want people to see it and read it. You can accomplish this much more readily if people know you are there! That is where building traffic comes in.

Create a Blogroll

You can share the love by including other websites and blogs in your *blogroll*, otherwise known as a links list. Adding others to your blogroll also lets them know that your blog exists. Everybody wins!

Create a Blogroll

Create a Blogroll

1 Click **Links** in the Dashboard's left menu bar.

The Links panel opens.

Note: Every new blog comes with a few links already listed. They vary according to the theme.

2 Click **Add New**.

The Add New Link window opens.

3 In the Name module, type the name of the link as you want it to appear in your blogroll.

4 Type the complete URL of the site in the Web Address module.

5 If you want, type a brief — as in four or five words — description of the site in the Description module.

6 Click **Blogroll** (☐ changes to ☑).

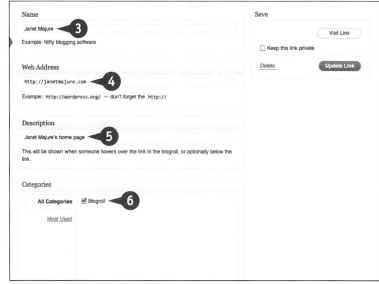

7 Scroll down to the Target module.

8 Click **_none** (◯ changes to ◉), which makes the target URL open in the same browser window or tab as your links list.

9 If desired, complete the relationship information.

10 Return to the top of the page and click **Add Link**.

WordPress saves the link and returns a new Add New Link screen.

Display Your Blogroll

1 After expanding the Appearance menu, click **Widgets**.

2 Drag the Links widget to one of the active widget areas on the right side of the Widgets panel.

3 Click your preferred display options (☐ changes to ☑).

4 Click **Save**.

WordPress saves your selections and displays your blogroll on your site.

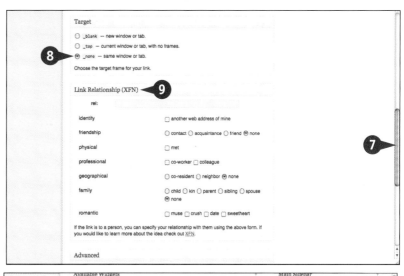

What are the Link Relationship and Advanced modules about?
The Link Relationship lets your links relay information about your relationship to the party you linked to. The Advanced options allow you to display an image right along with the link or add other information for your own use, such as RSS address, notes, and rating.

How do I organize my links into link categories?
You can create link categories on the Add New Link, Edit Link, or Link Categories panels. Then, when you edit individual links, you can assign the link to a category or categories. From the Link Categories panel, you also can edit category names, so that you can call yours Favorite Links rather than Blogroll and still have just one category. Currently, self-hosted blogs must use a plugin to sort their links by category. WordPress.com's Links widget gives some sorting flexibility.

Create a Comment Policy

Wordpress gives you the power to decide who can and cannot comment on your blog and under what conditions. You can even choose on a post-by-post basis whether people can comment on your blog. In other words, you can be the lone voice or the leader of a free-for-all. The choice is yours.

How Thick Is Your Skin?

Sharing opinions with readers sounds like a good idea until you get your first *flame*, a searingly critical comment, or *troll*, a commenter whose remarks are aimed at provoking argument, often by being nasty. If you love the kind of debate that those provoke, you may not need a comment policy. Otherwise, give it some thought.

Time Considerations

Moderating comments can be a time-consuming task, especially if you attract a lot of comments. Do you have time to manage that? Discussion Settings that give a pass to previous commenters, that ban words you specify, or that hold comments with numerous hyperlinks can reduce the load while making your blog somewhat less vulnerable to trolls.

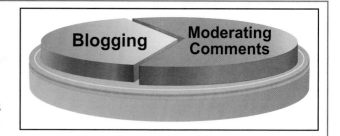

Consider Your Audience

Your policy should take into consideration not only your preferences but also those of your readers. If you are aiming at members of your church, you may want to block profanity. If you are aiming at American teens, you probably need to allow abbreviations commonly used in instant messaging and texting.

Aim for a Balance

Keep in mind that a major appeal of blogs for readers and publishers alike is the ability to interact by way of comments. Commenting that is too restricted or delayed, as when waiting for the moderator, can be frustrating for readers, but frequent malicious comments are a turnoff for lots of people. Try to strike a balance with your policy.

State Your Policy

Having a written comment policy is good for two reasons. One, creating it causes you to think about what is and is not acceptable to you. Two, it gives you something to point to when people complain about comments being deleted, edited, or excluded. Let your readers know where you stand.

1.30.2008

Comment Policy

The purpose of this blog is to facilitate an ongoing dialo in security, technology and the checkpoint screening pr encourage your comments; your ideas and concerns ar ensure that a broad range of travelers are active and ir in the discussion. TSA reserves the right to modify this

This is a moderated blog, and TSA retains the discretio which comments it will post and which it will not. That comments will be reviewed before posting. In addition, participants will treat each other, as well as our agency

Put It Where People Will Find It

Create a separate Comment Policy page, or put your policy on your About page, which is a good place because the About page is the most frequently viewed page on most blogs. If you have a self-hosted blog and are comfortable making a few adjustments with your theme, you could put your policy next to your comment form on your blog pages.

Home   Archives   Profile   Comment Policy   A

October 24, 2011

San Francisco's City CarShare Celebrates

When it comes to transportation, people want options. Everywhere I go, I Americans love their cars, but still prefer to ride transit for certain trips. Ot riders, but keep a car around for when they need to get somewhere that la simply can't afford to own a car, but like the freedom cars offer.

One innovative way of getting around urban and suburban areas that allow reducing emissions and congestion is car sharing. It's a phenomenon that the country.

What to Include in Your Policy

Make your policy clear and concise. It is a good idea to state who can comment — anyone or registered users only, for example — what you consider acceptable and unacceptable, and what your expected response is to unacceptable comments. Your response could be to edit or delete the comment or even to ban the writer via the Discussion settings. Your policy also might state if you close comments after a set number of days.

Comment on Someone Else's Blog

Commenting on others' blogs is a recognized means of attracting people to your blog. How? When others read your insightful remarks, they cannot wait to read what else you have to say. They therefore click the link in your comment that leads to your blog.

Comment on Someone Else's Blog

1 On the post that you want to comment about, click the link to the comments form.

Note: Comment link location and text will vary from one blog to another.

2 Type your name in the Name box.

3 Type your e-mail in the Email box if required.

4 Type your blog's URL in the Website box.

Note: Most blogs provide a link to your website with your comment.

5 Type your comment in the space provided.

Ⓐ Some blogs let you preview your post.

6 Type the words or letters of the *captcha* (or in this case ReCaptcha) box, if present.

Note: Captcha is a spam-avoidance tool, which you can add to self-hosted blogs with a plugin. See Chapter 7 to learn about using plugins.

7 Click **Submit Comment**.

Your comment is published or submitted for moderation.

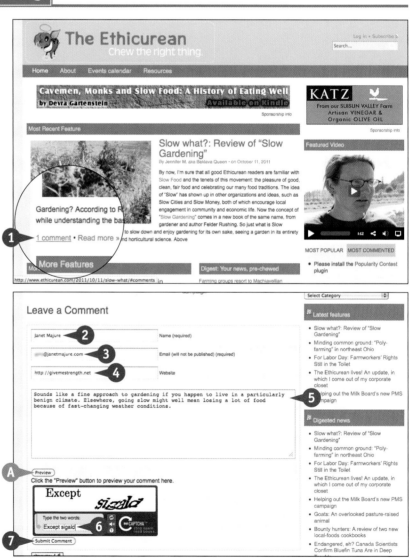

186

What to Say on Someone Else's Blog

Well-placed and considered comments prompt readers of other people's blogs to click to your website to read what else you have to say. Reading and commenting contributes to the blogging community and adds to your standing.

What to Say

Add something *useful* to the conversation. Useful might be anything from adding a bit of helpful advice based on your experience with the subject to sharing the good resources you know about. Useful also may mean to pose a question related to the blog post; pertinent questions expand the conversation. Also, you should see if the site has a comments policy and read it before commenting.

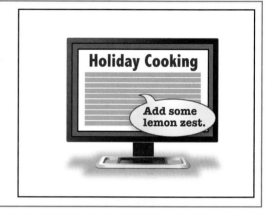

How to Say It

Whatever you say, keep it relevant to the topic of the blog post, keep it brief, and keep it polite. Break any of those rules and you lose most if not all the benefits that you might accrue by commenting. If you can provide a link to a useful resource, add it to your comment too. As always, proofread what you write; you may not be able to change it.

What Not to Say

New bloggers, eager to attract readers, often are tempted to visit numerous blogs and comment, "Great post!" or "Thanks for writing this!" Although such comments do little harm, they rarely have the desired effect — and they might be identified as spam. Self-promotional comments are rarely welcome, unless you really do have *the* solution to the problem being discussed.

Moderate Comments

Chances are you will need to moderate, or review, comments occasionally, even if you have a fairly wide-open comment policy. Doing so reduces comment spam and keeps the commentary within your comments policy. Remember you can choose which comments need to be moderated and how and whether you are notified with the Discussion Settings, as explained in Chapter 4.

Moderate Comments

Moderate an Individual Comment

1 Click **Comments** in the left menu bar of the administrative interface or Comments in the Dashboard's Right Now module.

The Comments panel opens.

Ⓐ The number of comments awaiting moderation appears here.

Ⓑ Comments awaiting moderation appear in the Recent Comments module with a note, *[Pending]*, and a pale yellow background.

2 Position your mouse pointer over the area of a comment awaiting moderation, which has a pale yellow background.

A set of options appears.

Note: Typos and lots of links are common in spam comments.

3 Click **Approve** to approve the comment.

The comment is published to your blog, and the background turns white.

Note: The other options are discussed later in this chapter.

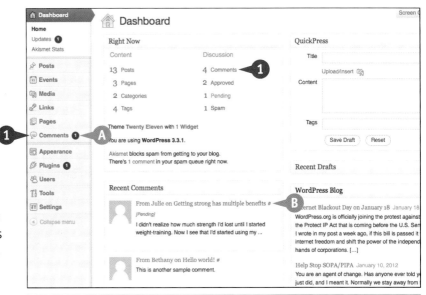

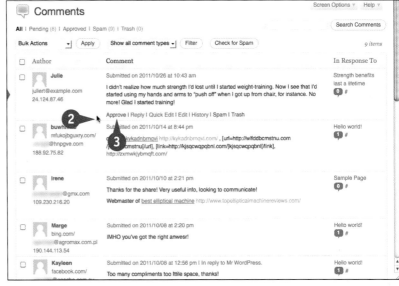

Moderate Multiple Comments

1 Click the comments you want to moderate (☐ changes to ☑).

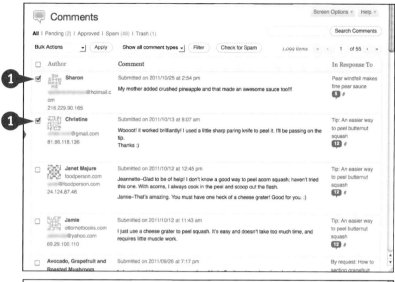

2 Click the drop-down menu next to Bulk Actions.

The Bulk Actions menu expands.

3 Click **Approve**.

4 Click **Apply**.

All checked comments are approved and published.

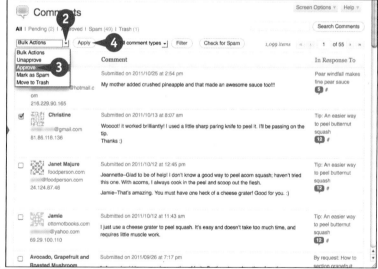

TIPS

What do I do about the e-mail I got asking me to moderate a comment?

Just click the appropriate link to approve the comment, delete it, or "spam it." Or, you can click the fourth link, which takes you to the moderation panel, otherwise known as the Edit Comments panel.

What is that information under In Response To on the Comments panel?

Ⓐ Shows name of post associated with the comment and links to Edit Post panel for that post.

Ⓑ Applies filter to show only those comments made on the post listed.

Ⓒ Links to published post associated with the comment.

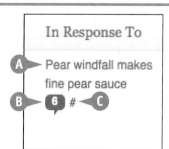

Edit a Comment

Editing comments lets you correct typos, tone down rhetoric, or make comments conform to your comment policy. Editing often is a nicer alternative to approving or deleting troublesome comments.

Edit a Comment

From the Edit Comment Panel

1 While you are logged on to your blog, click **Edit** next to the published comment you want to change.

The Edit Comment panel opens.

Note: Not all themes provide links from the comment display to the Edit Comment panel.

2 Make any changes you want, including spelling, grammar, and HTML formatting, in the HTML editing box.

Note: A WYSIWYG comment editor is not available at this time.

A Firefox's built-in spell-checker highlights possible misspellings.

3 Edit the publication time if desired.

4 Click **Update Comment**.

WordPress saves the changes and returns you to where you clicked Edit on the blog post or Edit Comments panel.

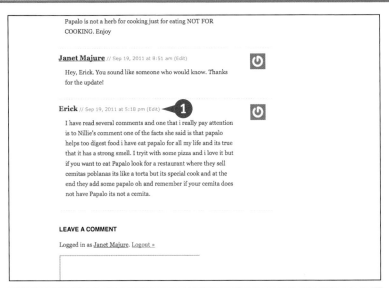

From the Quick Edit Pane

1 Position your mouse pointer over the comment you want to edit, and click the **Quick Edit** link that appears.

The Quick Edit pane expands.

2 Make any changes you want, including spelling, grammar, and HTML formatting, in the HTML editing box.

Note: Editing options in this pane are limited to the comment text, author, e-mail, and URL.

3 Click **Update Comment** when you are done.

The changes are saved, and the Quick Edit pane closes.

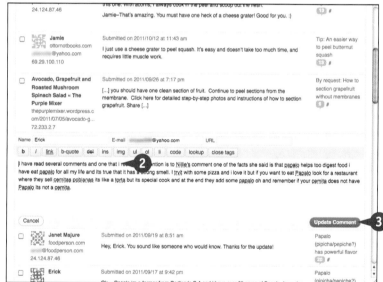

TIPS

Why would I want to edit the published time?

You may have occasions where you want to change the order in which comments appear. Editing the times can change the order.

Is there a way that commenters can edit their own comments?

If you have a self-hosted blog, you use the WP Ajax Edit Comments plugin or Edit Comments XT plugin to make that happen. See Chapter 7 for information about plugins.

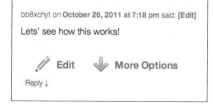

Respond to Comments on Your Blog

If you think blogs are all about conversation, then you will want to respond to your readers' comments. When you do, you also build readers' sense of involvement in your blog, which can increase loyalty and readership.

Respond to Comments on Your Blog

From the Blog Page

1 If you are logged in, simply type your response in the comment box.

2 When you are finished, click **Post Comment**.

Your comment is published to the site.

Note: If you are not logged in as administrator, you have to enter a name and e-mail address just as any other commenter would.

From the Dashboard

1 After going to the Comments panel by clicking **Comments** in the left menu bar, position the mouse pointer over the comment you want to respond to and click **Reply**.

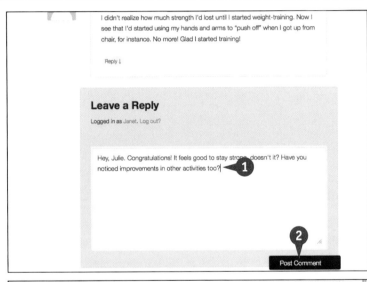

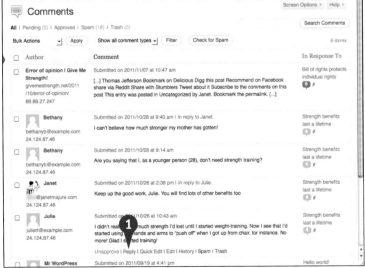

The Reply to Comment pane opens.

2 Type your response in the space provided.

3 Click **Reply**.

The Reply to Comment pane closes.

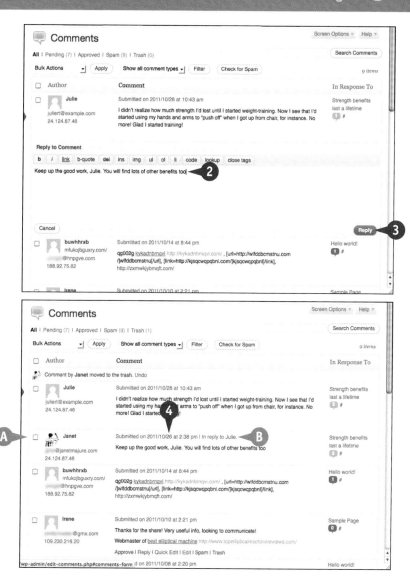

A The Comments panel lists the reply, which also is published to your blog site.

B The Comment details note that the comment is in reply to *Name,* where *Name* represents the commenter. If you have allowed threaded comments as discussed later in this chapter, the comment appears under that particular comment rather than as the newest comment.

4 Click the date and time display.

The link takes you to the published comment.

TIPS

Can I respond to several comments at once?

If you are looking for a bulk response option, none exists. What most bloggers do is to write one comment but refer to previous comments by the writers' names as shown on their comments. For example, you might write, "Susan, I agree with you. Bill, you make a good point, but I think . . ."

How do I link to a particular comment?

The date and time display with each comment on the Edit Comments panel has a permalink to the comment embedded in it. You can right-click the link and choose **Copy Link Location** to copy the comment's permalink. Then, use that permalink as needed. Or, click the date and time display, which takes you to the comment, and the permalink for that comment appears in your browser address bar.

Deal with Comment Spam

E ven after setting hurdles for commenters to clear, comment spam still gets through. Your blog will look better and be more appealing if you make sure that spam comments get zapped as soon as possible.

The Akismet tool covered in Chapter 7 is the primary means by which WordPress bloggers handle spam comments.

Deal with Comment Spam

Spam that Got Published

① After clicking **Comments** in the left menu bar to open the Edit Comments panel, find the offending comment in the list, position your mouse pointer over the comment to reveal the options, and click **Spam**.

The comment moves to the spam queue.

Ⓐ The marked comment is noted in the Comments list, along with an Undo link to click if you made a mistake.

Note: Spam comments do not otherwise appear in the ordinary Comments list after you click the **All** option under the Comments title.

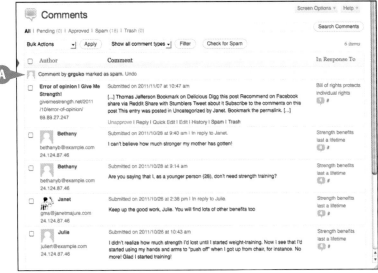

From an E-Mail Notice

1 After getting an e-mail notice to moderate a comment and clicking the link to "spam it," click **Spam Comment** in the Moderate Comment screen to confirm the item is spam.

WordPress sends the item to the spam comment list and notifies the Akismet database, which aids its spam-catching ability.

B You can click **No** if you realize the comment is not spam.

Review Spam Comments

1 Click **Comments**.

2 Click **Spam**.

The Comments panel reveals comments marked as spam. Review to make sure no valid comments are incorrectly identified as spam. You can position the mouse pointer over any valid comments and click the **Not Spam** link that appears, sending it to the regular comments list.

3 Click **Empty Spam**.

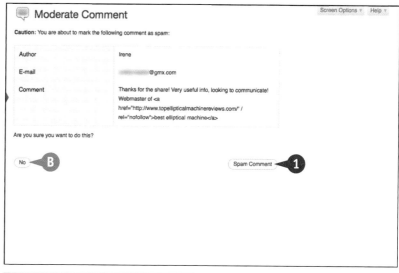

TIPS

How often do I need to review the spam list?
It depends on how active your blog is. You need to check it periodically, though, to make sure that your spam queue is not eating up your disk space and to make sure valid comments are not getting caught. Akismet automatically deletes comment spam after a month at WordPress.com and by default for self-hosted sites unless you told it differently. Click **Settings** for Akismet in the Plugins panel if you are not sure.

Why not just click Trash when a spam comment shows up in the Comments panel?
When you click **Trash** rather than **Spam**, you are not letting Akismet learn what senders and IP addresses are sending you spam comments. So, click **Spam** when you get a spam comment, and Akismet will start catching that sender for other WordPress users too.

Allow Threaded Comments

Y ou can reply — and let readers reply — directly to specific comments others make on your blog. The result is stair-stepped, or *threaded*, comments, and you can make them several levels deep.

Allow Threaded Comments

Enable Threaded Comments

1 Click **Settings**.

The General Settings panel opens and the Settings menu expands.

2 Click **Discussion**.

The Discussion panel opens.

3 Click **Enable threaded (nested) comments** (☑ changes to ☐).

4 Click the drop-down menu next to 5, the default level setting.

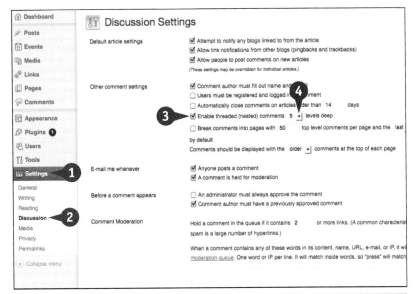

The level number drop-down menu opens.

5 Click the number of levels of threaded commentary you want.

6 Scroll to the bottom of the page and click **Save Changes**. A confirmation message appears.

7 After saving changes, click your blog name to visit the site.

Your blog opens for you to check the comments, and a Reply link appears with each comment in addition to with the post.

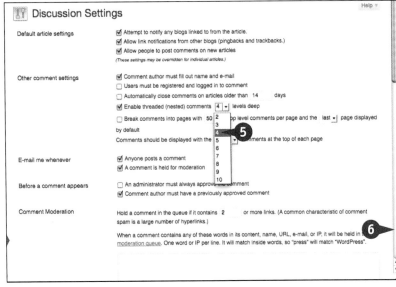

Reply to a Specific Comment from Post

1 After going to the comments on a post, click **Reply** in the comment box that you want to reply to.

The regular Reply box disappears, and a Reply box that combines with the comment appears.

2 Type your reply in the Leave a Reply box.

3 Click **Submit Comment** when done.

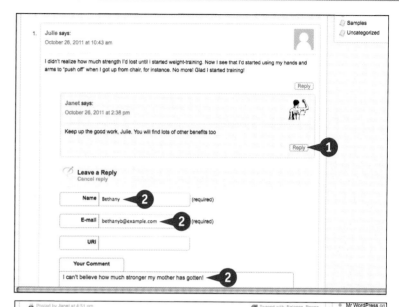

A The comment appears as a *subcomment* of the selected comment.

B Subcomments become threaded or nested.

C Comments made by clicking the Reply link in the post are *top-level* comments.

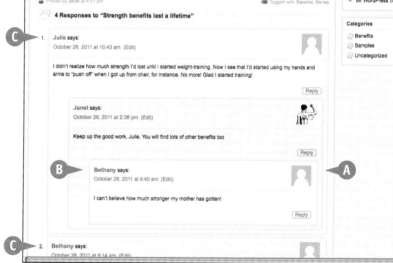

I am not finding the threaded comments option on my Discussion Settings panel.
Your theme may not support threaded comments. All themes at WordPress.com do, but a few themes for self-hosted sites may not. You can ask your theme developer to add threaded comments, or find out how to do it yourself at WordPress.org.

Can I create a threaded comment by clicking Reply on a comment in the Edit Comments panel?
Yes. Just click **Reply** under the appropriate comment. Note that if you want to add a top-level comment — a comment that is *not* threaded — you need to go to the blog post on the site, and create a new comment there.

Understanding Trackbacks and Pingbacks

Trackbacks and pingbacks automatically alert blogs when other bloggers have linked to them. When you publish trackbacks and pingbacks as miniature "comments," you also let readers see that your blog has credibility elsewhere.

Why Send Trackbacks and Pingbacks

Sending trackbacks and pingbacks to blogs that you have referred to builds community among bloggers and promotes your blog to the sites to which you link. It is a nice way to give credit and to let others know you exist.

Why Publish Trackbacks and Pingbacks

Publishing the trackbacks and pingbacks that other blogs have sent to your site similarly encourages community. It lets you and your readers discover other sites, and is a way of saying thank you to the blogs that have linked to your site.

How Trackbacks and Pingbacks Look

The appearance of trackbacks and pingbacks depends on the theme, but most themes style them a little differently than they do other comments. Typically, a theme displays a link to the post that links to yours and an excerpt from the pingback post. Some themes may allow you to publish pingbacks and trackbacks separately from other comments.

> **Ruby Red Grapefruit: Jewels in my Kitchen** // Nov 21, 2010 at 10:03 pm (Edit)
>
> [...] help sectioning a grapefruit? Here's a great step by step pictorial that is really [...]
>
> Reply
>
> **Avocado, Grapefruit and Roasted Mushroom Spinach Salad « The Purple Mixer** // Sep 26, 2011 at 7:17 pm (Edit)
>
> [...] you should have one clean section of fruit. Continue to peel sections from the membrane. Click here for detailed step-by-step photos and instructions of how to section grapefruit. Share [...]
>
> Reply

Trackbacks versus Pingbacks

Trackbacks are manual, and pingbacks are automatic if you have enabled them. With pingbacks, that means that if you link to another site, WordPress automatically sends a sort of mini-comment to the other site showing that you have linked to the site.

How to Enable Trackbacks and Pingbacks

Whether to routinely allow trackbacks and pingbacks is part of the default article settings mentioned in Chapter 5. The Attempt To Notify setting is for sending pingbacks, and the Allow Link Notifications setting is for publishing them on your site. You can change settings for individual posts, instead of site wide, in the Discussion module of the Edit Post panel.

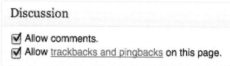

Discussion

☑ Allow comments.
☑ Allow trackbacks and pingbacks on this page.

How to and Why Send a Trackback

You may want to send a trackback when you mention or give credit to a blog but do not specifically link to it. To do so, enter the URL of the blog or blog post in the Trackback module of the Edit Post/New Post panel.

Send Trackbacks

Send trackbacks to:

(Separate multiple URLs with spaces)

Trackbacks are a way to notify legacy blog systems that you've linked to them. If you link other WordPress sites they'll be notified automatically using pingbacks, no other action necessary.

Stop Unwanted Self-Pingbacks

To prevent a pingback from appearing on an old post that you link to in a newer post, type only the part of the previous post's URL that comes after the domain as your

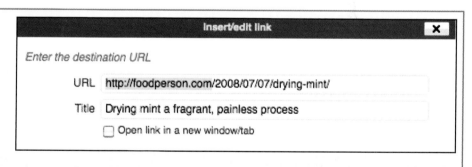

Insert/edit link   ✕

Enter the destination URL

URL   http://foodperson.com/2008/07/07/drying-mint/

Title   Drying mint a fragrant, painless process
        ☐ Open link in a new window/tab

link. In other words, instead of using *http://www.myblog.com/2012/03/12/oldpost/* as the link, use */2012/ 03/12/oldpost/*. If that fails, use the HTML editor to enter the link.

Understanding and Joining RSS Feeds

B y providing an RSS feed from your blog — which WordPress creates automatically — you are giving people who use feed readers ready access to your new content. Feed readers let someone read the updates of all of his or her favorite websites by going to a single location. When you read feeds, you too can keep up with your favorites.

What Is RSS?

RSS stands for *Really Simple Syndication*, and it really is simple to use. All it takes is a feed reader and feeds from your favorite sites. Blogs and news sites typically provide feeds. When you open your feed reader, you see content from each site that has been added since you last read that site's feed.

Feed Readers

Feed readers, also called aggregators, may be web-based, such as Google Reader and Bloglines. Some, such as FeedDemon for Windows, are *client* programs based on your local computer that download your feeds. Others are browser extensions. You can find a comparison list at http://en.wikipedia.org/wiki/Comparison_of_feed_aggregators.

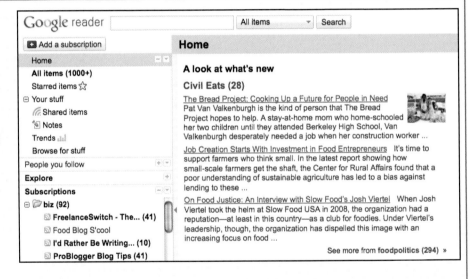

Identify Feeds

Internet Explorer and Firefox make it easy for you to identify pages that have feeds. IE shows the standard orange RSS logo in its toolbar. Firefox shows the logo in the address bar. In either case, clicking the logo opens a feed sign-up window. Also, many web pages display text or logo or both, inviting you to subscribe.

Subscribe to Feeds

Choose a feed reader for yourself, and then start subscribing to feeds. Subscribing to at least a few blogs in your topic area is a good idea to see what others are saying. Sign up for your feed, too, so that you can make sure that your feed is functioning properly.

Decide Feed Settings

Your blog's Reading Settings under Settings in the left menu bar specify whether your feed includes an entire post or a summary. If you choose summary, the feed sends an Excerpt if you wrote one on the Posts panel. If you did not, it sends a *teaser* — the words before a More tag. If there is no More tag, the feed sends the first 55 words of your post. WordPress.com blogs and plugins at self-hosted sites provide added options.

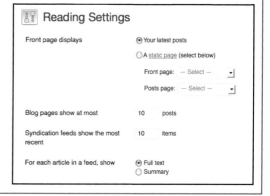

Invite Your Readers to Subscribe

You can do more to promote your blog's feed than rely on the RSS logos in browsers and perhaps within your theme. Consider writing a post from time to time specifically about your feeds — WordPress comes with one for your new posts and one for comments — or adding a line at the end of each post encouraging subscriptions or mentioning it in a sidebar.

Subscribe to my RSS feed!

Click here and start reading!

Track Feed Traffic

I f you wonder how many people are subscribed to your feed, you can get a pretty good idea by opening an account with FeedBurner, a service that Google acquired in 2007. You can get other helpful services through FeedBurner, too. If you have a WordPress.com blog, however, the host recommends using the Follow option on your site instead.

You need to have or create a Google logon to use FeedBurner.

Track Feed Traffic

Use FeedBurner

1 Type **feedburner.google.com** into your web browser, which takes you to the FeedBurner My Feeds page.

Note: If you are not already logged into your Google account, you first are asked to sign in.

2 Type your blog's URL into the Burn a Feed box.

3 Click **Next**.

The Identify Feed Source page opens. It lists all feeds available at your home page URL.

4 Click the feed you want to track (○ changes to ◉).

5 Click **Next**.

FeedBurner confirms the feed, and you click **Skip directly to feed management**, which opens a page saying that your feed is ready.

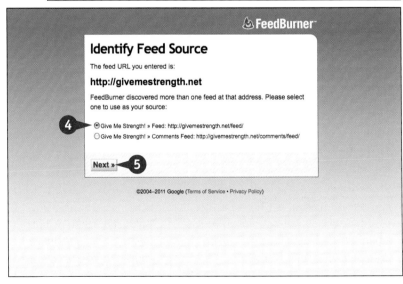

6 Scroll down on the page until you see WordPress logos.

7 Click **Use this plugin** under Self-Hosted WordPress.

A page opens that gives instructions for the FeedSmith plugin.

Note: Additional FeedBurner plugins are available through the Plugins panel on self-hosted blogs. Next time you go to FeedBurner, it displays your feeds and subscribers.

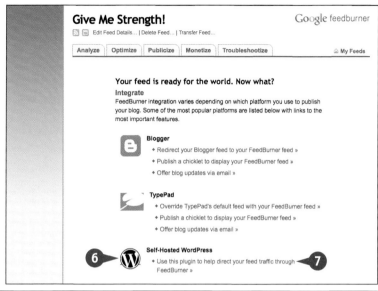

Follow at WordPress.com

1 With the Follow option available by default at WordPress.com, all you need to do is click **Site Stats** under the Dashboard menu, and then scroll down to see the Totals, Followers & Shares module.

A The total number of followers of your site appears here.

What if I want both my posts and my comments feeds tracked at FeedBurner?
Click the **My Feeds** tab at the top of the FeedBurner page when you are logged in. You can type another feed URL or put in your blog URL again, click **Next**, and then select the comments feed to track.

I do not see a link to sign up for RSS on my blog. How do I get one?
Because WordPress automatically creates two feeds — for posts and for comments — for your site, your browser's address bar shows it. With Internet Explorer, you see the orange feeds logo; click it to see the feeds on a page. At Firefox, you can click the Bookmarks menu or button, and choose **Subscribe**. The feed URL pops up. If you want your site to show a subscription link, see "Add an RSS Feed to Your Sidebar" later in this chapter.

Offer E-Mail Subscriptions

Not everyone wants go to the Internet to get blog updates. Fortunately, FeedBurner and WordPress.com let you offer e-mail subscriptions to your feed. It is simple to do, so you have no reason not to offer this service.

If you have a self-hosted site, you first need to set up an account with FeedBurner; see "Track Feed Traffic," the preceding section. WordPress.com has a widget for e-mail subscriptions.

Offer E-Mail Subscriptions

Through FeedBurner

1 After logging into your FeedBurner account, click the feed on which you want to offer e-mail subscriptions.

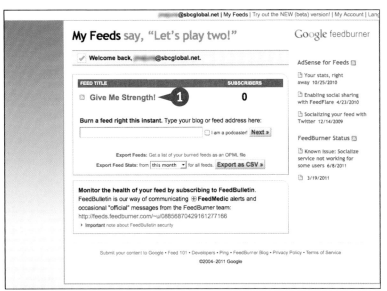

2 The Feed Stats page opens, where you click the **Publicize** tab.

3 When the Publicize Your Feed page opens, click **Email Subscriptions** in the left sidebar.

4 The Email Subscriptions page opens, where you click **Activate**.

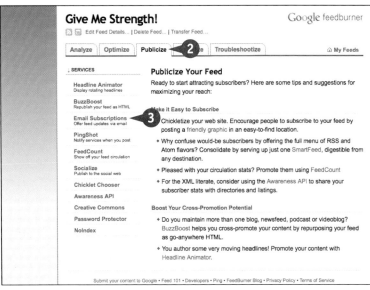

The Subscriptions Management panel opens and confirms your activation.

5 Click **Send me an email** if you want notification when people unsubscribe (☐ changes to ☑).

6 Copy all the code in the top code box to create a signup form for your site.

7 Put the code in a Text widget in your sidebar in your blog's Widget panel and save the widget, which publishes the form to your sidebar.

Note: You can use the code in the second box to create a signup link rather than a form.

At WordPress.com

1 After dragging the Follow Blog widget to a sidebar in the Widgets panel, review the standard text and make any change you want in it.

2 Click **Show total number** (☑ changes to ☐) until you have enough followers to boast about.

3 Click **Save**.

The Follow Blog widget is published to your site.

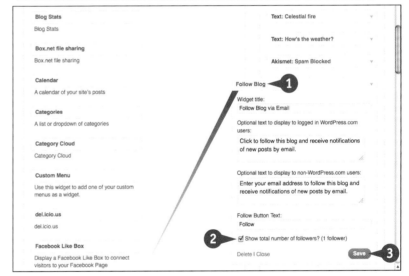

TIPS

Whose e-mail address shows as the sender from my FeedBurner-managed e-mail?

The e-mail address you used to sign up at FeedBurner appears, unless you prefer something else. If you want to change the "from" e-mail, click **Communication Preferences** under Email Subscriptions on the Publicize tab at FeedBurner. You also can change the standard confirmation e-mail text and subject line on that page. Remember to save changes.

After I set up the link and subscribed to my own feed, I put up a new post, but I have not gotten it in my e-mail. Did I do something wrong?

It may be a matter of timing. At FeedBurner click **Delivery Options** under Email Subscriptions in the Publicize panel, choose the time for your daily e-mail, and click **Save**.

Add an RSS Feed to Your Sidebar

You can continue to build community or keep your readers up to date with your favorite blogs by posting an RSS feed on your blog's sidebar. A WordPress widget simplifies this task once you choose what feeds to feature.

Add an RSS Feed to Your Sidebar

1 After you identify a feed you want to subscribe to, click its subscribe link to open a subscriptions page, and copy the URL in the address box.

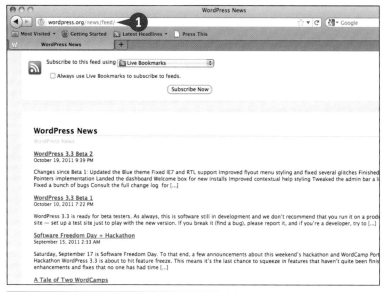

2 After going to **Widgets** under Appearance in the left menu of your Dashboard, scroll to the RSS widget, and click and drag the widget to the sidebar panel where you want the feed to appear.

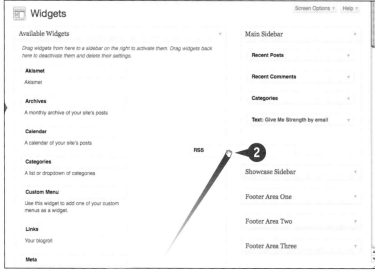

The widget opens.

③ Paste the URL of the feed in the first box.

Note: Be sure to include the protocol, http://.

④ Type a name for the feed.

⑤ Click the drop-down menu next to How Many Items and click to choose the number of feed items you want to display.

Ⓐ Check boxes let you add content, author, or date to the RSS display on your page.

⑥ Click **Save**.

⑦ Click **Close**.

The feed is published to your sidebar.

⑧ Click the blog title to go to your site.

⑨ Scroll down to view your RSS feed display.

⑩ Position your mouse pointer over one of the headlines to read the first part of that item's content.

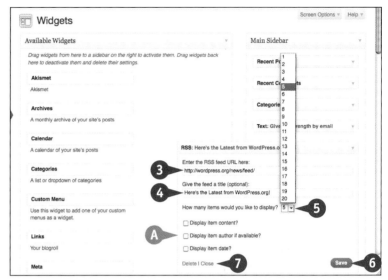

Can I publish my own feed this way on my blog?

No, you need to use the Recent Posts widget instead. You can read about standard widgets in Chapter 7.

Recent Posts

The most recent posts on your site

What is the difference between the RSS widget and the RSS Links widget?

The RSS Links widget, available as a default only on WordPress.com, lets you promote your own feeds in your sidebar. You can choose whether the links are text only, image only, or text plus image, and if you use image only, you can choose the color of the RSS logo. Similar plugins are available for self-hosted WordPress blogs.

Promote Your Blog via Social Media

Even if you are not a member of Facebook, LinkedIn, Twitter, MySpace, Digg, or other online communities, you can be sure some of your readers are. If you take advantage of that situation, you not only can promote your blog, but your readers can promote it, too. These social networks are evolving fast, so watch your WordPress news to see what new options are available. And remember that you can use social media both for incoming and outgoing content.

Social Networks and Bookmarks

At social networks such as Facebook and LinkedIn, people post personal updates and photos — and tell friends about favorite web pages they have read. Delicious, Digg, StumbleUpon, and other social *bookmarking* sites are specifically for users to store favorite links. All these sites can boost traffic to your blog, so it is nice to republish to these sites, tweet to the microblog Twitter, and make it easy for readers to recommend your post to their social networks.

Republish Your WordPress.org Posts

The easiest way to republish, or *crosspost,* your WordPress.org posts is via a plugin. Some plugins exist for a single service, such as Facebook. Others provide multiservice connections. Among the possibilities is the WordSocial plugin for Facebook, Twitter, and LinkedIn, or the Leenk.me plugin for those plus Google+ and FriendFeed.

The Publicize Tool at WordPress.com

The Publicize settings — available on the Sharing Settings panel under Settings in the left menu bar at WordPress.com — provide links to connect with and publish to Facebook, Twitter, Yahoo! Updates, Windows Live Messenger, and LinkedIn. Clicking the **Connect to** link for each service takes you through a series of screens that tells those services to publish an update with your latest WordPress.com post.

Let Readers Promote WordPress.org Posts

Numerous plugins are available that let your readers recommend your posts by clicking buttons that go to their social networking sites, such as Facebook, or their social bookmarking sites, such as StumbleUpon. Favorite plugins include AddToAny, Share and Follow, and Social Sharing Toolkit.

- improves balance
- maintains strong bones
- makes everyday tasks easier

Posted in **Benefits** | Tagged **Balance, Bones** | 4 Replies

The Share Buttons at WordPress.com

The Share Button options — on the Sharing Settings panel under Settings in the left menu bar at WordPress.com — let you select buttons for several social and bookmarking services to appear with your posts. To enable a service, drag it from the Available Services area (**A**) to the Enabled Services area (**B**). You also can choose: button display styles (**C**); the buttons' label (**D**); how to open links (**E**); and when to display buttons (**F**).

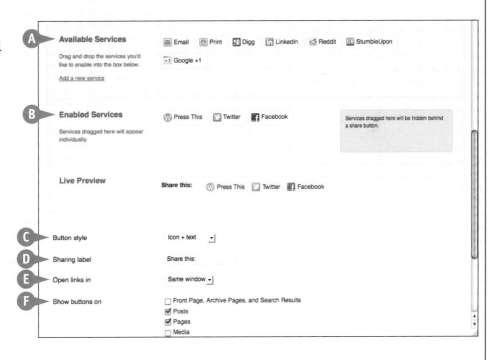

Bring Tweets to Your Blog

If you blog at Twitter — or follow other Twitter users — you probably want to bring tweets *to* your blog. WordPress and Twitter provide tools to do that easily, as explained in the next section.

Connect with Twitter

WordPress and Twitter let you communicate more than ever. Your blog readers can keep up with your Twitter feed right on your blog, and you can display other Twitter feeds of interest to your readers.

You need a Twitter account, available at http://twitter.com, to get started.

Connect with Twitter

Set Up Your Twitter Feed for WordPress.org Blogs

1 After logging in at Twitter.com, in your browser, go to http://twitter.com/about/resources/widgets.

2 Click **My Website**.

A list of widgets appears.

3 Click **Profile Widget**.

The Customize Your Profile Widget page opens, showing your username and latest Tweets.

4 Click **Dimensions**.

Dimension options appear.

5 Click **auto width** (☐ changes to ☑).

Note: You also can change colors and more by clicking **Preferences** and **Appearance**. You can click **Test settings** to see those option changes.

6 Click **Finish & Grab Code**.

The screen changes, and the code appears in a box.

7 Click in the box to select the code, and then copy and paste it in a new text widget on your WordPress.org site.

Set Up Your Twitter Feed at WordPress.com

1 After dragging a Twitter widget to a sidebar on the Widgets panel, type a title for the widget.

2 Type your Twitter username in the box.

3 Click **Hide Tweets pushed by Publicize** (☐ changes to ☑).

4 Click **Save**.

The Twitter feed is published to your blog sidebar, styled to match your theme.

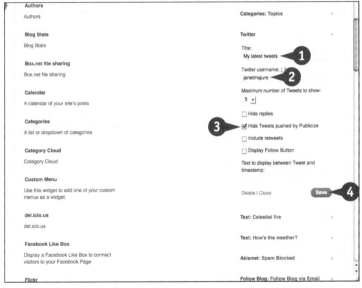

TIPS

I followed the directions, but nothing is showing up in the feed.
Make sure that the Twitter feed you want to show is public. Go to your Twitter settings, and see whether you have selected Protect My Tweets. The check box must be empty (☐). If it is not, click to clear the box, and then click **Save**.

Tweet Privacy	☐ Protect my Tweets
	Only let people whom I approve follow
	If this is checked, your future Tweets w
	previously may still be publicly visible

Can I post other people's Twitter feeds?
Yes. Just follow the same steps as for your own feed. Of course, the feed needs to be public.

211

Optimize Your Blog for Search Engines

You draw more readers to your blog when they are able to find it through search engines such as Google and Yahoo!. *Search engine optimization*, or SEO, means taking steps to help search engines do just that.

How SEO Works

Search engine companies do not reveal exactly the process they use to rank web pages found in their searches — and they change them periodically. Whatever their specific algorithm, you can be sure it is based largely on words. WordPress gives multiple opportunities for you to feature words that highlight your blog and specific posts. Go to www.google.com/webmasters/docs/search-engine-optimization-starter-guide.pdf to read the SEO suggestions straight from the leading search engine.

Use Keywords

Keywords are key to SEO. Think of keywords as words or phrases that people might use when searching for information that you have in your blog post. Therefore, if you have a post with great information about health problems in golden retrievers, use the term *golden retrievers* frequently, and not just your dog's name, *Bruno*.

Use Meaningful Blog Post Titles

Keywords need to appear in your blog post titles, or headlines, too. They are more search-engine friendly if they are specific rather than general. For example, a title reading *8 Easy-to-Care-For Tropical House Plants* is likely to get more search engine traffic than a title reading *My Favorite Plants*.

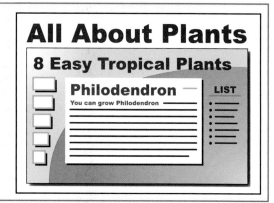

Choose Custom Permalinks

If you have a self-hosted blog, choose a post permalink structure that includes the post title or headline. You can do that on the Permalinks panel available under Settings in the left menu bar. (WordPress.com blogs automatically include the post title.) You can shorten the permalink when you create a post if you think it is too long.

 Permalink Settings

By default WordPress uses web URLs which have question marks and lots URL structure for your permalinks and archives. This can improve the aesth available, and here are some examples to get you started.

Common settings

○ Default   http://givemestrength.net/?

○ Day and name   http://givemestrength.net/2

Select Meaningful Category Names

Category names also provide words that search engines scan, or *crawl*. Again, specific names are better than general ones. Naming a category *Pet Care Books* is better than naming it simply *Books*, even if your blog topic clearly is pet care. Same thing for tags.

CATEGORIES

- Books about food
- Classes/education opportunities
- Digest
- Eating out

Other SEO Opportunities

Provide lots of high-quality content and update often, and your SEO will be fine. Still, you can and should use keywords in the alternate text of your images (see Chapter 6). At a self-hosted blog, you might consider an SEO plugin such as All in One SEO Pack or WordPress SEO. Provide opportunities for users to recommend your site as noted in this chapter in "Promote Your Blog via Social Media." Encourage visitors to stay on your site longer and click through to other pages. Site mapping, available via a plugin, also can be helpful.

Google Analytics WordPress

Track your WordPress site easily in Google Analytics

SEO No-No's

Although incoming links to your site help SEO, do not waste your money paying someone to build links to your site. Ignore outdated recommendations to stuff your site with lots of metadata and extra keywords. Search engines have become wise to those techniques.

Use Surveys and Polls

Surveys and polls get readers involved in your blog, and when readers feel involved, they want to come back for more. WordPress.com has a Polldaddy poll tool built in, and self-hosted blogs can get similar functions with a Polldaddy plugin. Other poll and ratings plugins also are available.

If your blog is self-hosted, first go to Polldaddy.com and register. Then install the Polldaddy Polls & Ratings plugin; you can read about plugin installation in Chapter 7. If your blog is at WordPress.com, click **Polls** and then auto-create an account at Polldaddy.

Use Surveys and Polls

Note: This example creates a poll. See the tip for more information about surveys.

1 Click **Polls** in the left menu of your Dashboard.

The Polls menu expands, and the Polldaddy Polls panel opens.

2 Click **Create a Poll Now**.

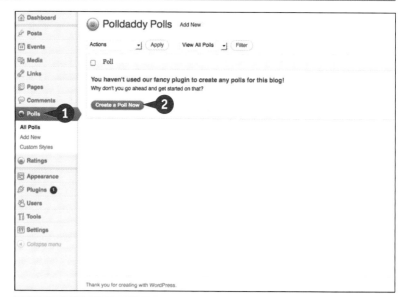

3 Type a question in the first box.

4 Type your proposed answers in the Answers boxes.

A You can click **Add New Answer** if you need more answer blanks.

5 Click **Allow other answers** (☐ changes to ☑) to create an answer called "Other" that has a box for users to type more information.

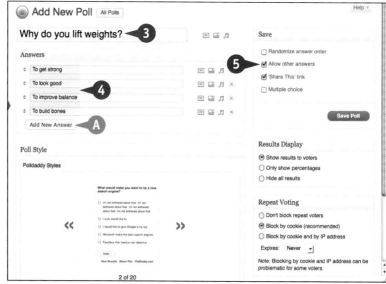

6 After scrolling down to reveal the Poll Style module, click the double arrows on either side of the sample poll until you find a design you like.

Note: Positioning your mouse pointer over the sample reveals the companion design for poll results.

7 Click the width of your choice.

8 After you are satisfied, click **Save Poll.**

The window name changes to Edit Poll and confirms a poll has been created. It is available for later editing in the Polldaddy Polls panel.

9 Click **Embed Poll in New Post** or copy the WordPress shortcode to place poll in an existing draft or post.

If you clicked Embed Poll, a New Post panel opens listing the shortcode. Otherwise, paste the shortcode into the draft or published post where you want the poll to appear.

When you save and publish your post, the poll appears, too.

TIPS

How do I put a poll in a sidebar?
Instead of using the shortcode in a post, paste it in a text widget in a sidebar of your site. Be sure to choose the narrow width option for better display.

How do I create a survey? This just looks like polls. And what are all those other options?
Polldaddy has lots of options, including creating surveys, but you have to go to Polldaddy.com, log in, and create your survey there. Also, you can get answers about the many options by going to http://support.polldaddy.com.

Let Readers Rate Content

If you start an account with Polldaddy, as explained in the preceding section, you also can let readers rate your posts, pages, and even comments. When readers are involved, they are more likely to stay and to return.

Self-hosted bloggers can choose a different plugin, such as WP-Post Ratings, if they want to offer ratings but do not want to include polls. This section covers only Polldaddy ratings and assumes you have installed the Polldaddy plugin or are blogging at WordPress.com.

Let Readers Rate Content

Set Up for Ratings

1 Click **Ratings** in the left menu bar.

The Ratings menu expands, and the Ratings Setup panel opens.

2 Click **Enable for blog posts** (☐ changes to ☑).

3 Click the drop-down menu and choose **Below each blog post**.

Note: The default ratings location is above the post.

4 Repeat steps **2** and **3** to allow ratings on posts on the front page.

5 Click **Save Changes**.

The selections are saved and an Advanced Settings link appears at the bottom of the panel.

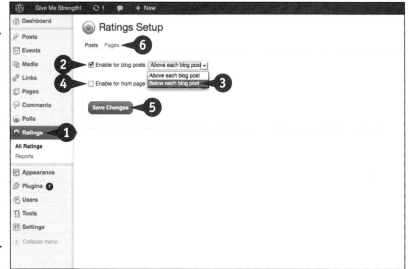

6 Click **Pages**.

The Ratings Setup Pages subpanel opens.

7 Repeat steps **2** and **3** to allow ratings on pages.

8 Click **Save Changes**.

9 Click **Comments**.

The Ratings Setup Comments subpanel opens, where you can repeat steps **2** and **3** to allow ratings on comments.

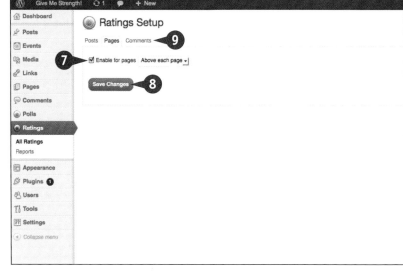

Advanced Rating Settings

1 Click **Advanced Settings**.

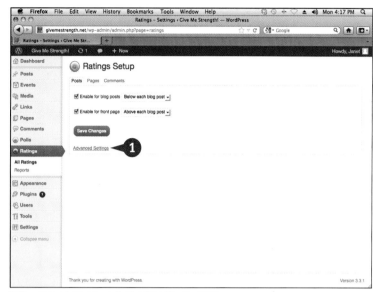

Advanced setting options appear at the bottom of the ratings panel.

A Lets you choose between 5-star ratings and Nero rating (for thumbs up or thumbs down ratings).

B Lets you change the size, color, and more for ratings graphics.

C Changes display of ratings graphics and text.

D Allows disabling of results popups and provides a ratings number, which you can use to identify posts to exclude from ratings.

E Previews display selections, including rating text and results popups if you move your mouse pointer over the preview module.

F Allows you to change or eliminate text that accompanies the ratings.

2 After making display selections, click **Save Changes**.

TIPS

How does the Custom Image option work?

It lets you select an image to use rather than stars for the ratings. Simply upload an image to your site as explained in Chapter 6 and then paste the image's URL in the Custom Image box. Now your ratings will show the flowers, birds, dots, or whatever else you choose. Make sure the image is scaled to the size you choose under Star Size.

What are the ratings reports?

After you have some ratings, the Rating Reports panel lets you see which posts, pages, and comments have the top ratings — and you can filter the report to see which are the best of all time or the best for the current month, among the many options.

CHAPTER 10

Tweak Your Theme

If you are like lots of people, you like your blog's theme but just a few little changes would make you like it *so* much better! Fortunately, you can make many adjustments to your WordPress theme, and most adjustments are quite simple.

Customize Your Header Art with a Built-in Tool

Using your own header art distinguishes your blog visually from others that use the same theme. The header art can be a photo, drawing, or other graphic. You can find themes with a built-in tool by using the Custom Header option when searching for a theme.

This example uses the Twenty Eleven theme for WordPress.com or WordPress.org blogs.

Customize Your Header Art with a Built-in Tool

Use Your Own Header Art

1 With your theme activated, click **Header** under Appearance in the left menu bar.

The Custom Header Image page opens.

2 In the Upload Image section, click **Browse** to find the image on your computer that you want in your header, and click **Open** in your browser's window to choose it.

A The file location appears in the box.

3 Click **Upload**.

The image is uploaded to your web host.

4 Stretch, shrink, or drag the crop box to crop the image.

5 Click **Crop and Publish** when you are satisfied.

Note: You can repeat steps **2** to **4** and upload multiple header images.

WordPress confirms the update, and the new header image is published to your blog.

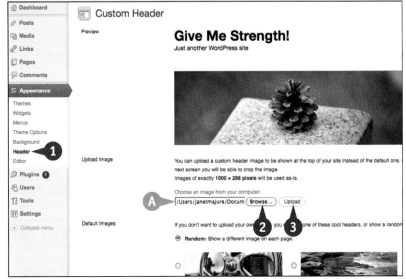

Choose Display Options

1 On the Custom Header panel, scroll down to reveal all available images.

B A selected radio button (●) indicates the active header image.

2 Click **Random** (○ changes to ●) to have WordPress display a different image on different pages.

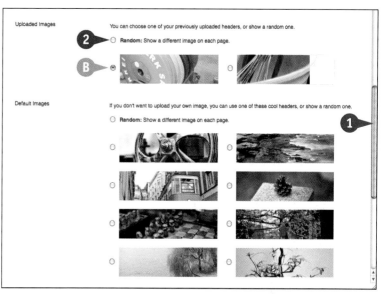

3 Scroll to the bottom of the page.

4 Click **Select a Color**.

A color selection tool opens.

5 Click in the circle to select the hue of the header text.

6 Click in the box to select the hue's tint, tone, or shade — that is, the amount of white, gray, or black to add to it.

Note: Scrolling to the top of the page reveals a preview of the color.

7 Click **Save Changes** to save the text color to your site.

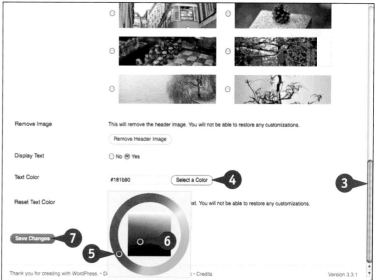

I do not like the way my image looks after it was resized for the header. Any suggestions?
To get the results you want, use a paint program or image editor to create your header image, and make it the size specified on the custom header page. You have more control that way.

I do not see a Header or Custom Header option under Appearance.
Different themes use different terminology, but the process is essentially the same. The popular Suffusion theme, for example, does not have a Header panel under Appearance, but if you click **Suffusion Options**, **Skinning**, and then **Header**, you will find more than a dozen options for your custom header. You may need to experiment, or go to your theme's home page for help.

Identify and Use Your Theme's Options

Atheme's options let you give your site a custom look. Besides simple header image changes discussed in the preceding section, options may include changing colors, sidebar arrangements, type styles, and more.

This section looks at Coraline, available on both WordPress.com and WordPress.org. It has many options to explore. Your theme may vary in its approach; check its home page for details.

Identify and Use Your Theme's Options

Identify and Use Your Theme's Options

1 Under the Appearance menu in the left menu bar, click **Theme Options**.

The Theme Options panel opens.

2 Click the Color Scheme drop-down menu, and click the color scheme you prefer.

3 Click the layout you prefer (○ changes to ●).

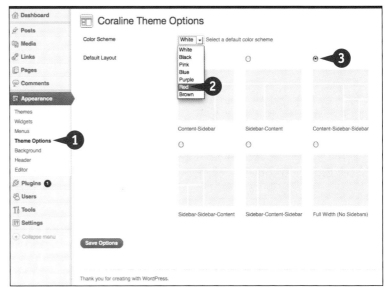

4 Click the Aside Category drop-down menu, and select a category to use for the theme's Aside posts.

5 If you want to use the theme's Gallery styling for a category with image galleries, click the Gallery Category drop-down menu and select a category.

Note: At this writing, the WordPress.com version does not offer the Aside and Gallery style options.

6 Click **Save Options**.

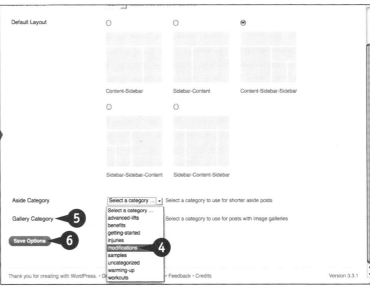

Change Background Color

1 Click **Background**.

2 In the Custom Background panel, click **Select a Color**.

3 Drag the dot in the circle to choose a hue.

4 Drag the dot in the square to select the tint, tone, or shade.

Ⓐ A preview of the color appears.

Ⓑ The color's *hexadecimal code*, or *hex code,* appears. The code defines colors on web pages.

5 Click **Save Changes** to save the color as your site's background color.

Change the Background Image

1 In the Custom Background panel, click **Browse** to find the image you want, and then **Upload**.

Ⓒ Before you click Upload, the file location appears in the Upload Image box.

Ⓓ A repeating. or *tiled,* pattern of your uploaded image appears.

2 Choose among the various display options.

3 Click **Save Changes** to publish your background image to your site.

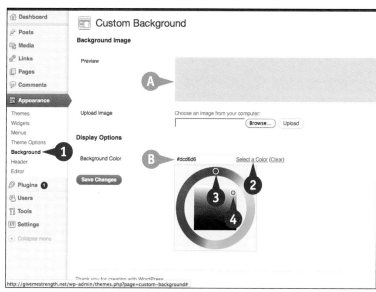

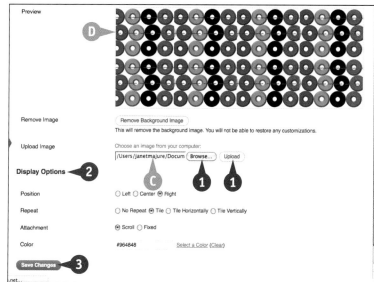

TIPS

My sidebar content changed when I changed the layout. What do I do?

Whenever you change the layout, whether with a new theme or within a theme, it is good practice to go to the Widgets panel and review what appears there. Different themes offer different widget options.

My background image looks terrible and I cannot read the text. Can I have a background that goes around the text?

If you do not want to change the theme, you can edit your image and apply a screen to significantly reduce the intensity of the background colors. Otherwise, you can choose a theme that, in effect, puts the background around the content areas, such as Skeptical at WordPress.com or Codium at WordPress.org.

Understanding the Theme Editor

If you do not mind getting your fingers a little dirty digging in the code (not for WordPress. com blogs), you can personalize your theme even more by making adjustments to your theme in the theme editor, listed as Editor under Appearance in the left sidebar. You do not have to be a programmer to make it happen.

Theme Editor Components

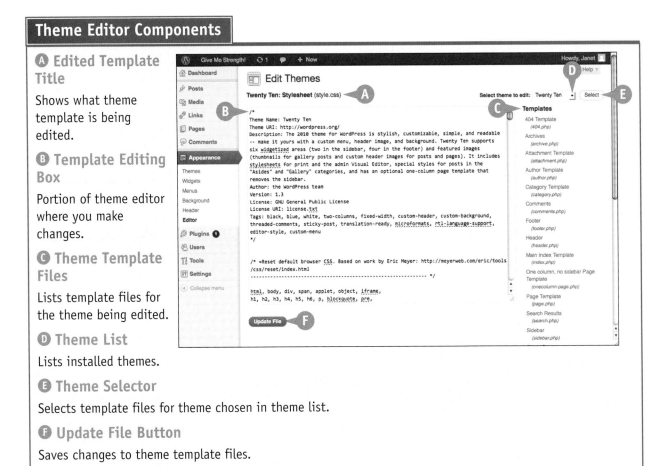

A Edited Template Title

Shows what theme template is being edited.

B Template Editing Box

Portion of theme editor where you make changes.

C Theme Template Files

Lists template files for the theme being edited.

D Theme List

Lists installed themes.

E Theme Selector

Selects template files for theme chosen in theme list.

F Update File Button

Saves changes to theme template files.

Theme Template Files

WordPress themes consist of several *PHP* templates, that is, files written in the PHP scripting language, plus at least one Cascading Style Sheet, or *CSS* file. All themes have a file called index.php, and almost all have such files as header.php, sidebar.php, footer.php, comments.php, and more. You can make changes — carefully — to any of them. If you want a good overview of how the files work, go to http://yoast.com/wordpress-theme-anatomy.

Templates

404 Template
(404.php)

Archives
(archive.php)

Author Template
(author.php)

Category Template
(category.php)

Theme Editor Alternatives

If you are not comfortable using the theme editor, you may edit theme files in a text editor on your computer and upload them to your theme's folder. If you save an unedited version of the files, you can reload them if your changes mess anything up. Free source code editors such as Notepad++ or Komodo Edit make editing the files easier.

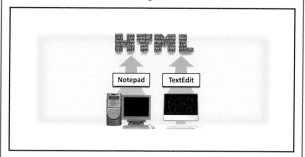

Common Changes

If you do not know PHP or HTML, keep changes simple. You may want to edit files to change text in templates or to insert code, such as from an affiliate advertiser, in a location, such as a footer, that does not have a widget to do it for you. CSS files also are commonly changed.

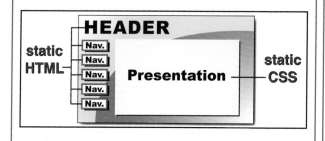

What to Change

It can be scary editing theme files. To be safe, *do not* change anything between a pair of angle brackets that start with `<?php`; *do not* change items beginning `<div` unless you know CSS; but *do* change text between common HTML tags such as `<h3>` and `</h3>`.

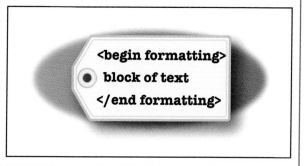

Add Copyright Information to the Footer

Adding a copyright statement to your blog's footer lets readers see at a glance what rights you retain, and you can use a plugin if you want for that purpose. Publishing the notice, though, is a good way to dip your toe into theme editing, because virtually all themes have a Footer template.

The example in this section uses the Twenty Eleven theme.

Add Copyright Information to the Footer

1 On your blog front page, scroll to the bottom to take note of how your footer looks and what it says, and decide where in that area you want your copyright notice to appear.

2 By positioning your mouse pointer over the text, you can see that:

Ⓐ The text is a link.

Ⓑ You can read the *tooltip*, the additional information box.

Remember or write down this information.

3 After going to the Dashboard and clicking **Appearance** and then **Editor**, click **Footer (footer.php)** under Templates.

Footer.php opens in the edit theme file box.

Ⓒ The text that appears in the footer.

Ⓓ The link associated with the text.

Ⓔ The tooltip text.

Ⓕ The HTML <a> tag that starts the hyperlink.

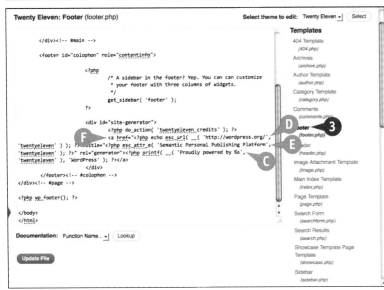

④ To insert plain text, click the mouse pointer just before `<a href=`, and type your copyright notice, such as **This site is licensed under the Creative Commons Attribution-Share Alike license, effective 2012 forward.**

⑤ Click **Update File**.

The changes are saved and published to your site.

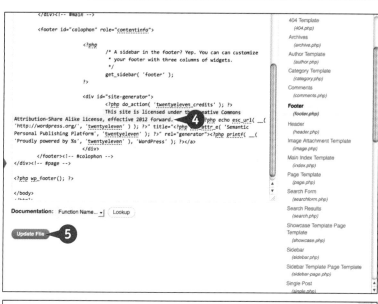

⑥ On your blog's front page, scroll to the bottom to review your changes.

TIPS

Can I make a link in the copyright statement?

Certainly. Just use the HTML to do so. It is `<a href="http://www.placetolink.com">link name </a>`, where *www.placetolink.com* is the place you want to link to and *link name* is the text you want to appear as a hyperlink.

Where can I find out more about copyrights? How about HTML?

You can get more information at www.copyright.gov. You also may be interested in the Creative Commons licenses, which you can read about at http://creativecommons.org. As to HTML, you can find many sources on the web, including www.w3.org, the HTML authority, or www.w3schools.com.

Add an Image to the Category Template

Another way to sample editing templates is to add an image to make the display of your category pages stand out. Note that a few themes do not have a category template.

First, you need to upload an image to your Media Library, as described in Chapter 6.

Add an Image to the Category Template

1 Click **Media** in the left menu bar.

The Media Library opens.

2 Click the image name.

Ⓐ You can also click **Edit** under the image name.

The Edit Media panel opens.

3 Select and copy the File URL for the image.

4 Click **Editor** under the Appearance menu to go to the Theme Editor.

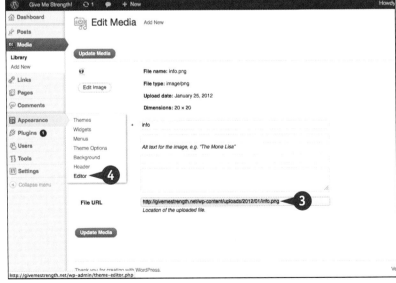

228

5 Click **Category Template**.

The code for the Category template appears in the editing box.

6 After inserting your cursor immediately after `<header class="page-header">`, type `<a href="` and then paste the URL for the image you want, followed by `">`.

7 After the URL, type `"><img src="`, paste the URL again, and then type `"></a>`.

8 Click **Update File**.

9 Go to your site's front page, click a category, and see the image at the top of the category page.

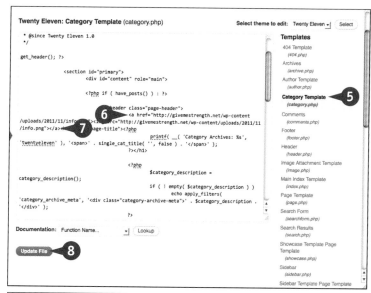

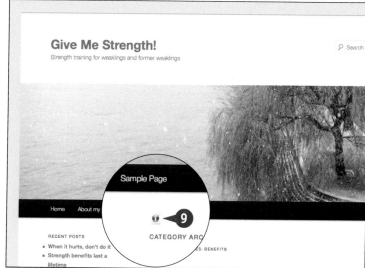

I tried this, and I did not get the results I expected. What did I do wrong?

Unfortunately, it is impossible to say because themes handle category displays differently. To do serious editing, you need to understand PHP and HTML. Avoid putting text or HTML between PHP commands — that is, between `<?php` and `?>` — and at the very least you will not mess anything up.

Can I change or add HTML tags to text in the theme files?

Yes. It should work just fine as long as you use proper opening and closing tags.

Understanding Post Formats

You can give your posts different looks by using different *post formats*. Not all themes support post formats, but if yours does you can take advantage of it from the New/Edit Post panel.

If you are code-savvy, you can add post format functionality to your WordPress.org theme. Get the scoop at http://codex.wordpress.org/Post_Formats.

Post Format Options

If your theme supports post formats, it lists available options in the Format module on the New/Edit Post panel. Particular themes style the formats differently, but WordPress intended them to be used as follows:

Standard	Basic post
Aside	Brief remarks
Link	For links
Gallery	Thumbnail on front page for post with image gallery
Status	Twitter-type personal updates
Quote	Highlighted quote
Image	Highlighted image

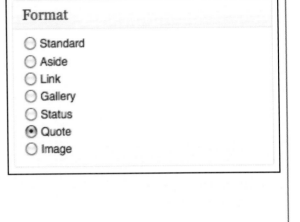

Post Format Styling

At this writing, few theme designers have taken full advantage of post format potential. Indeed, you may not see much difference in published posts. If you are interested in this feature, be sure to look at a theme's demo of the formats you want before you commit to the theme.

Use Post Formats

Make your status updates stand out from your regular posts by using the Status post format. It is among several options that post-format-enabled themes may offer. Although the formats have intended purposes as noted in the preceding section, you can use them any way you want.

Use Post Formats

1 Click **Add New** under Posts in the left menu bar.

   The Add New Post panel opens.

2 Write a headline.

3 Write your post.

4 Click the post format you want (○ changes to ⦿).

Ⓐ If Format module does not appear, click **Screen Options** and click **Post Format** (☐ changes to ☑).

5 Click **Save Draft**.

6 Click **Publish**.

   WordPress publishes the post.

7 Click the blog name to go to the front page.

Ⓑ The post format may leave off the headline you typed.

8 Click the date to go to the post's individual post page, which includes the headline.

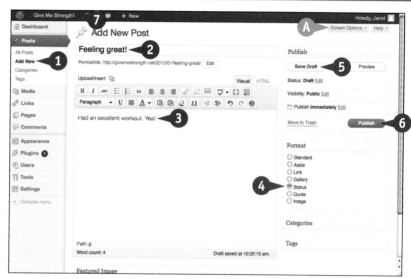

Create and Use a Page Template

By creating your own page templates, you can add pages to your theme that fit your needs. Perhaps you want a page that does not include a comments area. You can have it by creating your own page template.

This option is not available for users at WordPress.com. In this example, you create a template for a page without a footer section.

Create and Use a Page Template

1 Using your FTP program, save a copy of the page.php file from your theme directory to your computer.

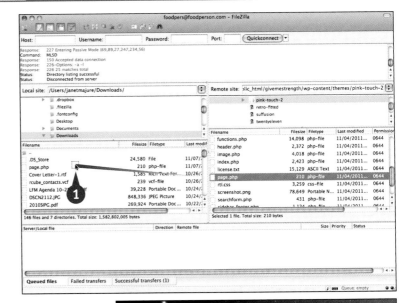

2 Open page.php with a text editor or a source code editor and save the file as no-footer.php, or a name of your choice, but it must have the .php ending.

3 Type `<?php /* Template Name: no-footer*/ ?>` at the top of the file.

4 Find and delete the line reading `<?php get_footer(); ?>`.

Save the file, and upload it to the directory where you found page.php.

5 In your WordPress Dashboard, expand the Pages menu and click **Add New**.

The Add New/Edit Page panel opens.

6 Click the drop-down menu next to Default Template to expand the templates menu.

7 Click **no-footer** to select the new template.

Note: The list of templates varies from theme to theme.

8 After typing a title in the title box and entering text or other content in the page box, click **Save Draft**.

9 When your page is ready, click **Publish**.

Your page is published and the Edit Page panel displays a View page link.

10 Click the **View page** link to go to the page published with the new template; you can see it has no footer.

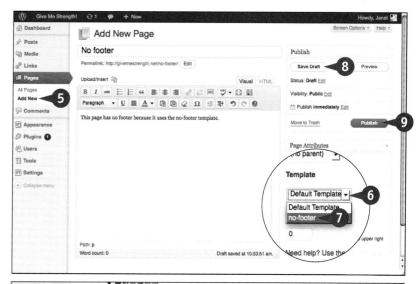

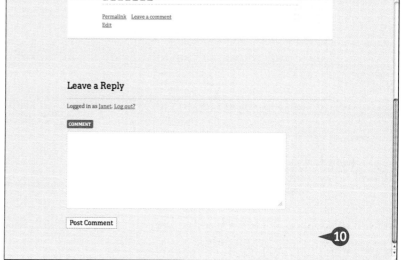

TIPS

Where do I find the page.php file?
You find it on your web host in your blog directory at wp-content\themes\ *your_theme*\page.php, where *your_ theme* is the name of the theme for which you want to create a page template.

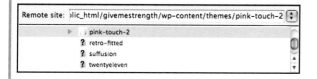

What else can I do with page templates?
Just about anything you want, but it is essential to know more about HTML, Cascading Style Sheets (CSS), and PHP if you want to do anything at all complicated.

Introducing CSS

Cascading Style Sheets, or CSS, allow you to create standard styles for your blog's appearance. Your theme comes with a style sheet file, called style.css, which stores those standards. By using your style sheet, you can change all aspects of your blog's look without changing the way it works.

You can use custom CSS on WordPress.com blogs only if you pay for the CSS upgrade.

What CSS Affects

Your style sheet determines what font you use, the colors of headlines and links, whether images have borders around them, how text is aligned on the page, how lists are shown, and just about anything else visual on your page — even the page layout.

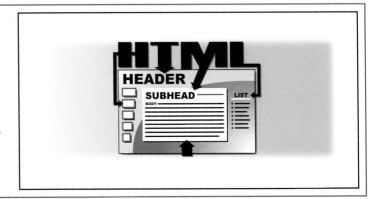

How CSS Works

Your WordPress theme is composed of a set of templates, and each template tells the web browser that displays your blog to get presentation information from your style sheet, which is exactly what happens.

Style Sheet Comments

You can open your style.css file in a text or source code editor. The file may have comments in it to help you understand its parts. Comments do not affect presentation. Comments appear between the characters /* and */.

Style Sheet Rules

Each CSS rule consists of a *selector*, or the HTML element you are defining, and a *declaration*, which is the rule you are applying to that HTML element. In the CSS rule `body {background-color:beige}`, `body` is the selector and `{background-color:beige}` is the declaration.

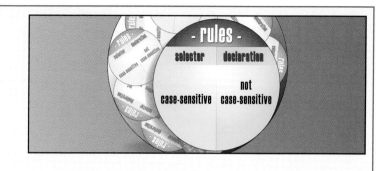

CSS Declarations

CSS declarations consist of a *property*:*value* pair, where *property* is the aspect of the element you want to define, and *value* is the definition. In the previous example, `background-color` is the property, and `beige` is the value.

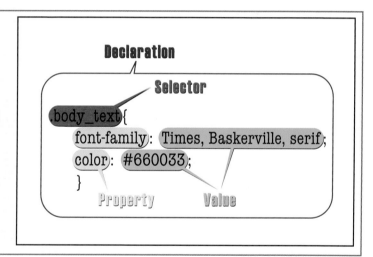

More CSS Information

If you want to learn CSS, which *can* get complicated, the authority is W3C, the World Wide Web Consortium. It has information on learning CSS at www.w3.org/Style/CSS/learning — in 40 languages! See also the excellent and free tutorials at www.yourhtmlsource.com and www.w3schools.com.

Try CSS with the Web Developer Toolbar

Fortunately, you can test CSS changes without being a CSS whiz. When you use the Firefox or Chrome extension called Web Developer Toolbar, you can see how changes to your blog's CSS affect your blog's presentation.

If you do not have the Firefox browser, you can download it from www.mozilla.org, and Chrome is available from www.google.com/chrome. This example uses Firefox.

Try CSS with the Web Developer Toolbar

1 With Firefox running as your browser, go to http://addons.mozilla.org, and type **Web Developer** into the search box.

A list of developer add-ons appears.

2 Click **Web Developer**.

A new page opens listing Web Developer by Chrispederick.

3 Click **Add to Firefox**.

4 A download window opens. Agree to the download and installation, and then restart Firefox as directed. Firefox restarts at a page that profiles the developer and invites you to make a contribution.

5 Under the Firefox View menu, click **Toolbars**, and click **Web Developer Toolbar**.

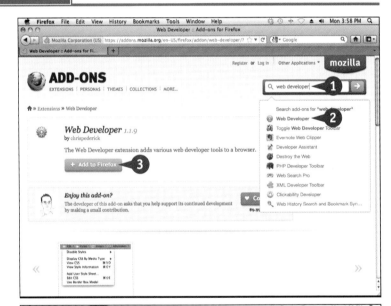

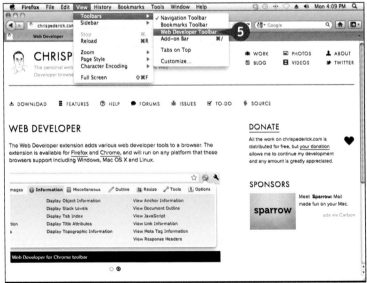

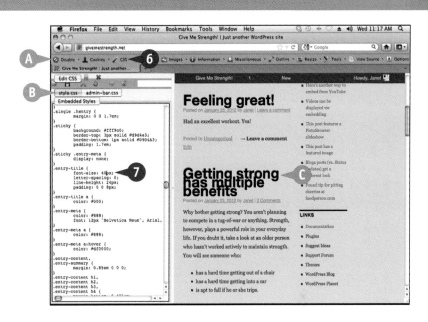

Ⓐ The Developer Toolbar appears.

❻ With your blog page open in Firefox, click **CSS** in the new toolbar, and then click **Edit CSS** in the menu that appears.

Ⓑ Your style.css file opens in the Edit CSS pane of your browser.

❼ This example changes the h2 entry-title size to 40px.

Ⓒ The type size changes instantly in the main part of your browser window.

Note: The browser displays what would happen if you changed the style sheet, but it does not actually change the style sheet.

TIPS

All I want to do is change the color of the headlines. How do I do that?

You need to specify the color in hexadecimal notation, such as #000000, which is black, or with one of 17 web standard names: aqua, black, blue, fuchsia, gray, green, lime, maroon, navy, olive, orange, purple, red, silver, teal, white, and yellow. Finding the right selector can be the trick. Fiddle around a bit with the Web Developer Toolbar and you will learn a lot about how CSS presents your site.

How do I find the selector?

The Web Developer Toolbar can help: Click the **Information** button on the toolbar and select **Display Element Information**. Now, click a headline whose color you want to change. A pop-up window displays information about the headline's styling. You also can use the Edit CSS search box to find all references to, say, h2 headings to find where the color may be defined.

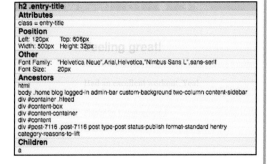

Add a Category RSS Feed Link

I f your blog has categories that may appeal to different audiences, you can set up separate feeds for those audiences. For example, you may have a needlework blog. You can create separate feeds for your knitting, needlepoint, crewel, and crochet categories. WordPress has the code built in; you just need to point your readers to it.

Add a Category RSS Feed Link

1 From your blog's administration pages, click **Posts**.

2 Click **Categories**.

The Categories page opens.

3 Select and copy the slug of the category to which you want to provide a feed link.

4 Click **Appearance**.

5 Click **Widgets**.

The Widgets page opens.

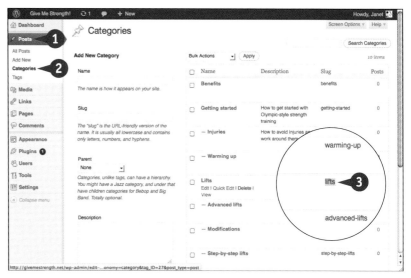

6 Drag a Text widget to a sidebar.

The widget pops open.

7 Give your widget a title.

8 Type an HTML link to the category feed, like so: `<a href="http://www.yourblog.com/category/category_slug/feed">link name</a>`, where *www.yourblog.com* (*yourblog*.wordpress.com) is your blog's URL; *category_slug* is the slug for the desired category; and *link name* is what you want your link to say.

Note: At WordPress.com the feed link would be `<a href="category/category_slug/feed">link name</a>`.

9 Scroll down and click **Save**.

The widget is published to your website.

10 On your blog's front page, find the new sidebar widget, and click the new subscription link.

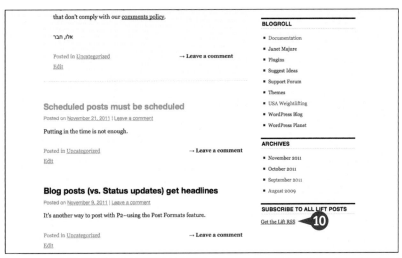

A feed subscription window opens.

11 Click **Subscribe Now** to subscribe to your own feed.

A subscription window appears and leads you through the steps.

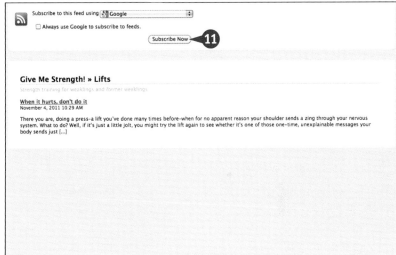

TIPS

Can I do this with tags too?

Yes. WordPress has feeds built in that you can use at any time. In addition to the main content and comments feeds discussed in Chapter 9 and categories as shown above, standard feeds are available for authors and for tags. Use the format above, except rather than `category/category-slug/` type `tag/tag_name/` or `author/author_name/`.

I entered the URL right, but when I click my new link to subscribe, it just shows my regular feed. What did I do wrong?

You may be using a plugin to manage feeds through FeedBurner, and the plugin is fouling things up. Try deactivating the plugin; if the link works then, go to the plugin's website, which you can find on your blog's Plugins panel, and look for FAQs. If that does not help, contact the plugin author for help.

CHAPTER 11

Content Management

Content management systems, or *CMS*, get much attention in web computing these days for the way they let multiple users work together or separately to create, edit, publish, and manage web content without having to fiddle with computer code. WordPress lets you manage authors, members, and content, and you can do even more if you are willing to touch code.

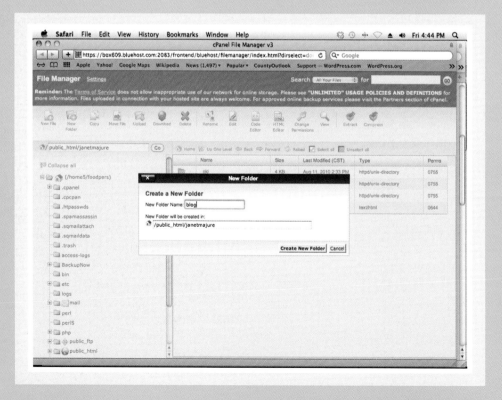

Understanding User Capabilities

As the site owner, you can decide who gets to write, edit, and publish content to your site. A critical aspect of using WordPress to manage content generated by multiple users is the permissions that you can assign to each user.

User Roles and Capabilities

WordPress provides a standard set of user *roles*, which specify what *capabilities*, or tasks, a user can perform. The standard roles are Administrator, Editor, Author, Contributor, and Subscriber/Follower. The Subscriber role is at WordPress.org; Follower is at WordPress.com.

Administrator Capabilities

If you set up the blog, you have Administrator capabilities. An Administrator can do anything, from writing posts to changing themes and adding users. In most cases, the blog owner runs the site as the Administrator, but more than one person can have the Administrator role. If you add an Administrator, make sure it is someone you absolutely trust!

Editor Capabilities

As implied by the role's title, the Editor role can write, edit, publish, and delete posts and pages by herself or by others. The Editor role also can moderate comments and manage categories, tags, and blogroll. An Editor can do a lot but cannot change themes, plugins, users, and the like.

This week's blog ~~post~~

Author and Contributor Capabilities

Authors can write, edit, publish, and delete posts that they wrote, but they cannot alter anyone else's posts. They also can upload images for their posts. Contributors can write and edit posts, but an Editor or Administrator must review and publish them. Authors and Contributors cannot create pages.

Subscriber/Follower Capabilities

If you have open registration available, Subscriber is the default role. Some blogs require registration to comment on blog posts, and when a reader registers, he gets the Subscriber role. A Subscriber can read blog posts, comment, and have a subscriber profile that defines his name, password, and so on. A WordPress.com registration fulfills that role for public WordPress.com blogs.

Determining Roles

If you own a blog and want to have several contributors, a good practice is to give any new users the fewest capabilities that they need to complete their jobs. Limiting broader capabilities to only the very few who need them deters both miscues and malicious changes.

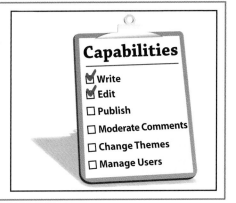

Add Authors and Contributors

You can turn your blog into a group blog by adding editors, authors, and contributors. At the same time, you can control — or not — when and how content is published by setting permissions to fit your blog's needs.

Add Authors and Contributors

In Self-Hosted Blogs

1 In the administrative pages, click **Users**.

The Users menu expands.

2 Click **Add New**.

The Add New User panel opens.

3 Type a username in the Username box.

4 Type the person's e-mail in the E-mail box.

5 Give the user a password and confirm it.

6 Click **Send Password** (☐ changes to ☑).

7 Click the Role drop-down menu, and click a role.

8 Click **Add New User**.

WordPress adds the user, sends the person an e-mail, and opens the Users list with the new user.

9 Click the username.

The Edit User panel opens, where you or the new user can add or change settings.

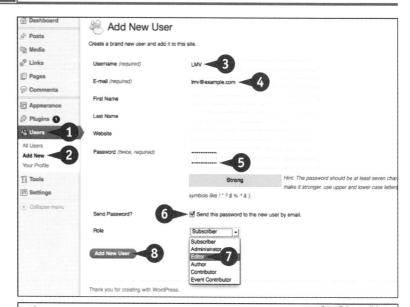

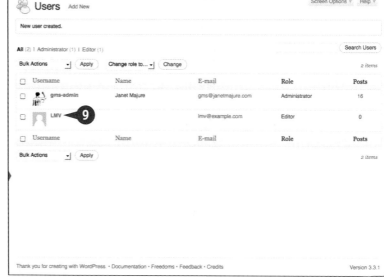

At WordPress.com

1 Click **Users** to expand the Users menu.

2 Click **Invite New**.

The Invite a New User to Your Blog panel opens.

3 Type an e-mail address or a WordPress.com member's username.

4 Click the Role drop-down menu, and click the role you want for that user.

5 Customize the invitation.

6 Click **Send Invitation**.

WordPress sends an e-mail to the person and adds her name to Your Past Invitations list. If your site is at WordPress.com, the recipient must accept the invitation to be added and be or become a WordPress.com member for any role except Follower.

7 Scroll down to see the status of your invitations.

A You can resend invitations or delete invitations from the list.

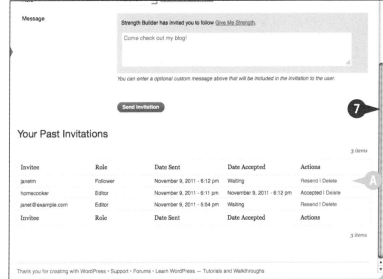

How do new users add content?
New members of your site can access your administrative pages with their username and password in the same way you do, probably by going to *mysite*.com/wp-admin or *mysite*.wordpress.com/wp-admin. The available admin pages and tasks they can do depend on what their role allows.

How do I change a user's role?
Click **All Users** under the Users menu, click the user whose role you want to change (☐ changes to ☑), and click the Change Role To drop-down menu. Click the role you want, and then click the **Change** button.

You can avoid the formality of creating authors by letting people register and post with the P2 theme or plugins such as Mingle. Be forewarned, though, that opening your blog to the world may invite *unwanted* contributions. At self-hosted blogs, using a plugin may be a safer way to go.

Create a Simple Member Community

Use a Theme

1 After installing and activating a theme listed in the WordPress.org theme directory as having a front page post form, such as P2, click **Settings** to open the General Settings pane.

Note: At this writing, P2 is the only front page post theme at WordPress.com. Four others are available at WordPress.org.

2 Click **Anyone can register** (☐ changes to ☑).

3 Click **Save Changes**. Any visitor now can register as a subscriber, allowing him to write and publish posts.

Note: Steps **1** to **3** are not necessary at WordPress.com.

4 Click **Theme Options**.

5 In the P2 Options panel, click **Allow any registered member to post** (☐ changes to ☑).

6 Type a color code or choose a color by clicking **Pick a Color**.

7 Type a prompt that viewers will see to encourage posting.

8 Click **Update Options**.

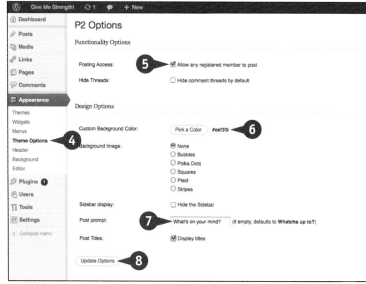

9 On the Widgets panel, drag the Meta widget to a sidebar.

10 Give the widget a title to encourage members to sign up or sign in.

11 Click **Save**.

The widget is published to your sidebar.

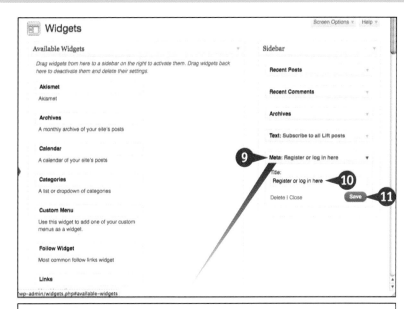

Create a Post

1 When you or a member is signed in, go to the site's front page, click, and type in the post entry box.

Note: P2 defaults to the Status Update post format, which includes no headline. If you want a headline, click the **Blog Post** button. Click the **Quote** and **Link** buttons for special boxes for quotes and links.

2 Add a tag if you like.

3 Click **Post it**.

The post is published immediately to your front page as you watch.

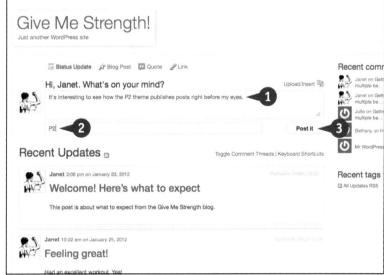

Can each contributor have an author's page, and maybe front-page login too?
If you click an author's name, a page with all her posts appears. If you want more, WordPress.com has a widget that posts a grid of author avatars or a list of author posts. Also, plugins such as WP-Members for self-hosted blogs give the functions you want.

Can I get the social networking function with ordinary themes?
You can if your site is self-hosted, with plugins such as WP Symposium Social Network or WP Mingle. In addition, read about BuddyPress in the next section.

Create a BuddyPress Social Network

Your own complete social network is possible with BuddyPress, which is owned by Automattic of WordPress fame. This complex plugin has plugins that extend its functions. Be advised that BuddyPress is probably best for advanced — or patient — users, because of its complexity and limited documentation.

The first step in creating a BuddyPress network is to install the plugin, as explained in Chapter 7. BuddyPress is not available at WordPress.com.

Create a BuddyPress Social Network

1 After installing and activating the BuddyPress plugin and clicking **installation wizard** on the confirmation screen, review each item in the BuddyPress Setup panel's Components tab, and click any you do not want (☑ changes to ☐).

2 Click **Save & Next**.

The Pages tab opens, where you leave the default page settings, and click **Save & Next**.

The Permalinks tab opens.

3 If you are satisfied with your permalinks, click **Save & Next**.

Note: You should not change permalink structure after your site is established.

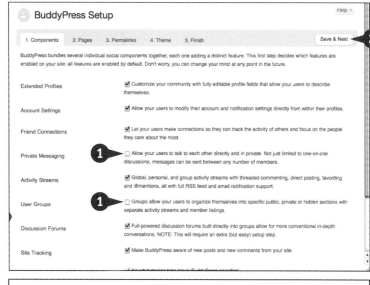

The Theme tab opens with the
BuddyPress Default theme
selected.

④ Click **Save & Next**.

Ⓐ If you prefer, you may select a
BuddyPress-compatible theme
that you already have installed.
If you are not an advanced
user, do not choose to install
the BuddyPress Template Pack
for your current theme.

WordPress confirms your
setup selections.

⑤ Click **Finish & Activate**.

WordPress activates the
BuddyPress plugin and theme
you selected.

BuddyPress is not working the way I expected it to. How do I fix it?
The ins and outs of BuddyPress could fill a book and are beyond what
can be covered here. Your best bet is to read documentation at http://
codex.buddypress.org and to
search or post at the BuddyPress
support forums, at http://
buddypress.org/support.

Should I try BuddyPress?
Go to http://testbp.org to
get a taste of what running
a site with BuddyPress might
be like. In addition, try
reviewing the information
at the links in the preceding
question to get a sense of
what you are getting into.

Add a Forum to Your Blog

If a blog does not provide enough commentary to satisfy you, you can add a forum. Doing so allows visitors to start topics and respond to other people's topics, even if the visitors are not regular contributors. Among solutions at self-hosted blogs is Mingle Forum.

Start by installing the Mingle Forum plugin following the Chapter 7 installation instructions.

Add a Forum to Your Blog

1 Click **Add New** under the Pages menu in the left menu bar.

The Add New/Edit Page panel opens.

2 Type **Forum** in the title box, or type a different title if you prefer.

3 Type **[mingleforum]** in the text box.

4 Click **Allow comments** and **Allow trackbacks** (☑ changes to ☐).

Note: If you do not see those options, make them visible by clicking **Discussion** (☐ changes to ☑) under Screen Options at the top of the page panel.

5 Click **Save Draft**.

6 Click **Publish**.

7 Click **Settings** in left menu bar.

The General Settings panel opens.

8 Click **Anyone can register** (☐ changes to ☑).

9 Click **Save Changes**.

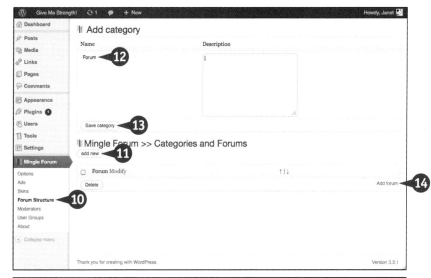

10 Click **Forum Structure** under the Mingle Forum menu in the left menu bar, which was added when you activated the plugin.

The Mingle Forum>> Categories and Forums panel opens.

11 Click **add new**.

The Add Category module opens.

12 Type **Forum**, or another name, under Name.

Note: You can add a description, but it is visible only to the site's administrator.

13 Click **Save category**.

The panel confirms that the category has been added.

14 Click **Add forum**.

The Add Forum panel opens.

15 Type a name.

16 Type a description, which readers can see.

17 Click **Save forum**.

The forum is set up and ready.

TIP

Can I add a forum for my WordPress.com blog?
Not directly, but you can do so in indirect ways. First, do a Google search on *free forum hosting*, and then set up a forum at the site of your choice. Then, create a link to your forum in a Text widget on your WordPress.com site.

TALK IT OUT AT MY FORUM!

Get it by clicking GMS Forum.

Manage Documents

You can use your WordPress site as a portal to assorted documents that you want to store online and make accessible to others. Using the same technique as uploading images, you can upload word processing documents, spreadsheets, and PDFs for sharing.

For this example, you make a page just for documents.

Manage Documents

1 Create a new page by clicking **Pages** then **Add New**.

2 On your page, type the categories of the documents you want to upload.

3 Click where you want a link to your first document to be listed.

4 Click the **Add Media** button (🖻).

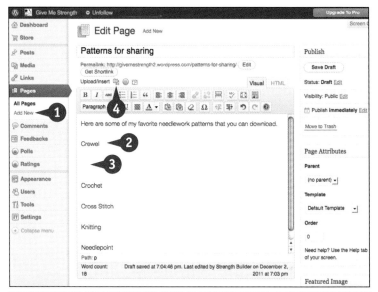

The Add Media window opens.

5 Click **Select Files**.

Note: You can drag the file to the window if you prefer.

6 A file selection window opens. When you locate the file you want to upload, click the filename.

7 Click **Open**.

WordPress uploads the file and displays information about it in the Add Media window.

8 Change the title, which by default is the filename, to what you want the link to the document to say.

9 Click **Insert into Post**.

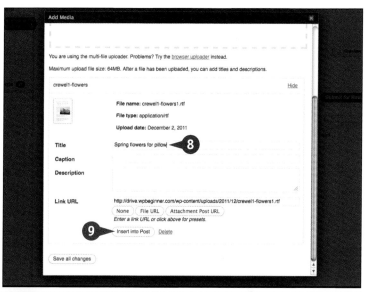

A A link to the file is inserted into the page where you positioned your cursor earlier.

10 Click **Save Draft**.

The page draft is saved.

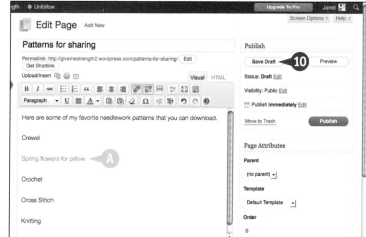

Is there a way I can upload several documents at once?

Yes. After you click **Select Files** and the file selection window opens, you can click multiple files as long as they are in the same folder on your computer. Press and hold Ctrl (⌘ on a Mac) as you make your selections. After all the files are uploaded, click **Show** next to each one to change the title and insert into your file.

I tried to upload an RTF file, but it would not let me. Why not?

WordPress.com has some restrictions on the file types you can upload, and it does not allow RTFs. Use one of the file types listed near the top of the Add Media window at WordPress.com.

> **"crewel1-flowers.rtf" has failed to upload due to an error**
> Sorry, this file type is not permitted for security reasons.

Use WordPress.com in Languages Besides English

Localized versions of WordPress are available in dozens of languages, from Afrikaans to Welsh, and the software was written to make localized versions easier. At WordPress.com, you just need to choose from a menu.

Use WordPress.com in Languages Besides English

At the WordPress.com Site

1 At WordPress.com, click the Language drop-down menu.

The languages menu expands.

2 Click the language of your choice.

The WordPress.com pages now read in the language you selected.

Note: If you click **More Languages**, a page opens with dozens of languages you can choose among.

For Your Blog

1 At the Dashboard, click **Settings**.

The General Settings panel opens.

2 Click the Language drop-down menu.

The Language menu expands.

3 Click the language of your choice.

4 Click **Save Changes**, and the language for your blog entries changes.

5 Click **modify the interface language**.

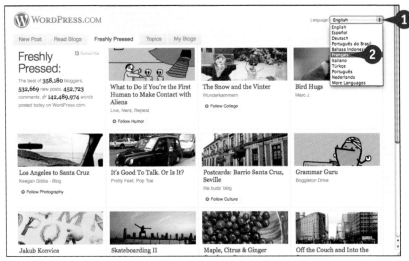

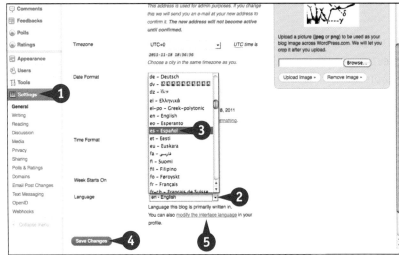

254

The Personal Settings panel opens.

6 Scroll down to Interface Language, and click the drop-down menu.

7 Click the language you want to read in your administration pages.

8 Scroll to the bottom of the page, and click **Save Changes**.

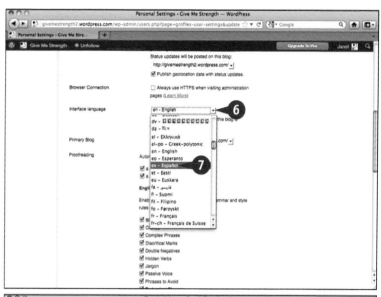

Transliterate/Type in a Non-Roman Script

1 Go to http://google.com/ transliterate in your browser.

2 Choose the transliterated language from the drop-down menu.

3 Type Roman letters the way the word *sounds* in the target language.

When you press ⟨Spacebar⟩ after each word, the site changes the word to the target alphabet.

4 Copy the transliterated words, and paste them into your WordPress.com post using the Paste from Word button (📋).

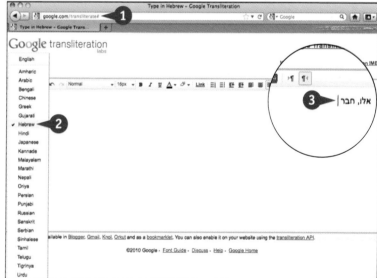

Can I use more than one language at a time?

Yes. If you want, you can have the administrative panels in one language and the user interface — such as the menus your readers see — in a different language.

LAISSER UN
COMMENTAIRE

Strength benefits can

OCTOBRE 24, 2011

I changed the settings, but my posts are still in English. Why?

These settings change what WordPress does; it is up to you to write in the language of your choice.

Self-Hosted WordPress Blogs in Languages Besides English

Translations of WordPress are not built in to the standard self-hosted WordPress installation, but scores are available. You need to find the .mo file in your language and follow a few directions. WordPress users also welcome those who can help with translations.

Find Your Language

In your browser, type http://codex.wordpress.org/WordPress_in_Your_Language, and look for your language. Some languages have complete, translated versions of the WordPress software, and you can find a link to translated support pages. Those languages include Basque, Catalan, Danish, Dutch, French, German, Indonesian, Korean, Portuguese, Sinhala, Sudanese, Swedish, Thai, Ukrainian, and Uighur. Other languages have *add-on language files* with an *.mo* extension that work with the English-language original software.

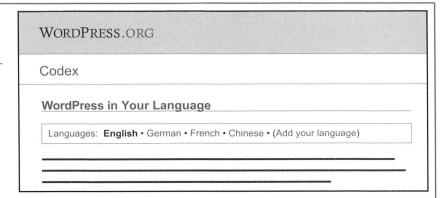

WORDPRESS.ORG

Codex

WordPress in Your Language

Languages: **English** • German • French • Chinese • (Add your language)

Add Language Files

After finding a link to an add-on language file at the above URL, go to the .mo file and download it to your computer. If directions for installation are not available, go to http://codex.wordpress.org/Installing_WordPress_in_Your_Language for further instruction. If you do not find a translation but are willing to help create one, read the information at http://codex.wordpress.org/Translating_WordPress and get started!

WORDPRESS.ORG

Codex

Manually Installing Language Files

Languages: **English** • German • French • Chinese • (Add your language)

Get Support in Your Language

At http://codex.wordpress.org/ Codex:Multilingual, you can find links to more-or-less complete translations of the WordPress documentation, or Codex, in numerous languages, though not in as many languages as the software.

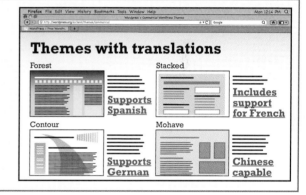

WORDPRESS.ORG

Codex

es:Antes de instalar

Localization through Themes

A few themes are available that have built-in translations for some widely spoken languages. Go to the WordPress themes directory at http:/wordpress.org/ extend/themes, and use *localization* or the language of your choice as the search term.

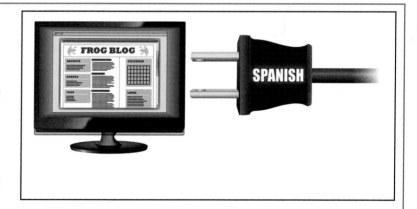

Localization through Plugins

Assorted plugins are available that can help you either install a language to your WordPress site or provide translations. Options include WP Native Dashboard, xili-language, and Plugins Language Switcher for changing the language on your site. If you would rather keep your English site but provide translations, a plugin such as Transposh provides translation in many languages; the reader chooses.

Use a Static Page as Your Home Page

You can give your site an entirely different feel by making your front page a static page, rather than the usual reverse-chronological presentation of blog posts. When people go to your domain, they see photos, text, or whatever else you want to display.

Use a Static Page as Your Home Page

1 Click **Pages** in the left menu bar.

2 Click **Add New**.

The Add/Edit Page panel opens.

3 Type **Home** in the title box.

4 Click **Save Draft**.

5 Click **Publish**.

The new page is published.

6 Click **Add New**.

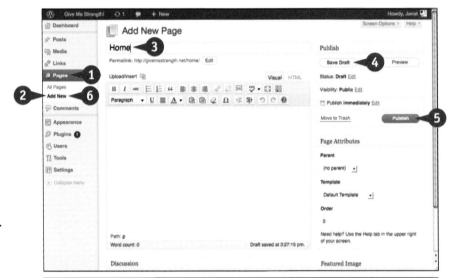

A new Add/Edit Page panel opens.

7 Type **Blog** in the title box.

8 Click **Save Draft**.

9 Click **Publish**.

The new page is published.

10 Click **Settings**.

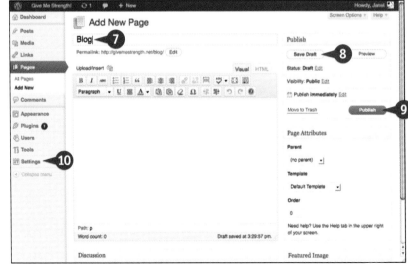

The Settings menu expands.

11 Click **Reading**.

The Reading Settings panel opens.

12 Click **A static page** (○ changes to ◉).

13 Click the Front Page drop-down menu.

14 Click **Home**.

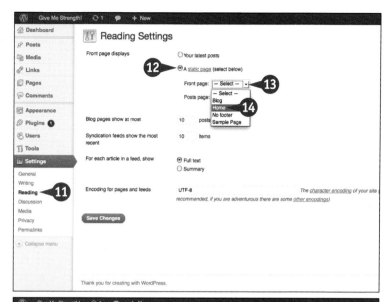

15 Click the Posts Page drop-down menu.

16 Click **Blog**.

17 Click **Save Changes**.

Visitors to your domain name now land on the page called Home and must click **Blog** to read blog posts.

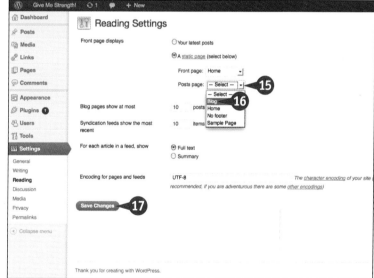

Why is my home page blank except for the sidebar and comments box?

You still must add the content you want — words, images, and so on — to your home page. Do it as you would create content for any other static page.

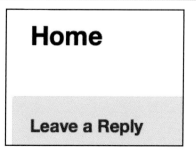

Do I have to name the blog page Blog?

No. You can name it whatever you want. If Blog does not fit the tone of your site, you can always call it News or Announcements or something else altogether.

You can add a WordPress blog to your existing website with very little effort. That way, you get to keep the website you are known for while adding the dynamic content you can easily create with WordPress.

You can add a self-hosted blog via a subdirectory or subdomain, but if your blog is hosted at WordPress.com, you must use a subdomain at your main site.

Add a Blog to an Existing Static Website

Use a Subdirectory for Self-Hosted Blogs

① Create a subdirectory, or folder, called *blog* or some other name, in the root directory of your existing site.

Note: This example uses the cPanel file manager. You can use FileZilla for the same purpose.

② Install WordPress into the blog directory.

Note: See Chapter 3 for installation information.

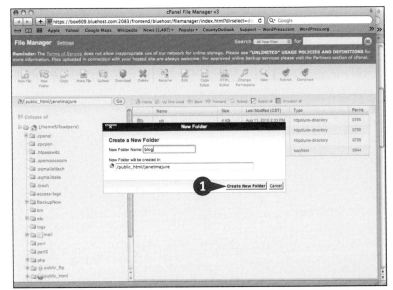

③ In your browser, type the subdirectory name in the address bar using the format **http://www.*yourdomain*.com/ *blogdirectory***, where *yourdomain.com* is the domain of your website and *blogdirectory* is the name of the new subdirectory.

Note: Do not forget to create a link to your blog from your site's home page.

Your blog page appears in your browser.

Use a Subdomain

1 Type **blog** as the subdomain in your web host's subdomains tool.

Note: This example uses the cPanel Subdomains tool.

A This field shows the directory where your blog content is stored.

2 Click **Create**.

A subdomain called *blog. yourdomain.com* is created. For a self-hosted blog, install WordPress into the subdomain's directory, and you are ready to blog.

Map a Subdomain to WordPress.com Blog

1 After you have created a subdomain, create a new CNAME record at your domain registrar. It will look something like this: `blog.yourdomain.com. IN CNAME myblog.wordpress. com.` — where *myblog* is your WordPress.com username.

2 Go to your WordPress.com Dashboard and click **Store**.

3 Click **Mapping** and follow the steps to add the subdomain and buy the mapping upgrade.

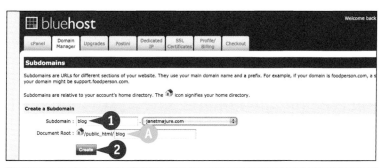

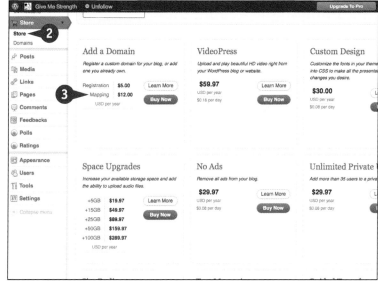

I am trying to direct my subdomain to my WordPress.com blog, and it is not working for me.
You may find the instructions at http://en.support. wordpress.com/domain-mapping/map-subdomain helpful. If not, contact your web host or post a question on the WordPress.com support forums at http://en.support.wordpress.com.

I added WordPress to a subdirectory at my site, but I cannot log on to the administration panels.
Your WordPress blog works just as if it were a stand-alone self-hosted blog, using http://www.*your domain.com/blogdirectory/wp-admin* to get to the administration pages. Be sure to use the logon information you use for your WordPress administration pages, not your web host logon information.

Use Sticky Posts to Control Page Content

You can make your blog's home page partly static and partly *dynamic*, or changing, thanks to sticky posts. Just mark one or more posts as *sticky*, and it or they stay at the top of your front page, with your latest blog post right after them. Sticky posts are a great way to welcome readers or announce policies.

Use Sticky Posts to Control Page Content

From the Edit Posts List

1 Click **Posts** to expand the Edit Posts lists.

2 Click the Quick Edit link that appears when you position the mouse pointer over the desired post, which expands the Quick Edit pane.

3 Click **Make this post sticky** (☐ changes to ☑).

4 Click **Update**.

The post is published to the top of your home page, the Quick Edit pane collapses, and *Sticky* appears with the title in the Posts list.

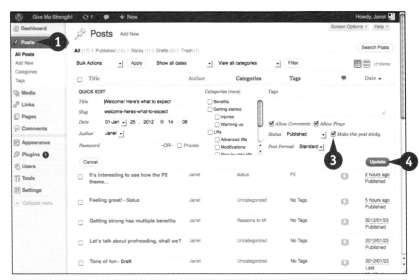

From the Edit Post Panel

1 With the Edit Post panel open for the post you want to change, click **Edit** next to the Visibility setting.

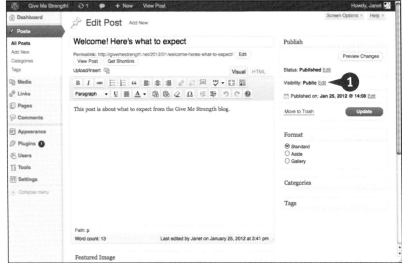

The Visibility pane opens.

2 Click **Stick this post to the front page** (☐ changes to ☑).

3 Click **OK**.

4 Click **Update**.

The post appears at the top of the blog front page, and *Sticky* appears with the post title in the Posts list.

Suppress the Date on Sticky Posts

1 Under Appearance, click **Editor**.

The Edit Themes panel opens to the style sheet, style.css.

Note: Your theme may have a different .css filename.

2 Find the code reading `.entry-meta...}`, and type `.sticky .entry-meta {visibility: hidden;}`.

3 Click **Update File**.

Your sticky posts do not show the original posting date.

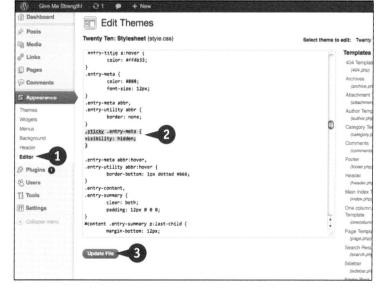

Is there a limit to how many sticky posts you can have?

You can have multiple stickies, but if you wind up with a whole front page of static posts, consider using a page for the

front and blog posts elsewhere as described in the section "Use a Static Page as Your Home Page" earlier in this chapter.

I tried to suppress the dates on the sticky posts as you suggested, but it did not work. What to do?

It works with the Twenty-Ten theme and others, but you may need to do things differently with your theme. Check with the theme developer or WordPress forums.

Create a Portfolio of Your Photos or Art

The easiest and probably best way to create a portfolio blog of your photos or art is through your choice of theme. Your portfolio or photoblog site is more than a blog with pictures, but a blog where the images are the focus, rather than illustrations of the words.

Create a Portfolio of Your Photos or Art

1 Click the **Appearance** menu, which opens to the Manage Themes panel.

2 Click the **Install Themes** tab at the top of the page.

3 Click **Photoblogging** (☐ changes to ☑).

Note: This option is not available at WordPress.com, but you can use the search term *photoblogging* or *photography* to find suitable themes.

4 Scroll to the bottom of the page and click **Find Themes**.

Ⓐ A selection of themes appears, which you can preview.

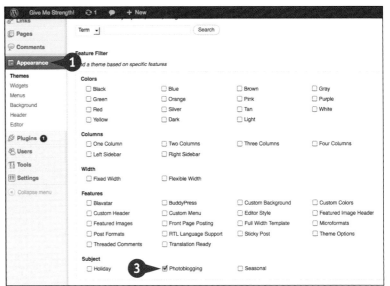

5 Click **Install** to install the theme of your choice.

The Install window opens, where you confirm that you want to install the theme. After the theme is installed, activate it.

Note: At WordPress.com, you merely activate your chosen theme.

Considerations for Your Portfolio

When you are choosing a theme or a plugin to operate your photoblog, consider ease of use, whether it resizes photos for you, and whether it displays your photos to best advantage. After all, that is why you have a photoblog! On the other hand, you *can* put other themes to work for photos.

Portfolio Theme Design Considerations

You can present photos — and other visual art — on a blog in more than one way, and you need to decide what works best for you: One great photo highlighted on the front page? A full-screen image on the front page? Perhaps you want to draw viewers in with a selection of photos on your front page. A theme generally makes all these options possible. If you only occasionally want to splash a big photo or gallery on your front page, you do not need a photoblogging theme; simply post a big photo or a gallery for an individual post as needed.

WordPress.com Themes to Consider

If you go to the Theme Showcase, http://theme. wordpress.com/themes, you get more theme search options than via your Manage Themes panel. The showcase lets you search by *subject*, with options including Art, Photoblogging, and Photography, all good options for theme selection. If you do not like any of those, however, you can take a different approach: Choose a plain theme such as Blogum, set the Reading settings to display just one post per page, and insert images.

WordPress.org Themes to Consider

Your self-hosted blog offers numerous photoblogging themes. Search at http://wordpress.org/extend/themes/tag-filter. Among the free themes are AutoFocus, with a slick front page display; HoPE, which has an easy, built-in image link to your Picasa or Flickr photostream; and Duotone, which changes background color based on your images. Popular premium themes include Photocrati, which has an e-commerce function as well as multiple formats.

Place Ads on Your Blog

If making money is part of your blog plan, you have plenty of company, and a lot to learn. Entire books have been written about making money on your blog, but here is an introduction to ways your blog can use advertising to earn income.

Advertising Possibilities

Advertising essentially is a means by which someone pays you for displaying their ad on your blog. You can contract directly with advertisers, sign up for an ad service or network, or use affiliate programs. Payments may be made for clicks on ads; for *impressions,* or the number of times the ad was viewed; or as sales commissions.

WordPress.com Limits

You can place any ads you want on your self-hosted blog. WordPress.com, however, significantly restricts advertising. Read the WordPress.com Terms of Service or contact support at WordPress.com if you have questions. Generally, Amazon Associate links are acceptable, but only if they are part of an original commentary about the item you are linking to.

Advertising Networks or Services

The most popular ad system is Google's AdSense, which offers text and display ads. Other popular ad systems include Text Link Ads, Chitika, and Adbrite. Most often, these networks select ads to place on your site based on the content of your site.

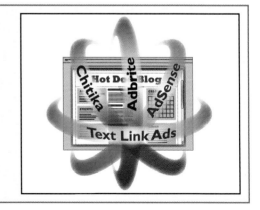

Affiliate Programs

Numerous individual businesses offer affiliate programs, with Amazon being the best known. Many smaller businesses offer affiliate programs through affiliate networks, such as Commission Junction, LinkShare, or ShareASale. With affiliates, *you* choose the merchant or product to advertise, rather than the ad network choosing for you.

How They Work

Typically, ad networks provide a bit of code that you place on your site via a widget or by inserting it into your theme's files. The code keeps track of impressions, clicks, or both. Various plugins are available that you can use to manage ads, including ads that you sell directly to blog sponsors.

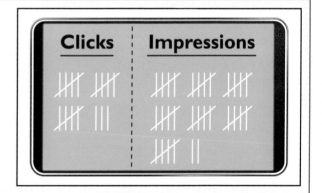

Ad Considerations

Some blogs make a lot of ad income, but most do not. Before you decide whether to include ads on your site, you may want to consider whether they are worth the effort to include and whether ads will detract from your blog content.

Add Google Ads to Your Site

Placing Google AdSense ads on your site lets you earn a few cents every time someone clicks an ad. Google lets you choose among a variety of ad types, and you can customize the ads to make them fit in with your blog design.

As a first step, you need to have or create a Google account and log on. WordPress.com does not allow use of Google AdSense.

Add Google Ads to Your Site

1 Go to www.google.com and click **Advertising Programs**.

2 The Advertising Programs page opens, where you click **Get Started With AdSense**.

The Google AdSense page opens.

3 Type your site's complete URL.

4 Select a language from the drop-down menu.

5 Click to agree to Google's terms (☐ changes to ☑).

6 Provide the information requested in the Contact Information section.

7 Scroll down to complete all the information, agree to the Policies, and click **Submit Information**.

8 Answer the questions on the confirmation page, and click **Continue**.

9 Google sends an e-mail asking you to confirm your e-mail address. Click the link in it to complete your application.

10 After your application is approved, which may take two to three days, sign in at google.com/adsense.

11 Click the **My ads** tab.

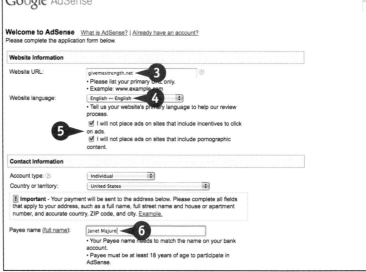

12 Click the **New Ad Unit** button.

The Create New Ad Unit page opens.

13 Type a name for your ad display.

14 Selected an ad size from the drop-down menu.

15 Choose whether to have text only, text and image/rich media, or image/rich media ads only.

Note: Not all ad types are available for all ad sizes.

16 Click the ad style you prefer.

17 When your ad selections are complete, scroll to the bottom of the page, and click **Save and get code**.

The Ad Code box appears.

18 Click in the box to select the code, and then copy the code.

19 On your blog Widgets panel, create a text widget, and paste the code into it. Ads start appearing in the widget space after a few minutes.

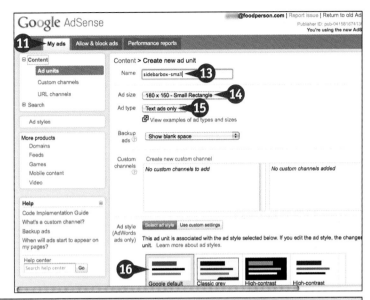

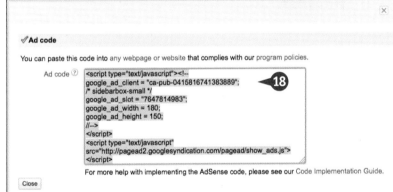

TIPS

I tried to put AdSense on my site at WordPress.com, where I bought my own domain, but the ads do not appear. Why not?

As noted above and on WordPress.com, you cannot put Google ads on your WordPress.com site, even if you paid for the domain upgrade. This question arises regularly but the answer is always *no* unless WordPress.com changes its policies, or unless you have a high-traffic VIP site, a *paid hosting* option WordPress.com offers to a select few.

Is a widget the only way to implement AdSense?

No. You can incorporate it into your blog's theme templates by pasting the code in the location where you want the ads, such as in a footer or sidebar template. Another option is to paste the code into a sticky post.

Add Amazon Affiliate Ads to Your Site

If you find yourself recommending products on your blog, you can make a little money by providing a link to a place where someone can purchase them — and earn a commission for you through an affiliate program. Amazon.com Associates is the most popular such program, and you may be able to use it at WordPress.com. See "Place Ads on Your Blog" earlier in this chapter.

As a first step, go to https://affiliate-program.amazon.com and sign up.

Add Amazon Affiliate Ads to Your Site

1 After signing in, click the **Links & Banners** tab to expand the drop-down menu.

2 Click **Product Links**.

Ⓐ The Get Started Now button provides an introduction for new associates.

Ⓑ Search here to find a URL to add a text or image link on your site.

3 The Product Links page opens, where you search for the item you want to link to. When you find the item in the search results, click **Get Link**.

The Customize and Get HTML page opens.

4 Click the **Text Only** tab.

The page changes to display text link information.

5 Click **Highlight HTML**.

6 Press Ctrl+C (⌘+C on a Mac) to copy the code.

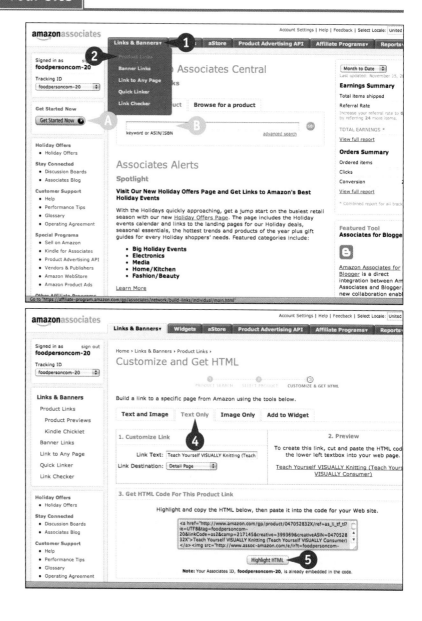

7 After logging into your blog's administration pages and creating a new post where you want to add the text link, click **HTML** to go to the HTML post editor.

8 Paste the code in the place where you want the link to appear.

9 Click **Save Draft**.

The draft is saved with the text link to the product you recommend.

Note: The process is the same for adding a text link to an existing post. Simply open the post, click the HTML tab, and paste the link.

10 Click **Preview** to see what your link looks like.

 The coded Amazon link appears as a hyperlink.

11 Click **Edit** or click the **Edit Post** tab to resume writing your post.

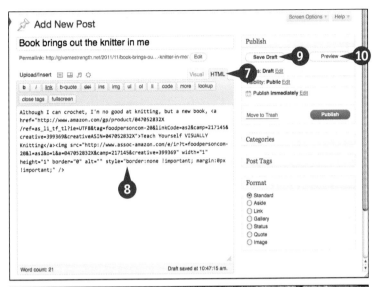

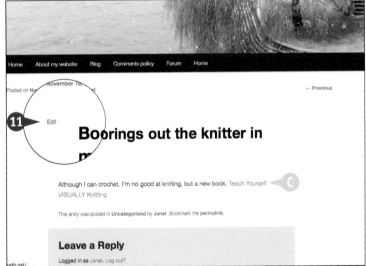

Can I use the other kinds of ads and links that Amazon offers?
Yes, you can, at least if your site is self-hosted. You also can put Amazon and other affiliate ads in your sidebar. Many bloggers like the text links because they are unobtrusive, and WordPress.com frowns on image ads.

What are the Amazon widgets?
They are a form of dynamic ad. Find out more about them and other Amazon Associates products and issues at the Help page, https://affiliate-program. amazon.com/gp/associates/ help/main.html.

Get Set for E-Commerce

You can get going with online sales through a free or premium e-commerce plugin, a theme, or a separate e-commerce provider that you incorporate into your site. As you consider options, keep in mind how many and what type of products you want to sell, how much time or money you can spend, and what solution you are most comfortable with. Adding e-commerce definitely increases the complexity of your website.

E-Commerce Plugins

An e-commerce plugin may be the quickest way to get a shop on your website and may be the best solution for you if you have just a handful of products to sell. Plugins, with the possible exception of eShop, may not have as much support as you would like and may require a lot of hands-on involvement in getting started.

E-Commerce WordPress Themes

Themes created specifically for e-commerce hold out the prospect of having seamless integration between your e-commerce and website management functions. At this writing, nearly all e-commerce themes require payment for use, but the prices tend to be modest. The respected WooThemes' WooCommerce framework is a good option with various themes.

WOO THEMES   Home   Themes   Pricing

An e-commerce toolkit that helps you sell anything. Beautifully.

Transform your WordPress website into a thoroughbred online store. Delivering enterprise-level quality & features whilst backed by a name you can trust. Say hello to WooCommerce.

E-Commerce Hosting

You also can choose to use a separate e-commerce host and integrate that store into your WordPress site via a subdomain. Or you can add your WordPress site to your e-commerce site — the only way to have e-commerce with a WordPress.com blog. The process is the same as adding a blog to a static site as explained in "Add a Blog to an Existing Static Website." This might be the best approach if you have a large number of products. This option generally costs most but offers the most support. Well-regarded providers include Volusion, Shopify, and BigCommerce.

V volusion   Features   Pricing

Open a successful online store

All-in-one ecommerce solution

V volusion   Orders

Set Up an E-Commerce Plugin

Self-hosted WordPress users can set up e-commerce using familiar plug-in tools, but be prepared for lots of questions! This example uses the eShop plugin.

To get started, install and activate the eShop plugin following the methods described in Chapter 7, and create a new page, My Shop. This section merely introduces you to the possibilities. See http://quirm.net/wiki/eshop for details.

Set Up an E-Commerce Plugin

1 Click **eShop** under Settings in the left menu bar.

The eShop Settings panel opens.

2 Type an e-mail address for e-mails to be sent from your shop.

3 Scroll down and change any settings you want to change.

4 Click **Save Changes**.

5 Click **Merchant Gateways**, and then each of the other tabs, reviewing the settings on each.

6 Click **Add New** under the Pages menu.

7 Type the name of a product in the title field.

8 Upload and insert an image if desired.

9 Type a product description.

10 Choose **My Shop** as the parent of your product page.

11 Scroll down and complete additional product information.

12 Click **Save Draft**.

13 Click **Publish**.

Your product is published and appears under the My Shop menu.

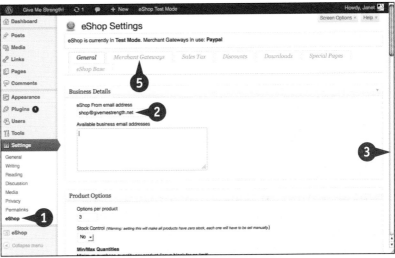

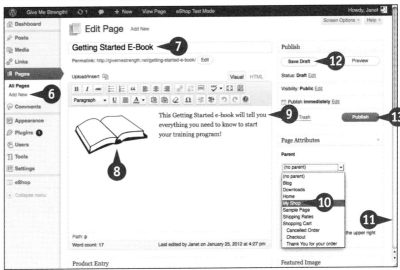

CHAPTER 12

Maintain Your WordPress Blog

Now that your WordPress blog is up, running, and getting readers, you want to make sure that it continues to work smoothly. Although WordPress.com users have fewer maintenance tasks than do self-hosted bloggers, everybody can benefit from a little blog upkeep.

Understanding WordPress Backups

If you have a self-hosted blog, you are responsible for backing up your website. Doing regular backups assures that you do not lose data — or at least not much — should your database become corrupted or your host crash for whatever reason.

What to Back Up

You need to back up the MySQL database that you created when you installed WordPress because the database stores all your blog posts and comments. You also need to back up the *site*, however. It contains your plugins, themes, uploads, scripts, and a few other files as well as the core WordPress files.

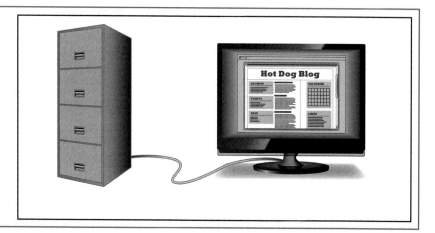

When to Back Up

You are wise to back up your files on a regular schedule so that you do not forget. Some people do it daily, others monthly. Frequency depends on how active your site is — or how much you are willing to lose. In addition, you should always back up before updating to a new version of WordPress.

Backup Methods

There are several backup methods for you to consider. You can use a plugin, such as WordPress Backup; a backup tool provided by your web host; or a manual backup method. You may want to try more than one method to see what works best for you.

Web Host Tools

Web hosts that use the cPanel control panel have a tool set called Site Backup & Restore. Others provide phpMyAdmin, an interface you can use for backing up your site and database. Find more information by searching on *backups* at http://codex.wordpress.org.

How Long to Save Backups

Some people discard old backups when they create a new one. WordPress experts recommend keeping the latest three backups, just in case something has gone wrong along the way. Let your risk aversion be your guide.

Backup Instructions

Most web host tools are fairly self-explanatory, but contact your web host if you have questions. WordPress.org provides step-by-step instructions for backups using phpMyAdmin and MySQL tools. If you have trouble, also consult the WordPress.org forums.

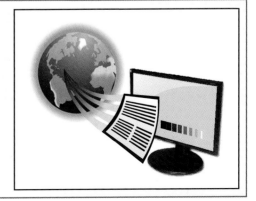

Get to Know WordPress Support Options

The multiplicity of WordPress support options means you are almost certain to find the answer to your particular question. You can find it quicker if you go to the right places: WordPress.org sites for self-hosted bloggers, and WordPress.com if your blog is hosted there.

The WordPress.org Codex

A *codex* is a bound manuscript, and that is the name that WordPress.org chose for its set of support articles, which you can find at http://codex.wordpress.org. Note that numerous contributors write Codex articles, and some are definitely better and more up to date than others.

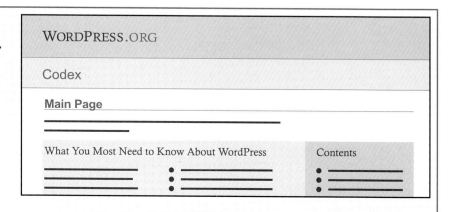

Official WordPress.com Support

Compared with those at WordPress.org, the support pages at WordPress.com are more consistent in style and timeliness. You can find them at http://en.support.wordpress.com. The main page lists topics that you may find helpful. Occasionally, WordPress.com Support articles may be helpful even to self-hosted bloggers.

Search for Answers

Both the WordPress.org Codex and the WordPress.com Support pages have search options, and both allow you to search the documentation as well as the forums. If you do not identify what you need by browsing the documentation, search the documentation and the forums. You are likely to find an answer.

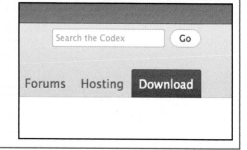

Do Not Miss WordPress.TV

WordPress has numerous instructional and informational videos you may find useful. You will find them at http://wordpress.tv. Although many of the videos focus on WordPress.com, you also can find videos from WordCamps, conferences for WordPress enthusiasts of all descriptions.

Pose a Question

If you fail in your attempts to find an answer, you are welcome to post a question to the thousands of WordPress users who read the forums. You need to be logged in to post a question — or an answer.

Search the Support Forums

Enter a few words that describe the problem you're having.

[   ] Search

Posting Etiquette

Things that might be considered bad manners on the forums:

- Posting a question that has been answered many times before. Search first!

- Posting a *.com* question on the *.org* forum or vice versa.

Good manners include posting a link to your site, being specific, and using standard grammar and spelling.

WORDPRESS.COM

8 Things To Know Before Posting in WordPress.com

✔ FAQ   ✔ Linking   ✔ Remember...
✔ Search   ✔ Be polite   ✔ It's free!
✔ Be specific ✔ www.myblog.com

Update WordPress Automatically

If you have a self-hosted blog, you need to keep up with WordPress updates, a task that WordPress.com does for its users. Updating WordPress is a simple process, and it assures that you have the latest features and the latest security measures installed.

You will see an alert on your Dashboard when an update is available. If you click it, which takes you to the updates panel, it provides a link to information about backing up your site.

Update WordPress Automatically

1 After backing up your site, click **Updates** in the left menu bar.

The WordPress Updates panel opens.

2 Click **Update Now**.

WordPress presents a progress screen as it downloads and installs the update.

The Welcome to WordPress screen appears.

③ Read through What's New to ease your transition to the new version.

My automatic update failed. Now what?

You are among the unlucky few. Worry not; you still should be able to update successfully. If an automatic update does not work, you can update manually. Here are some troubleshooting tips. Note that you must update manually if you are updating from a version earlier than WordPress 2.7.

Automatic Update Troubleshooting	
Error	**Likely Solution**
Installation Failed message	Simply try again; you may have had some Internet connection interruption.
First message says *WordPress Updated Successfully*, but another message says *An automated WordPress update has failed to complete — please attempt the update again now.*	Using your FTP program, open the directory or folder where WordPress is installed — that is, the folder that contains the WP-Admin folder. Look for and delete a file named .maintenance. Then, try the automatic update again.
Fatal Error message	Go to your plugins list and deactivate all plugins. Then, try the automatic update again. When the update is complete, reactivate the plugins. If you still get the message, again deactivate all the plugins and then activate them one at a time, going to the site after each activation, until you identify one that may be causing the error.
Repeated failure	Review the information at http://codex.wordpress.org/Updating_WordPress for ideas. Then, ask at the WordPress.org forums for help, or do a manual update, as described in the next section.

Update WordPress Manually

M aybe you are a hands-on kind of person, or maybe you have had trouble with the automatic update. In any case, you can orchestrate a WordPress update manually. Be sure to back up your site first, and it is good practice to check your host's services against the minimum requirements listed at http://codex.wordpress.org/Updating_WordPress.

Update WordPress Manually

1 After backing up your site, click **Updates** in the left menu bar.

The WordPress Updates panel opens.

2 Click **Download 3.3** (or whatever is the latest version).

Your browser opens a download window.

3 Click **Open with Archive Utility** (○ changes to ◉) if not already selected.

Note: Your computer may use a different program for extracting the Zip file.

4 Click **OK**.

Your browser downloads the file to your computer and extracts the Zip file.

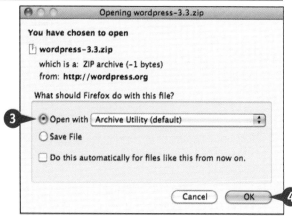

5 Click **Plugins**.

The Plugins panel opens.

6 Select all plugins (☐ changes to ☑).

7 Click the Bulk Actions drop-down menu and select **Deactivate**.

8 Click **Apply**.

The plugins are deactivated.

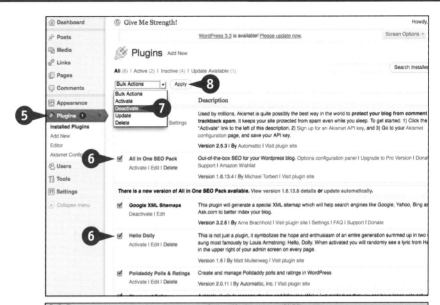

9 Using your FTP access, delete the files called wp-admin and wp-includes from your site's root directory.

10 Upload the new wp-admin and wp-includes from your extracted WordPress folder.

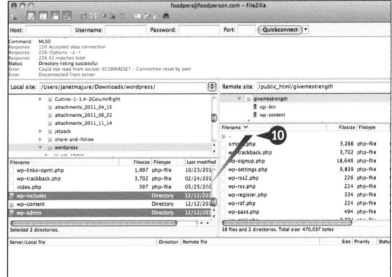

TIPS

Can I just upload the new folders and write over the old ones?

You can, but it is safer to delete and then upload, to make sure all old files are removed.

My web host used Simple Scripts to do my initial installation. Does that affect what method I use to update?

It should not. You can check with your host and Simple Scripts to see if it has an update ready. If it does, you can use it. If not, you can use either the automatic or manual updates described in this and the previous sections.

continued ▶

anual updating usually takes much longer than automatic updating, so allow time to upload the many files needed. If you need more help, go to http://codex.wordpress.org/Upgrading_WordPress_Extended.

Update WordPress Manually (continued)

11 Upload the contents — not the folder itself — from the new wp-content folder to your existing wp-content folder.

Note: Overwrite any old files with the same names as the new files, but do not delete any other files in your old wp-content folder.

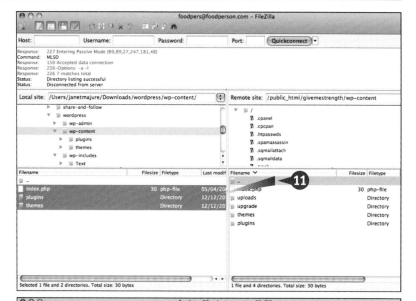

12 Upload the other remaining files from the download into the root directory of your site.

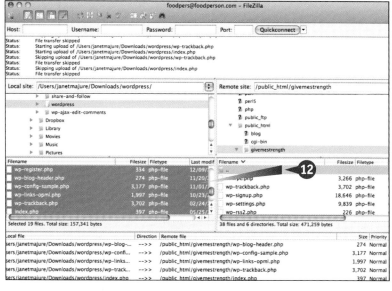

⑬ Go to your site's Dashboard at www.*yoursite*.com/wp-login and click **Plugins**.

The Plugins panel opens.

⑭ Click the plugins you want to activate (☐ changes to ☑).

⑮ Click the Bulk Actions drop-down menu and select **Activate**.

⑯ Click **Apply**.

The plugins are activated.

Note: Some users prefer to activate plugins one at a time, checking the site after each, to detect any plugin conflicts with the new software.

⑰ Click the website name and visit the updated site.

⑱ Navigate around your site to see whether everything seems to be working correctly.

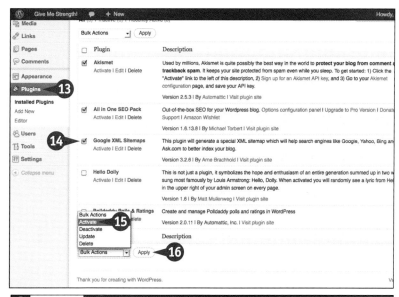

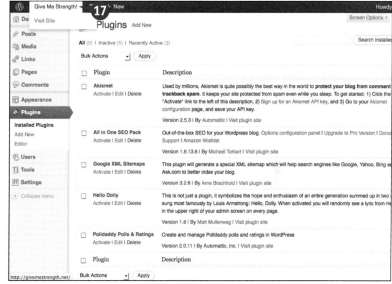

When I tried to return to the Dashboard, I got a notice that said "Database Update Required." What should I do?
WordPress has detected that your database needs some updates to work with the updated WordPress installation. Go ahead and click **Update WordPress Database**.

Since my update, the layout looks weird. What do I do?
Make sure you have the latest versions of all your plugins. If you still have a problem, turn off all plugins. Then, activate each plugin one at a time, checking your blog's performance after each activation. If you identify a problem plugin, leave it deactivated and contact the plugin developer to see whether an update is available. If it is not, you may need to seek a different plugin.

Clean Out Outdated Drafts

Keeping your blog up-to-date also involves clearing out detritus that can distract you from your purpose, not to mention that it can take up space unnecessarily on your web host. Take a few minutes to get rid of it!

Clean Out Outdated Drafts

1 Click **Posts** in the left menu bar.

The Posts menu expands, and the Posts list opens.

2 Click **Drafts**.

The Edit Posts list filters out all except draft posts.

3 Click **Title** to select all drafts (☐ changes to ☑).

4 Choose **Move to Trash** from the drop-down menu.

5 Click **Apply**.

WordPress confirms the move to Trash and provides an Undo link.

6 Click the **Trash** link under the confirmation message.

The Edit Posts list filters out all but the posts in Trash.

7 Click the drafts and other trash you want to remove (☐ changes to ☑).

8 Choose **Delete Permanently** from the drop-down menu.

9 Click **Apply**.

WordPress confirms that the posts you selected are permanently deleted.

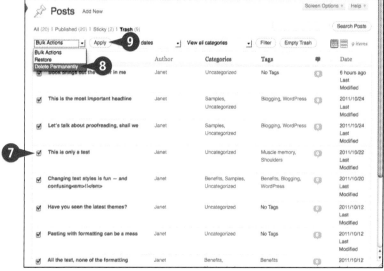

TIPS

Should I review the drafts before I delete them?
That would probably be a wise step, although if your blog is like most people's, chances are that drafts that have been sitting for more than six months are out of date — or you are not able to remember what your point was!

Do I have to delete all drafts?
Of course not. Feel free to review and delete drafts one at a time.

Check Your Site for Outdated Links

You know you hate it when you click a link and get a *Page Not Found* message, so you can assume your readers will not like it if they find a broken link on your site. Fortunately, finding and fixing broken links is fairly simple. Try it occasionally! Even better, schedule it regularly.

Check Your Site for Outdated Links

1 Go to http://validator.w3.org/checklink in your web browser.

2 Type your URL in the box.

3 Click **Check linked documents** (☐ changes to ☑), and type **4** in the box next to recursion depth.

The depth setting takes the link checker into directories beyond the home page directory.

4 Click **Check**.

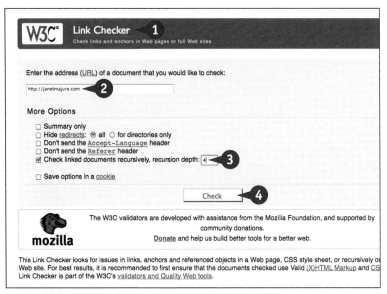

The link checker goes to work reviewing your site's links.

5 When the validator is done, click **the results**.

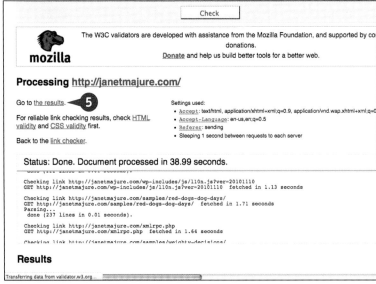

Lists of broken links and other issues appear.

6 Review the problem links. You may click them to see what happens.

Note: Some links may work but are flagged because they do not comply with the World Wide Web Consortium standards.

Ⓐ Details of issues and repair suggestions appear under each page's list of problem links.

7 Scroll down to see more results.

8 Above the list of broken links is the URL of the page link where the broken link or links appear. Click the link.

The page with the broken link appears in your browser.

9 When you have found the broken link, correct it or delete it in the Edit Post or Edit Page panel.

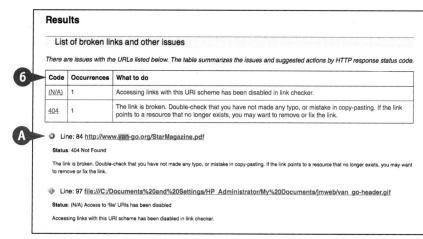

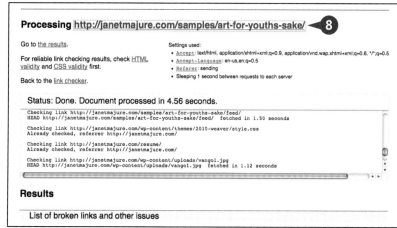

TIP

Are there any other link trackers?
Yes, several. Perhaps you would prefer Xenu's Link Sleuth, a free program you can download for Windows, or the LinkChecker add-on for the Firefox browser. The Broken Link Checker plugin is an option for self-hosted blogs.

Sign Up for a Statistics Tracker

You can find out how many people are looking at your blog, which posts are getting the most attention, how people made their way to your blog, and much more information with a statistics tracker. WordPress.com users have a tracker built in. Self-hosted WordPress users, though, have to add one, such as Google Analytics.

The WordPress.com-type statistics tracker is included in the Jetpack set of plugins.

Sign Up for a Statistics Tracker

1 In your browser, go to www.google.com/analytics.

2 Click **Sign Up Now**.

3 A new page opens, where you can sign in with existing Google account information or, if you do not have a Google account, you can sign up for one.

4 Proceed through the pages until you agree to terms and conditions; then, click **Create Account**.

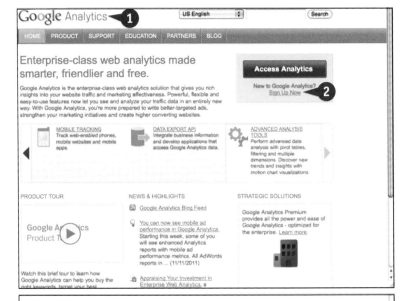

The tracking instructions page opens to the Tracking Code tab of your account.

5 Make sure the radio button is selected (●) next to your domain or domains to be tracked.

6 Click in the box to select the code, and then press Ctrl+ C (⌘+C on a Mac) to copy the code.

7 Click **Save** at the bottom of the page.

8 In your blog's administrative pages, click **Appearance**.

The Appearance menu expands and the Manage Themes page opens.

9 Click **Editor**.

The Edit Themes panel opens.

10 Click **Footer (footer.php)**.

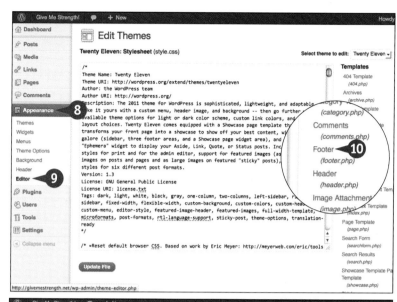

The footer template opens.

11 Scroll to the bottom of the Edit Themes box, click to insert your cursor in front of `</body>`, and then press `Ctrl`+`V` (`⌘`+`V` on a Mac) to insert the analytics code.

The code appears in the box just before `</body>`.

12 Click **Update File**.

The Google Analytics code is inserted.

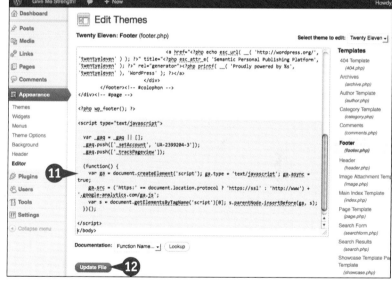

TIPS

I cannot find </body> in my footer.php file. Where do I put the code?

You can put it just before the `</head>` tag, usually found in header.php. Or you can check your other template files for the `</body>` code. Look for a template that you know appears on every page, and it likely has the `</body>` tag.

Is there another way to insert the code?

You can find a theme that integrates Google Analytics into it. You could get a plugin, of which there are several, at http://wordpress.org/extend/plugins. Or, you can skip Google and use a tool from your web host.

Understanding Your Statistics

With your website being tracked with one tool or another, you can get a lot of information about your site visitors, popular posts, and much more. Checking that information periodically can help you see trends and refine your blog content.

Visitor Counts

Your statistics tracker undoubtedly shows numbers of visitors, visits, and page views. *Visitors* (or *unique visitors*) is a count of visits from a unique IP address (an ID assigned to everything connected to the Internet) to your blog. *Visits* is a count of uninterrupted sessions on your site, and *page views* indicates the number of pages viewed.

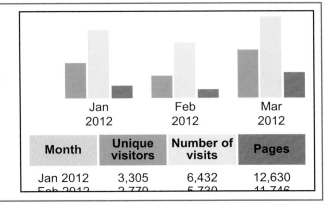

Month	Unique visitors	Number of visits	Pages
Jan 2012	3,305	6,432	12,630
Feb 2012	2,779	5,730	11,746

Traffic Sources

You also may receive information on your tracker about where your visitors came from, both geographically and *virtually*. That is, it tells you the page from which visitors clicked to arrive on your site, or the search engine that pointed to your site — or how many visitors entered your URL directly into their web browser.

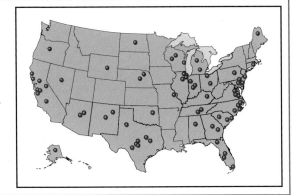

Content Popularity

Do you want to know what posts or pages get read the most? Your tracker tells you. It also tells you at which pages visitors arrived, or *landed*, and from which pages visitors left. It also tells you what search terms people used to find your content.

Pages-URL (Top 25)

152 different pages-url	Viewed	Average size	Entry	Exit
drying-mint	1,404	67.84 KB	749	711
tuscan-bread	1,264	35.50 KB	761	710
butternut-squash	1,028	47.63 KB	916	731
papalo-power	658	59.05 KB	251	169
vegetable-dish	168	45.70 KB	81	93

More Statistics

Most statistics trackers provide more information than you know what to do with. They tell you what browser people used, for example, and what links visitors clicked on. They tell you how long visitors stayed on your site and how many pages they viewed on average.

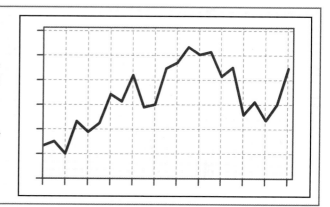

Look for Trends

What do you do with all those statistics? If you are blogging for pleasure, you can ignore them entirely. If you want popularity, you may aim for an ongoing traffic increase as judged by statistics trends. You might gauge whether a particular *type* of content draws traffic or if certain search terms work for you, and then use that knowledge to shape content.

A Cautionary Note

The truth is that website statistics are imperfect. None can give you an exact count of much of anything, and one tracker may give different information from another. Your time is far better spent creating great blog content than in watching your statistics.

Install Plugin Updates

To keep your plugins running smoothly, you need to keep them up to date. Happily, WordPress alerts you to available updates, and with most plugins, you can complete the updates in just a click or two.

If an automatic update is not available, follow instructions provided by the plugin developer.

Install Plugin Updates

1 Click **Plugins** in the left menu bar.

The Plugins panel opens.

A A number in a circle or square, depending on your browser, indicates how many plugins have updates available.

2 Click **update automatically**.

B If you have several updates, you can filter the plugin list by clicking the **Update Available** link.

The Update Plugin panel opens and displays update progress.

3 When the update is complete, click **Return to Plugins page**, and update other plugins as needed.

Read Blogs that Focus on WordPress

or better or worse, WordPress, like most successful computer programs, is always a work in progress. If you prefer, you can simply update your blog as needed, or you can keep abreast of what is going on so that you are not taken by surprise!

Official Blogs

WordPress developers maintain blogs that apprise readers of new developments. At WordPress.com, keep the What's Hot module active and near the top of your Dashboard to see headlines of the latest official blog posts. If you are a self-hosted blogger, you can keep the WordPress Development blog active on your Dashboard. Or subscribe to either feed for your feed reader or to get posts by e-mail.

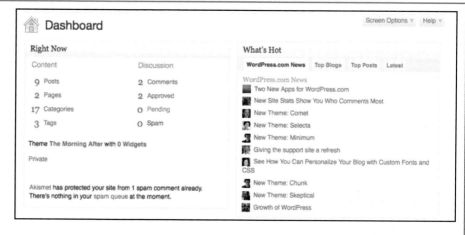

WordPress Help Blogs

Several bloggers write much useful information about WordPress. Check out http://planet.wordpress.org, which aggregates the blogs of several WordPress bloggers, including the helpful blogs at http://wp-community.org; http://lorelle.wordpress.com and http://onecoolsitebloggingtips.com, which cover both the hosted and self-hosted versions; and http://weblogtoolscollection.com.

Make a Suggestion

Have you noticed that your blog would work just about *perfectly* if only it would do that one thing that you want? If you are certain that the widget or plugin you know you need is not available, you can always ask for it!

Make a Suggestion

Send a Suggestion to WordPress.com Support

1 Log in to WordPress.com, and go to http://en.support.wordpress.com/contact in your web browser.

2 Type your suggestion in the text box.

A An advisory about response time appears.

B Links to possibly similar information appears.

3 Click **No** (☐ changes to ☑) if the related information did not show your idea.

4 Provide the information requested in the boxes that appear, and click **Contact Support.**

Post an Idea in the Forums

1 Go to http://en.forums.wordpress.com/forum/ideas in your web browser.

2 Click **Add New.**

The New Topic box appears.

3 Type your suggestion in the New Topic box, add tags, such as *themes* or *organization,* to describe your suggestion, and then click **Submit.**

Your idea appears in the Ideas forum.

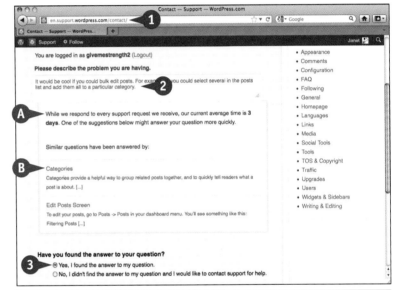

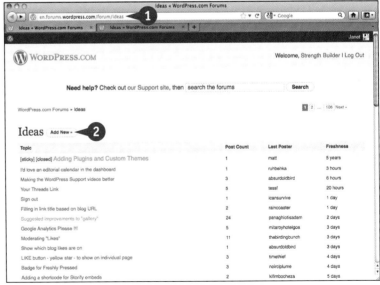

Make a Suggestion at WordPress.org

1 Go to http://wordpress.org/extend/ideas in your web browser.

2 Scroll to the bottom of the Ideas page, and type a subject in the One Line Summary box.

3 Describe your idea in the Description box.

4 Type a keyword or two as tags.

5 Choose a category from the pop-up list.

6 Click **Submit Idea**.

Your idea is submitted for consideration.

Rate an Idea

1 After reading other people's ideas, click one you like or dislike, and then click a star to rate the idea.

Note: For ideas under consideration, you also can type a reply to add to the consideration.

C More ideas can be reviewed by their status.

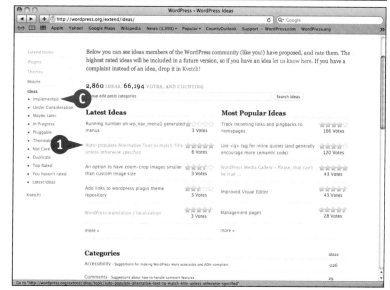

Is there a way to propose something privately at WordPress.org?
Yes, the Kvetch page: http://wordpress.org/extend/kvetch, which is largely for complaints.

How can I tell if my suggestion is being considered?
On the right sidebar of each idea's display is a status line indicating that the idea is being considered, has been addressed with a plugin, or has been implemented.

Status

Good idea! We're working on it

Steps to Take When Your Blog Breaks

Blogs do break or crash, but they can be recovered. Most often, problems involve plugins or updates to your WordPress software — or even updates to your host's software. Because you cannot get into the code at WordPress.com, the host must resolve crashes there, but see the table in this section for some issues common to both WordPress types.

Remain Calm and Take Notes

Take a deep breath and write down exactly what happened. Note any error message you saw or see, and when possible take screenshots. Try to recall what you did just before everything went wrong.

Turn Off Plugins

Even if you have not altered plugins lately, deactivate all plugins, and see if your blog works. If it does, you may well have a plugin conflict. Turn one plugin on and view your blog. Repeat with the next plugin and so on until the crash recurs. Then, deactivate that last plugin.

Install the Default Theme

Themes, too, can cause strange behavior. The default theme, Twenty Eleven, is guaranteed to run on the latest version of WordPress. If you activate the default theme and the blog works okay, then you need to identify what is wrong with the theme you were running.

Reinstall the Plugin or Theme

Sometimes the code for the problem plugin or theme becomes corrupted. Using your FTP program — not the administrative panels — delete the plugin from the Plugins folder on your server, or the theme from the Themes folder. Then, reinstall the plugin or theme, either manually or through the administrative panels.

Support Forums

If your problem is a plugin or theme, you can contact the developer or post on the plugin or theme forum if one exists. For other problems, go to the forums at WordPress.org. When you post a question to the forum, be sure to provide your URL and the error message or other behavior you are getting.

If All Else Fails

You may need to restore your site from a backup. Your web host should have a utility to help you do that, or you can find instructions at http://codex.wordpress.org/Restoring_Your_Database_From_Backup. You may need only to restore your database, or you may need to restore your site's files as well. These files include the WordPress software, plugins, themes, and so on. If you have been using a backup plugin such as XCloner-Backup and Restore, it also may be able to restore your data and files.

Troubleshoot Common WordPress Problems

As with any computer program, WordPress poses problems for its users now and then.

Problem	Possible Explanation	What to Do
I forgot my password!	Brain freeze.	Go to your blog's logon page — http://*yourblog*.com/wp-admin (or http://*yourblog*.wordpress.com/wp-admin) — and click the lost password link. You still need to know your username and e-mail address. A password will be e-mailed to you.
Page does not display.	Server is down or your web connection is interrupted.	Check to make sure you can access other websites. If you can, your web connection is okay, so it may be a server at your web host, including WordPress.com. Wait 15 minutes and try again.
Page still does not display, although you have Internet connectivity.	Server is still down after waiting 15 minutes.	Contact your web host.
I made changes to my theme, but when I check it, nothing happened.	Your site is *cached* in your browser (meaning a previous version is showing up).	Refresh your browser by pressing and holding `Ctrl` (`⌘` on a Mac) and clicking the **Refresh** button on your browser.
I need to talk to a *live person!*	You are frustrated.	Try live chat. Read about it at http://codex.wordpress.org/WordPress_IRC_Live_Help. If your blog is hosted at WordPress.com, you can contact support at http://en.support.wordpress.com/contact. You may get a quicker response by going to www.justanswer.com or http://wpquestions.com, but you will need to pay a small fee.
No answers to my forum question.	You posted it in the wrong forum, you did not give it any tags, or your question was too vague.	Make sure you post WordPress.com questions at WordPress.com, and self-hosted blog questions at WordPress.org forums. Note that WordPress forums are subdivided into categories such as Installation and Plugins. Use descriptive tags, such as *comment plugin*, rather than *I cannot figure out why this is not working!*
Scheduled post did not appear.	You forgot to click **Schedule**.	After you save a draft to be published at a future date, you not only need to save the draft and okay the time for publication, but you also need to click **Schedule** to make it happen. When you do, the Status will read *Scheduled*.
Blog looks funny on different machine.	Different browser, different monitor.	The nature of web design is that pages' appearance varies according to the monitor and the browser being used. You can get an idea of it at home by viewing your blog with different browsers or changing the display settings, such as resolution, for your monitor.

Index

A

account management, 25
Add Media window, 116–117, 124–125
Add New Post panel, 82–90
Admin Bar, 20, 24–25, 57
Administrator user, 242
AdSense, Google, 5, 266, 268–269
advertisements
    affiliate ads, 5, 266, 267, 270–271
    blocking, 32
    placing on blog, 5, 266–271
    WordPress.com compared to WordPress.org, 5
affiliate ads, 5, 266, 267, 270–271
After the Deadline plugin, 161
aggregator (feed reader), 200
alignment
    image, 125, 127
    text, 84
Allow Link Notifications setting, pingbacks and trackbacks, 199
alternate text for image, 124, 164, 213
Amazon.com Associate links, 266, 270–271
Analytics, Google, 290–291
API key, 19
appearance, 5, 60. *See also* theme
Attachment Page option for gallery image, 129
Attempt to Notify setting, pingbacks and trackbacks, 199
audio file, linking to, 136–137
Author list, 83
Author user, 242, 243, 244–245
Automattic Inc., 27
Autosave version of post, 93
avatar, 29, 75

B

background image, 223
backordering a domain name, 14
backup of data, 154, 276–277
blavatar, 29
blockquote format, 84, 163
blog. *See also* traffic on your blog
    adding to existing website, 260–261
    content planning, 10–11
    inviting viewers to, 77
    terminology, 9
    title, 12–13, 20, 28, 212

topic choice, 6–7
    viewing options, 20–21
Blogger, 108–109
blogging client, 106–107
blogroll, 21, 182–183
bookmark sites, social, 208
bookmarklet, defined, 104
Browser Connection setting, 35
browser uploader, 117
browsers, 105, 112, 130, 236–237, 299
BuddyPress social network, 248–249
bulk editing of categories and tags, 175
bulleted lists, 163

C

cached web pages, clearing, 299
captcha, defined, 186
caption, image, 124, 164
cascading style sheet (CSS), 32, 225, 234–237
categories
    child/parent structure, 169, 170, 177
    creating, 170–171
    default setting, 72
    function, 168–169
    introduction, 20
    posts, applying to, 174–175
    slug for, 171
    tags, converting to/from, 176–177
    template image for, 228–229
    as traffic enhancers, 213
Categories Box, post panel, 82
category-based RSS feed links, 238–239
child category, 169, 170, 177
child page, 94–95
codex, WordPress.org, 5, 278
color
    admin page scheme, 58
    background, 223
    text in post box, 85, 91
    theme, changing, 66–67
comments
    comment policy, 184–185
    commenting on other sites, 186–187
    Discussion settings, 74–75, 83
    editing, 190–191
    e-mail notifications of, 74, 189
    link to, 20, 193

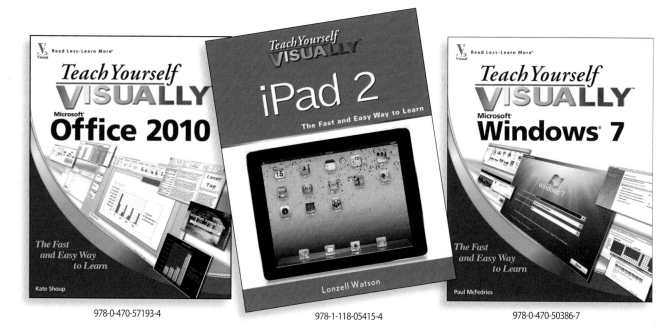